Voices From The Kitchen: A Collection of Antebellum and Civil War Era Recipes
From Period Receipt Books

Volume II

David W. Flowers

Dedications

To my Wife, Monica, who stands beside me, supports and loves me in sickness and in health. I thank God that He gave you to me to love.

To my Son, David. Your ancestors gave you your history, your family. Their stories made you. The future belongs to you. Learn from those who came before you and teach your children the ways of the people who have loved you.

To my Mom and Dad, Melody and John Wayne Flowers. You taught me how to love, how to be a good Dad.

To my Grandparents, John Marshall and Lula Mae Flowers. You gave me my past, taught me things that I have passed on to my son. I wish he could have known you. You'd be proud!

To my Grandparents Milton and Helen Michal. From you, I have learned love, the "old" ways, laughter and good cooking!

To my Sisters Lisa, Denise and Carrie. Thanks for letting me be "me"! May God bless you and your families as they grow!

To my Mother-In Law, Dorothy Rowland. We loved each other and had some good times sharing meals, family and family history. I miss you.

To my Second Cousin Mike Flowers. A great fisherman and Coon Hunter. I miss fishing with you and your laugh.

To my Aunty Wanda (Flowers) Patterson. Time spent researching genealogy, hunting cemeteries and bringing our past back to life, led to many good meals that you cooked!

To my Pards in Scott's Tennessee Battery. My Brothers In Arms. My friends who sustain me.

To my Civil War Soldier Ancestors:
My Great-great Grandfather, Henry V. Flowers, Sgt, Co. A, 6th TN (Federal) Cavalry, from McNairy County, Tennessee.

My Great-great Grandmother's, Henry's wife, brothers, Pvts. William Curtis, Henry Curtis and Charles Curtis Co. A, 6th TN Cavalry (Federal) from McNairy County, Tennessee.

My Great-great Grandfather, Pvt. John Wesley Jenkins and his brother Pvt. Ira Jenkins, 49th Alabama (Confederate) Infantry, from Blount County, Alabama.

CONTENTS

Introduction   12

1 Breakfasts   15

Apple Pancakes, Buckwheat Cakes, Cream Pancakes, Crepes, Soft Crullers, Walnut Hill's Doughnuts, Dutch Pancakes, Fried Eggs and Bacon, Eggs and Bread, Eggs A La Maitre D'Hotel, Eggs with Brown Butter, Eggs Stewed with Cheese, Ham and Eggs Fried, Fried Ham and Eggs, Slices of Ham or Bacon, Hashed Beef, Indian Batter Cakes, Kedgeree, Kentucky Batter Cakes, Oeufs Au Plat, or Au Miroir, Omlette, Oyster Omelet, Plain Omelet, Omlette Souffle, Young Corn Omelet, Poach Eggs, Common Pancakes, Fine Pancakes, New-England Pancakes, Pancakes of Rice, Richer Pancakes, Rye Batter Cakes, Potato Omelette

2 Soups   28

Bacon and Cabbage Soup, Baked Soups, Barley Soup, Bean Soup, Bouillabaisse Soup, Bouillon, Broth Made From Bones for Soup, Cabbage Soup, Carrot Soup, Catfish Soup, Celery Soup, Chantilly Soup, Chicken Broth, Chowder, Clam Soup, Cocoa-Nut Soup, Cottage Soup, Crayfish Soup, Egg Soup, Fish Stock No. 192, French Vegetable Soup, Green-Peas Soup, Hessian Soup, Maccaroni Soup, Macaroni Soup (Mrs. F.'s Receipt), Medium Stock (No. 105), Mullagatawny Soup, Ochra Soup, Onion Soup, Plain Green Pea Soup, Plum Broth, Potato Soup, Rich Brown Soup, Soup à-la-sap, Soup De L'Asperge, Soup Italienne, Soup Maigre, Spinach Soup, Tomato Soup, Vegetable Soup, Winter Vegetable Soup

3 Main Courses   42
Beef   42

Beef a-la-Mode, Beef Bouilli, Beef-Collops, Beef With Baked Potatoes, Beef Stew, Chitterlings or Calf's Tripe, Broiled Beef-Steaks or Rump Steaks, Broil Beef Steaks, French Beef, Calf's Heart, Fry Calf's Liver, To Stuff and Roast A Calf's Liver, English Dish of Beefsteak and Onions, Fried Steaks, Beef À La Braise, Beef Steaks, A La Francaise, Beef Steaks A La Parisienne, Fry Beefsteaks, Fried Steaks and Onions, Beef Steaks With Mushrooms, Beef Steaks Rolled and Roasted, Fried Rump-Steak, Beef-Steaks with Fried Potatoes, Italian Beef-Steaks, Jerked Beef, Larded Calf's Liver, Mock Hare, Beef-Steak Pie, Beef Ragout, Roast Beef, Stew a Rump of Beef, Beef Steaks, Broil Beefsteaks, Rump of Beef Stew, Stewed Rump Another Way, Beef, or Veal Stewed with Apples, Stew Cold Corned Beef, Salt Beef, Scotch Kail

Pork   57

Black Puddings, Broiled Rashers of Bacon, Cure Hams, Bake A Ham, To Stuff A Ham Economical Dish, French Ham Pie, Fillet of Pork to Resemble Veal, Melt Lard, Liver Pudding, Tongue Pie, Leg of Pork Roasted, Roast A Loin of Pork, Pig's Feet Fried, Spare Rib, Roast a Spare Rib, Roast a Sucking Pig, Stew Pork, Pork Cheese, Pork Chops Grilled or Broiled, Pork Chops, Pork Cutlets, Pork Cutlets, Pork Cutlets or Chops, Pork Steaks, Sausages, Sausage to Eat Cold, Tongue Toast

Chicken and Fowl   68

Chicken Croquets and Rissoles, Chicken or Fowl Patties, Chicken Gumbo, Chickens Stewed Whole, Curried Fowl, Fricasseed Chickens, Fried Fowls, French Chicken Cutlets, French Chicken Pie, Fowl A La Hollandaise, Poulet A La Marengo, Chicken Pudding, A Favourite Virginia Dish, Pull Chickens, Rice Chicken Pie, Roast Chickens

Fish   75

Anchovy Toast, Baked Carp, To Stew Carp, Baked Fish, Chowder, Clam Pie, Cod's Head and Shoulders, Halibut Cutlets, Fry Fish, Fry Fish, Lobster, Boiled Lobster, Matelote of Fish (English), Soused Mackerel, Stew Fish White, Fried Oysters, Oyster Loaves, Oyster Pie, Stew Oysters, Perch Stewed With Wine, Perch With Wine, Bake Pike, Baked Salmon-Trout, Baked Salmon, Salmon Baked In Slices, Roasted Salmon, Roast Shad-(Sea-Shore Receipt), Bake Smelts, Fry Smelts, Fry Trout, Stewed Trout

4   Side Dishes and Salads   87

Asparagus Loaves, Asparagus Pudding, Baked Beans-Yankee Fashion, Baked Potatoes, Baked Tomatoes, Beet Roots, Boiled Cauliflowers, Brain Balls, Buttered Parsnips, Buttered Swedish Turnips, Cabbage, Cabbage, Carrots In The German Way, Cauliflower Dressed Like Macaroni, Cauliflower Maccaroni, Cauliflowers With Parmesan Cheese, Cauliflower in White Sauce, Cold Slaw, Cucumbers A La Poulette, Cucumbers Stewed, Egg Balls, Egg Plant, French Spinach, Fricassee of Parsnips, Fried Artichokes, Fried Cauliflower, Fried Celery, Fry Potatoes, Greens, Green Corn Pudding, Green Peas A La Francaise, Lettuce Peas, Macaroni As Usually Served, Macaroni Gratin, Onion Custard, Peas and Bacon, Boiled Salad, Potato Salad, Roast Onions, Russian or Swedish Turnips, Squashes, Sour Kraut, Spinach, Stew Celery, Stewed Eggplant, Stewed Green Peas, Stewed Red Cabbage, Succotash, Succotash, á La Tecumsah, Turnips, Warm Slaw

5   Wild Game   104

A Nice Way of Cooking Game, To Boil Ducks With Onion Sauce , To Make Onion Sauce, Hashed Duck, Ragout A Duck Whole, Roast Ducks, Salmis of Wild Duck, Stew Canvas-Back Ducks, Stew Ducks, Stewed Wild Ducks, Boil Fowl with Rice, Braise (Fowl), Davenport Fowls, Fowl and Oysters, Game Soup, Baked Goose, Roast Goose, Hare, Rabbit, or Partridge Soup, Jugged Hare, Roasted Hare, Roast Hare, Partridges In Pears, Stew Pigeons, Pheasant Cutlets, Roast Pheasants, Cook Pigeons, Pigeons, Boiled Rabbit, Fricaseed Rabbits, Boned Turkey, Venison, Stewed Venison, Venison Pasty

6   Ketchups, Sauces, Gravies, Salad Dressings   118

Apple Sauce, for Goose and Roast Pork, Benton Sauce, for Hot or Cold Roast Beef, Bread Sauce for A Roast Fowl, Brown Onion Sauce, Camp Ketchup, Caper Sauce, Celery Sauce, Chestnut Sauce, Cold Sweet Sauce, Cucumber Catchup, Egg Sauce for Roast Fowls, Fish Sauce, Brown Gravy for Fowl, Ham Gravy, Ham Sauce, A L'Hollandaise, Horseradish Sauce, Kitchiner's Fish Sauce, Lemon Catchup, Liver Sauce, La Magnonnaise, Marinade to Baste Roast, Meats, Mayonnaise, Melted Butter, Mint Sauce for Veal or Mutton, Mushroom Catsup, Very Fine Mushroom Sauce for Fowls, or Rabbits, Very Rich Mushroom Sauce for Fowls or Rabbits, French Mustard, To Make Mustard, Orange Gravy Sauce, Parsley Sauce, Parsley Sauce, Peach Sauce, Pink Sauce, Quin's Sauce, Roux, Sauce for a Pig, Scotch Sauce, Superlative Sauce, Tomato Catsup, Tomato Ketchup, Tomato Ketchup, Tomato Sauce, Tomata Soy, Sauce for Wild Fowl, Wine Sauce, Wine Sauce for Mutton, or Venison, Wow Wow Sauce, for Stewed Beef or Bouilli, A Good Sauce for Steaks, Soy, Tarragon Sauce, Basil Vinegar or Wine (No. 397), Vinegar for Salads (No. 395), Walnut Ketchup, White Onion Sauce

7   Jams, Jellies and Preserves   135

Apple Jam, Apple Jelly, Apple Marmalade, Apricot Jam or Marmalade, Blackberry Jam, Calf's Foot Jelly, Cherry Jelly, Clear Apple Jelly, Crab Apples, Cranberry and Rice Jelly, Currant Jelly (Red), Currant Jelly, Damson Jam, Fruit Jelly, Four Fruit Jelly, Gooseberry Jelly, Brandy Grapes, Preserved Mulberries, Orange Butter, Orange Jelly, Peaches Preserved In Brandy, Very Fine Preserved Peaches, Preserve Pears, Pineapple Preserve, Purple Plum.--No. 1, Purple Plum.--No. 2, Preserved Pumpkin, Raspberry Jam.--No. 1, Raspberry Jam.--No. 2, Rhubarb Jam, Jellies Without Fruit, Strawberries, Preserved Strawberries In Wine, Tomato Marmlade, Preserve Watermelon Rind

8 Breads and Biscuits   149

Almond Bread, Batter Bread, Biscuit, Bread, Bread, Bread Muffins, Soyer's Brioche Rolls, Common Bread, Corn Muffins, Crackers, Crumpets, Damascus Biscuits, French Rolls, Ginger Crackers, Hard Biscuits, Johnny Cake, Johnny Cakes, Journey or Jonny Cakes, Johnny Cakes, Rice Journey or Johnny Cake, Kentucky Corn Dodgers, Light Buns, Milk Biscuits, Molasses, Gingerbread, Muffins, Plain and Very Crisp Biscuits, Plain Buns, Rocks, Rolls, Rusks, Rye and Indian Bread, Soda Biscuits, Soda Bread, Spiced Gingerbread, Sour Milk Biscuit Tea Biscuit, Wheat Muffins, To Make Yeast

9 Drinks   163

Non-Alcoholic   163

Apple Water, Boy's Coffee, Carbonated Syrup Water, To Make Chocolate, Chocolate Cream, Ciders-Artificial, OR Cider Without Apples, Cocoa, Cream Nectar Imperial, Cream Soda Without A Fountain, Currant Ice Water, Ginger Pop, Portable Lemonade, Delicious Milk Lemonade, Nectar, Pistachio Cream, Simple Syrup, Sarsaparilla, Spanish Gingerette, Summer Draught

Coffees and Teas   170

Tea Parties, Tea Parties and Evening Company To Make Tea, Apple Tea, Cranberry Tea, Coffee, Coffee, Coffee, To Roast, Making Coffee, Very Simple Method of Making Coffee, Essence of Coffee, Milk Coffee, Substitute for Milk or Cream In Tea or Coffee

Alcoholic Drinks   178

How To Brew Your Own Beer, Anniseed Cordial, Champagne-Cup, Codlin Cream, Corn Beer Without Yeast, Country Syllabub, Ginger Wine, Hippocras, Hydromel, Or Mead, Lemon Brandy, Orange Brandy, Excellent Orange Cream, Raspberry Brandy, Raspberry Cordial, Rhubarb Wine, Sassafras Beer, Strawberry Cordial, Whiskey Cordial

10   Holidays   187

Pound Cake, Broiled Fowl or Rabbit, New-Year's Cookies, Secrets, Lavender Water, Scented Bags, Violet Perfume, Chocolate Custard, To Corn Beef In Hot Weather, Lent Potatoes, Cross-Buns, Pancakes for Shrove Tuesday, Passover Cakes, Election Cake, To Roast A Turkey, Cranberry Sauce, Egg Nog, Fruit Cake, Practical Housewife's Christmas Ham, Christmas Goose Pie, Christmas Pie, Christmas Plum Pudding, Sweet Pudding Sauce, Roast Chestnuts

11   For the Sick   204

Mutton Stewed and Soup for One Hundred Men, Beef Soup, Beef Tea, Six Pints, Thick Beef Tea, Chicken Broth, Rice Water, Barley Water, Crimean Lemonade, Citric Acid Lemonade, French Raspberry Vinegar (for a Cold), Gargle for Sore Throat, Rice Gruel (for Bowl Complaints), Chronic Gout-To Cure, Lemonade, Nourishing, For Fever Patients, Prof. Hufeland's Drink for Fever Patients OR Excessive Thirst, 3 Ways To Purify Air In A Sick Room, Camphor Ice-For Chapping Hands or Lips, Warts and Corns-To Cure In Ten Minutes, A Soothing Ointment, For A Headache, For A Cold, Relief of Sore Throat, Corns, Egg Gruel for Dysentery

| 12 | Dishes The Soldiers Ate | 214 |

Sloosh (Coosh), Coffee for One Hundred Men, One Pint Each, Fresh Beef Soup for One Hundred Men, Soyer's Stew For One Hundred Men, Suet Dumplings, To Fry Meat, To Cook Salt Beef or Pork, Salt Beef or Pork With Mashed Beans, For One Hundred Men

Measurements and Definitions	218
Bibliography	222
Index	228

INTRODUCTION

"Everything was propitious, the most perfect of days and the old place in great beauty. Those large rooms were delightful for dancing; we had as good a dinner as mortal appetite could crave; the best fish, fowl, and game; wine from a cellar that can not be excelled."
-Mary Boykin Chesnut

Food sustains us. The fact that we enjoy the way it tastes is a gift from God. The diversity of food, from how it is prepared, spiced and seasoned is an art. This art can be replicated by anyone with the proper utensils, a fire and the ability to follow directions. This book is written with the desire that it be used to enjoy and teach the culinary history and flavors of our ancestors. In other words, it is written for curious cooks looking for something "new", for people interested in history, for novice cooks, experienced cooks, hunters and fishermen. It is written for those who grow their own gardens to make simple to elegant side dishes or salads. It is written for growers of fruits who find making their own jelly to be a thing of pride. In short, it is written for anyone interested in cooking, period!

In this volume, as in the first, dishes for breakfasts, soups, main courses, side dishes, drinks, ketchups and sauces, breads and dishes the soldiers ate have all been expanded upon. In addition to those subjects, recipes for Wild Game, Jams and Jellies and Foods and Remedies for the Sick are explored. With an eye on Civil War era society, instruction for Tea Parties and evening guests, from period sources, has been included. Another interesting item is the instruction for brewing beer in the Nineteenth century. As hunting was a primary way to put food on the table, it became necessary to include recipes for wild game.

As with the first volume of *Voices From the Kitchen,* this book is not a comical "Hillbilly" recipe compilation as hawked in souvenir shops for tourists. All recipes come from a variety of period cookbooks. None are contrived. To "make up" recipes is to be misleading. As such, with each recipe, I have cited the period source from which it is taken. This gives credibility to the research involved. Also included is a "Measurements and Definitions" section. This is necessary so as to provide the reader with, for example, the temperature definition of a "Slow Oven", as well as various conversions of 19th century weights and measures compared to the "modern" understanding of those terms. It is believed that this will encourage readers to prepare the recipes. After all, this book is meant to be used.

While the "Heart" of this book is in the recipes, the "Soul" is in the "Voices" of the soldiers and civilians from whom the quotations are taken. They lived the cruel hardships of war. Some survived, forever scarred by their experience. Some died in the defense of freedom. As you read the quotes, I hope you feel, in your heart, the context, celebration and pain of their recollections. Remember their hunger, their distance from families, the monotony of camp life, their unimaginable participation in the horrors of combat. In short, remember the fact that they once lived, giving us a history, making us who we are today, not only as a Nation, but as individuals. "They" are "us". They made us. We honor them by never forgetting them and by keeping history, their memory, alive.

"I am sorry to hear that the yanks have been through our country again but I hope they have left you all enough to live on yet."- Corporal Burr J. Caldwell, Co. D, 22nd Mississippi Infantry, July 22, 1864, near LaGrange, Georgia. Letter to his wife Sarah (Sallie).

"Aunt Betsy & Uncle Harvey wanted me to see if you all could spare them a barrel of salt." -Pvt. James F. Currie (of Lauderdale County, Tennessee) of Co. M, 7th Tennessee (Confederate) Cavalry (a.k.a. "Duckworth's Cavalry"), Abbeville, Mississippi, June 2, 1864. Letter to his wife, Kate. There is some possibility that James Currie was killed before the end of the Civil War.

The seeds of the idea for this book were planted by my father, John Wayne Flowers, when he and my mother Melody took me to Tennessee for the first time when I was six years old, visiting a family that had been in the South since the 1600's. In subsequent trips, we continued to eat fantastic home cooked meals, visit historical sites and fish the Hatchie and Mississippi Rivers and Cold Creek in Lauderdale County, Tennessee. As I grew, I began to appreciate the Southern style of cooking from my grandmother, Lula Mae Flowers, who could make Fried Chicken, biscuits, Cornbread, Bread Pudding, etc., from memory, the way her mother taught her as she learned it from her mother, born around the time of the Civil War. Food is my connection to history!

About fifteen years ago, I became a Civil War reenactor, rising to the rank of Corporal in Scott's Tennessee Battery. Doing this blessed me with "Pards", guys that I've campaigned with in intense heat, bitter cold and snow, rain and sunshine. We've shared many a great, period correct meal, an abundance of laughs, numerous 150th Civil War Battle anniversary National events and hundreds of "local" events. We have become good friends outside of the reenacting world; Brothers In Arms that I can count on when I need a Pard to share a tear or to celebrate a life event. They've always been there when I needed them, I hope they can say the same of me.

Notes on Font and Spelling

All direct quotes from soldiers and civilians are in italics with quotation marks. All other text in italics reflect an author's note.

In quotations and in all recipes, I have kept the spelling as I found it from the original source. This was done in order to preserve the integrity of the original writing and to illustrate to the reader what may have been either common spellings or errors (i.e from diary/letter writing) of the day in which they were written.

1. Breakfast

"As soon as we arrived Lieutenant Brown directed me to inform the men that they could either have their rations issued to them and cook them themselves, or pay for our breakfasts at the hotel. The men unanimously elected to pay for their breakfasts, which was served in about an hour." – Pvt. T. Roberts Baker, Second Howitzer Company of Richmond, Va. May, 1861. Diary entry

"All have plenty to eat and a better, satisfied crowd I never saw. The rations that we draw are plenty and I have heard no complains at all……. As far as suffering for anything to eat is concerned, its all foolish talk. There is not a man but what has as much as he wants. Yesterday morning for breakfast, one of the mess baked splendid cornbread and fried a pan full of No. 1 meat, and I enjoyed it as well as any meal I ever eat." – Pvt. Augustus Alexander Clewell, Company B, 1st Battalion Sharpshooters Regiment North Carolina, Camp 1st North Carolina Battery, Kingston, North Carolina, April 7, 1864. Letter to his mother

Apple Pancakes
From "The Practical Housekeeper; A Cyclopedia of Domestic Economy", By Elizabeth Fries Ellet, 1857

Mix two large spoonfuls of flour in a cup of milk or wine; when smooth add eight eggs, some pounded cinnamon, grated lemon-peel, a handful of currants, and six or eight apples peeled and chopped: mix it all well together; melt some butter in a frying-pan; when hot pour the whole mass in, and fry it on both sides: serve it stewed with pounded cinnamon and sugar very hot.

Buckwheat Cakes
From "The Practical Housekeeper; A Cyclopedia of Domestic Economy", By Elizabeth Fries Ellet, 1857

Mix a quart of buckwheat flour with a pint of lukewarm milk, (water will do, but is not as good,) and a teacup of yeast--set it in a warm place to rise. When light, (which will be in the course of eight or ten hours if family yeast is used, if brewer's yeast is used they will rise much quicker,) add a teaspoonful of salt --if sour, the same quantity of saleratus dissolved in a little milk, and strained. If they are too thick, thin them with cold milk or water. Bake them with just fat enough to prevent their sticking to the griddle.

Cream Pancakes
From "The Complete Cook", By J. M. Sanderson, 1864

Mix the yolks of two eggs, well beaten, with a pint of cream, two ounces of sifted sugar, a little nutmeg, cinnamon, and mace. Rub the pan with a bit of butter, and fry the pan cakes thin.

Crepes
From "The Practical Housekeeper; A Cyclopedia of Domestic Economy", By Elizabeth Fries Ellet, 1857

Make a batter with flour, milk and eggs, adding brandy and orange-flower water. In two or three hours afterwards, melt a piece of butter or lard, the size of a walnut, in a frying-pan, pour in some batter, and shake it over the pan. "When done on one side, turn it over; when the other side is done, dish it and keep hot till the others are done, sifting sugar over each.

Soft Crullers
From "The Lady's Receipt-Book; a Useful Companion for Large or Small Families", By Eliza Leslie, 1847

Sift three quarters of a pound of flour, and powder half a pound of loaf-sugar. Heat a pint of water in a round-bottomed sauce-pan, and when quite warm, mix the flour with it gradually. Set half a pound of fresh butter over the fire in a small vessel; and when it begins to melt, stir it gradually into the flour and water. Then add by degrees the powdered sugar, and half a grated nutmeg. Take the sauce-pan off the fire, and beat the contents, with a wooden spaddle or spatula, till they are thoroughly mixed. Then beat six eggs very light, and stir them gradually into the mixture. Beat the whole very hard, till it becomes a thick batter. Flour a paste-board very well, and lay out the batter upon it in rings, (the best way is to pass it through a screw funnel.) Have ready, on the fire, a pot of boiling lard of the very best quality. Put in the crullers, removing them from the board by carefully taking them up, one at a time, on a broad-bladed knife. Boil but a few at a time. They must be of a fine brown. Lift them out on a perforated skimmer, draining the lard from them back into the pot. Lay them on a large dish, and sift powdered white sugar over them.

Soft crullers cannot be made in warm weather.

Walnut Hill's Doughnuts
From "Miss Beecher's Domestic Receipt Book",
By Catharine Esther Beecher, 1850

One tea-cup of sour cream, or milk. Two tea-cups of sugar. One tea-cup of butter. Four eggs, and one nutmeg. Two teaspoonfuls of saleratus. Flour enough to roll.
Cut into diamond cakes, and boil in hot lard.

Dutch Pancakes
From "The Practical Housekeeper; A Cyclopedia of Domestic Economy", By Elizabeth Fries Ellet, 1857

Mix one pound of flour with a half a pound of sugar and a table-spoonful of cinnamon in powder; make it into a paste with ten eggs and two glasses of white wine, or one each of wine and brandy; when well mixed, roll it out and fry like other pancakes.

Fried Eggs and Bacon
From "A Plain Cookery Book for the Working Classes", By Charles Elme Francatelli, 1852

First, fry the rashers of bacon, and then break the eggs into the frying-pan without disturbing the yolks, and as soon as these are just set, or half-done, slip them out on to the rashers of bacon which you have already placed in a dish.

Eggs and Bread
From "A Poetical Cookbook", By Maria J. Moss, 1864

Put half a handful of breadcrumbs into a saucepan, with a small quantity of cream, sugar, and nutmeg, and let it stand till the bread has imbibed all the cream; then break ten eggs into it, and having beaten them up together, fry it like an omelet.

Eggs A La Maitre D'Hotel
From "The Book of Household Management", By Isabella Beeton, 1861

1/4 lb. of fresh butter, 1 tablespoonful of flour, 1/2 pint of milk, pepper and salt to taste, 1 tablespoonful of minced parsley, the juice of 1/2 lemon, 6 eggs.

Put the flour and half the butter into a stewpan; stir them over the fire until the mixture thickens; pour in the milk, which should be boiling; add a seasoning of pepper and salt, and simmer the whole for 5 minutes. Put the remainder of the butter into the sauce, and add the minced parsley; then boil the eggs hard, strip off the shells, cut the eggs into quarters, and put them on a dish. Bring the sauce to the boiling-point, add the lemon-juice, pour over the eggs, and serve.

Time-5 minutes to boil the sauce; the eggs, 10 to 15 minutes.

Eggs with Brown Butter
From "A Plain Cookery Book for the Working Classes", By Charles Elme Francatelli, 1852

Cook the eggs as directed in the foregoing Number, and when you have slipped them out on to a dish, put a piece of butter into the frying-pan, and stir it on the fire until it becomes quite brown (not burnt); then add two table-spoonfuls of vinegar, pepper, and salt; boil
for two minutes, and pour this over the eggs.

Eggs Stewed with Cheese
From "A Plain Cookery Book for the Working Classes", By Charles Elme Francatelli, 1852

Fry three eggs in a pan with one ounce of butter, seasoned with pepper and salt, and when the eggs are just set firm at the bottom of the pan, slip them off on to a dish, cover them all over with some very thin slices of cheese, set the dish before the fire to melt the cheese, and
then eat this cheap little tit-bit with some toast.

Ham and Eggs Fried
From "The Practical Housekeeper; A Cyclopedia of Domestic Economy", by Elizabeth Fries Ellet, 1857

Cut some nice slices of ham, put them in a frying-pan; cover them with hot water, and set the pan over the fire. Let it boil up once or twice; then take out the slices and throw out the water; put a bit of lard in the pan; dip the slices in wheat flour or finely rolled crackers, and when the fat is hot, put them into the pan; sprinkle a little popper over; when both sides are a fine brown, take them on a steak dish; put a little boiling water into the pan, and put it in the dish with the meat. Now put a bit of lard the size of a large egg into the pan; add a salt-spoonful to it; let it become hot; break six or eight eggs carefully into a bowl; then slip them into the hot lard; set the pan over a gentle fire. When the white be gins to set, pass a knife-blade, so as to divide an equal quantity of white to each yolk; cut it entirely through to the pan, that they may cook the more quickly, When done, take each one up with a skimmer spoon, and lay them in a chain around the edge of the meat on the dish. Fried eggs should not be turned in the pan.

Fried Ham and Eggs (A Breakfast Dish)
From "The Book of Household Management", By Isabella Beeton, 1861

Ham; eggs.
Cut the ham into slices, and take care that they are of the same thickness in every part. Cut off the rind, and if the ham should be particularly hard and salt, it will be found an improvement to soak it for about 10 minutes in hot water, and then dry it in a cloth. Put it
   into a cold frying-pan, set it over the fire, and turn the slices 3 or 4 times whilst they are cooking. When done, place them on a dish, which should be kept hot in front of the fire during the time the eggs are being poached.
Poach the eggs, slip them on to the slices of ham, and serve quickly.
Time-7 or 8 minutes to broil the ham.

Slices of Ham or Bacon
From "The Complete Cook", By J. M. Sanderson, 1864

Ham or bacon may be fried, or broiled on a gridiron over a clear fire, or toasted with a fork; take care to slice it of the same thickness in every part. If you wish it curled, cut it in slices about two inches long (if longer, the outside will be done too much before the inside is done enough); roll it up, and put a little wooden skewer through it; put it in a cheese-toaster, or dutch oven, for eight or ten minutes,

turning it as it gets crisp. This is considered the handsomest way of dressing bacon; but we like it best uncurled, because it is crisper and more equally done. Slices of ham or bacon should not be more than half a quarter of an inch thick, and will eat much more mellow if soaked in hot water for a quarter of an hour, and then dried in a cloth before they are broiled. If you have any cold bacon, you may make a very nice dish of it, by cutting it into slices of about a quarter of an inch thick; grate some crusts of bread, as directed for ham, and powder them well with it on both sides; lay the rashers in a cheese-toaster--they will be brown on one side in about three minutes--turn them, and do the other. These are delicious accompaniaments to poached or fried eggs. The
bacon having been boiled first, is tender and mellow. They are an excellent garnish round veal cutlets, or sweetbread, or calf's head hash, or green peas, or beans, &c.

Hashed Beef
From "Directions for Cookery, in its Various Branches" By Eliza Leslie, 1840

Take some roast beef that has been very much under-done, and having cut off the fat and skin, put the trimmings with the bones broken up into a stew-pan with two large onions sliced, a few sliced potatoes, and a bunch of sweet herbs. Add about a pint of warm water, or broth if you have it. This is to make the gravy. Cover it closely, and let it simmer for about an hour. Then skim and strain it, carefully removing every particle of fat.

Take another stew-pot, and melt in it a piece of butter, about the size of a large walnut. When it has melted, shake in a spoonful of flour. Stir it a few minutes, and then add to it the strained gravy. Let it come to a boil, and then put to it a table-spoonful of catchup, and the beef cut either in thin small slices or in mouthfuls. Let it simmer from five to ten minutes, but do not allow it to boil, lest (having been cooked already) it should become tasteless and insipid. Serve it up in a deep dish with thin slices of toast cut into triangular or pointed pieces, the crust omitted. Dip the toast in the gravy, and lay the pieces in regular order round the sides of the dish.

You may hash mutton or veal in the same manner, adding sliced carrots, turnips, potatoes, or any vegetables you please. Tomatas are an improvement.

To hash cold meat is an economical way of using it; but there is little or no nutriment in it after being twice cooked, and the natural flavour is much impaired by the process.

Hashed meat would always be much better if the slices were cut from the joint or large piece as soon as it leaves the table, and soaked in the gravy till next day.

Indian Batter Cakes
From "Directions for Cookery, in its Various Branches" By Eliza Leslie, 1840

Mix together a quart of sifted Indian meal, (the yellow meal is best for all purposes,) and a handful of wheat flour. Warm a quart of milk, and stir into it a small tea-spoonful of salt, and two large table-spoonfuls of the best fresh yeast. Beat three eggs very light, and stir them gradually into the milk in turn with the meal. Cover it, and set it to rise for three or four hours. When quite light, bake it on a griddle in the manner of buckwheat cakes. Butter them, cut them across, and send them to table hot, with molasses in a sauce-boat.

If the batter should chance to become sour before it is baked, stir in about a salt-spoonful of pearl-ash dissolved in a little lukewarm water; and let it set half an hour longer before it is baked.

Kedgeree For Breakfast
From "The Practical Housekeeper; A Cyclopedia of Domestic Economy", By Elizabeth Fries Ellet, 1857

Boil two tablespoonfuls of rice, add any fish previously cooked (salmon or turbot is preferable), and nicely picked; beat up an egg well, and stir it in just before serving. The egg must not boil.

Kentucky Batter Cakes
From "The Lady's Receipt-Book; a Useful Companion for Large or Small Families", By Eliza Leslie, 1847

Sift a quart of yellow indian meal into a large pan; mix with it two large table-spoonfuls of wheat flour, and a salt-spoonful of salt. Warm a pint and a half of rich milk in a small sauce-pan, but do not let it come to a boil. When it begins to simmer, take it off the fire, and put into it two pieces of fresh butter, each about the size of a hen's egg. Stir the butter into the warm milk till it melts, and is well mixed. Then stir in the meal, gradually, and set the mixture to cool. Beat four eggs, very light, and add them, by degrees, to the mixture, stirring the whole very hard. If you find it too thin, add a little more corn-meal.

Have ready a griddle heated over the fire, and bake the batter on it, in the manner of buckwheat-cakes. Send them to table hot, and eat them with butter, to which you may add molasses or honey.

Oeufs Au Plat, or Au Miroir, Served on the Dish in which they are Cooked
From "The Book of Household Management", By Isabella Beeton, 1861

4 eggs, 1 oz. of butter, pepper and salt to taste.
Butter a dish rather thickly with good fresh butter; melt it, break the eggs into it the same as for poaching, sprinkle them with white pepper and fine salt, and put the remainder of the butter, cut into very small pieces, on the top of them. Put the dish on a hot plate, or in the oven, or before the fire, and let it remain until the whites become set, but not hard, when serve immediately, placing the dish they were cooked in on another. To hasten the cooking of the eggs, a salamander may be held over them for a minute; but great care must be taken that they are not too much done. This is an exceedingly nice dish, and one very easily prepared for breakfast.
Time-3 minutes.

Another Omlette
From "The Great Western Cook Book, or Table Receipts, Adapted to Western Housewifery", By Anna Maria Collins, 1857

Boil the eggs ten minutes, and let them lie a little while in cold water. Then roll them lightly on the table, and they will peel without breaking; cut them in half, and have ready a sauce, made of two ounces of butter and flour rubbed together on a plate, and put it in a stewpan with three-quarters of a pint of new milk. Set it on the fire, and stir it till it boils. If it is not quite smooth, strain it through a sieve. Chop some parsley and a clove of eschallot very fine, and put it in your sauce. Season it with salt, to your taste; put in a little mace and lemon-peel. Place the eggs on a dish with the yolks upward, and pour the sauce over them.

Oyster Omelet
From "The Lady's Receipt-Book; a Useful Companion for Large or Small Families", By Eliza Leslie, 1847

Having strained the liquor from twenty-five oysters of the largest size, mince them
small; omitting the hard part or gristle. If you cannot get large oysters, you should have forty or fifty small ones. Break into a shallow pan six, seven, or eight eggs, according to the quantity of minced oysters. Omit half the whites, and, (having beaten the eggs till very light, thick, and smooth,) mix the oysters

gradually into them, adding a little cayenne pepper, and some powdered nutmeg. Put three ounces or more of the best fresh butter into a small frying-pan, if you have no pan especially for omelets. Place it over a clear fire, and when the butter (which should be previously cut up) has come to a boil, put in the omelet-mixture; stir it till it begin to set; and fry it a light brown, lifting the edge several times by slipping a knife under it, and taking care not to cook it too much or it will shrivel and become tough. When done, clap a large hot plate or dish on the top of the omelet, and turn it quickly and carefully out of the pan. Fold it over; and serve it up immediately. It is a fine breakfast dish. This quantity will make one large or two small omelets.

Clam omelets may be made as above.

An omelet-pan should be smaller than a common frying-pan, and lined with tin. In a large pan the omelet will spread too much, and become thin like a pancake.

Never turn an omelet while frying, as that will make it heavy and tough. When done, brown it by holding a red-hot shovel or salamander close above the top. Excellent omelets may be made of cold boiled ham, or smoked tongue; grated or minced small, mixed with a sufficiency of beaten eggs, and fried in butter.

To Make A Plain Omelet
From "The Book of Household Management", By Isabella Beeton, 1861

6 eggs, 1 saltspoonful of salt, 1/3 saltspoonful of pepper, 1/4 lb. of butter. Break the eggs into a basin, omitting the whites of 3, and beat them up with the salt and pepper until extremely light; then add 2 oz. of the butter broken into small pieces, and stir this into the mixture. Put the other 2 oz. of butter into a frying-pan, make it quite hot, and, as soon as it begins to bubble, whisk the eggs, &c. very briskly for a minute or two, and pour them into the pan; stir the omelet with a spoon one way until the mixture thickens and becomes firm, and when the whole is set, fold the edges over, so that the omelet assumes an oval form; and when it is nicely brown on one side, and quite firm, it is done. To take off the rawness on the upper side, hold the pan before the fire for a minute or two, and brown it with a salamander or hot shovel. Serve very expeditiously on a very hot dish, and never cook it until it is just wanted. The flavour of this omelet may be very much enhanced by adding minced parsley, minced onion or eschalot, or grated cheese, allowing 1 tablespoonful of the former, and half the quantity of the latter, to the above proportion of eggs. Shrimps or oysters may also be added: the latter should be scalded in their liquor, and then bearded and cut into small pieces. In making an omelet, be particularly careful that it is not too thin, and, to avoid this, do not

make it in too large a frying-pan, as the mixture would then spread too much, and taste of the outside. It should also not be greasy, burnt, or too much done, and should be cooked over a gentle fire, that the whole of the substance may be heated without drying up the outside. Omelets are sometimes served with gravy; but *this should never be poured over them*, but served in a tureen, as the liquid causes the omelet to become heavy and flat, instead of eating light and soft. In making the gravy, the flavour should not overpower that of the omelet, and should be thickened with arrowroot or rice flour.

Time-With 6 eggs, in a frying-pan 18 or 20 inches round, 4 to 6 minutes.

Omlette Souffle
From "The Great Western Cook Book, or Table Receipts, Adapted to Western Housewifery", By Anna Maria Collins, 1857

Take six eggs, separate the yolks and the whites, and beat half a pound of crushed sugar into the yolks. Beat them well, and put in enough essence of lemon to flavor them. Let the whites of twelve eggs be beaten to a froth; beat it all together till quite light, put it in a buttered dish that it will just fill, and bake it fifteen minutes. It must be used immediately, before it falls.

Young Corn Omelet
From "The Lady's Receipt-Book; a Useful Companion for Large or Small Families", By Eliza Leslie, 1847

To a dozen ears of fine young Indian corn allow five eggs. Boil the corn a quarter of an hour; and then, with a large grater, grate it down from the cob. Beat the eggs very light, and then stir gradually the grated corn into the pan of eggs. Add a small salt-spoon of salt, and a very little cayenne. Put into a hot frying-pan equal quantities of lard and fresh butter, and stir them well together, over the fire. When they boil, put in the mixture thick, and fry it; afterwards browning the top with a red-hot shovel, or a salamander. Transfer it, when done, to a heated dish, but do not fold it over. It will be found excellent. This is a good way of using boiled corn that has been left from dinner the preceding day.

To Poach Eggs
From "Directions for Cookery, in its Various Branches" By Eliza Leslie, 1840

Pour some boiling water out of a tea kettle through a clean cloth spread over the top of a broad stew-pan; for by observing this process the eggs will be nicer and more easily done than when its impurities remain in the water. Set the pan with the strained water on hot coals, and when it boils break each egg separately into a saucer. Remove the pan from the fire, and slip the eggs one by one into the surface of the water. Let the pan stand till the white of the eggs is set; then place it again on the coals, and as soon as the water boils again, the eggs will be sufficiently done. Take them out carefully with an egg-slice, and trim off all the ragged edges from the white, which should thinly cover the yolk. Have ready some thin slices of buttered toast with the crust cut off. Lay them in the bottom of the dish, with a poached egg on each slice of toast, and send them to the breakfast table.

Common Pancakes
From "A New System of Domestic Cookery", By Maria Eliza Ketelby Rundell, 1807

Make a light batter of eggs, flour, and milk. Fry in a small pan, in hot dripping or lard. Salt, or nutmeg and ginger, may be added.
Sugar and lemon should he served to cat with them. Or, when eggs are scarce, make the batter with flour, and small beer, ginger, &c. or clean snow, with flour, and a very little milk, will serve as well as egg.

Fine Pancakes, Fried without Butter or Lard
From "A New System of Domestic Cookery", By Maria Eliza Ketelby Rundell, 1807

Beat six fresh eggs extremely well; mix, when strained, with a pint of cream, four ounces of sugar, a glass of wine, half a nutmeg grated, and as much flour as will make it almost as thick as ordinary pancake batter, but not quite. Heat the frying-pan tolerably hot, wipe it with a clean cloth; then pour in the batter, to make thin pancakes.

New-England Pancakes
From "A New System of Domestic Cookery", By Maria Eliza Ketelby Rundell, 1807

Mix a pint of cream, five spoonfuls of fine flour, seven yolks and four whiles of eggs, and a very little salt; try them very thin in fresh butter, and between each strew sugar and cinnamon. Send up six or eight at once.

Pancakes of Rice
From "A New System of Domestic Cookery", By Maria Eliza Ketelby Rundell, 1807

Boil half a pound of rice to a jelly in a small quantity of water; when cold, mix it with a pint of cream, eight eggs, a bit of salt and nutmeg: stir in eight ounces of butter just warmed, and add as much flour as will make the batter thick enough. Fry in as little lard or dripping as possible.

Richer Pancakes
From "The Book of Household Management", By Isabella Beeton, 1861

6 eggs, 1 pint of cream, 1/4 lb. of loaf sugar, 1 glass of sherry, 1/2 teaspoonful of grated nutmeg, flour.

Ascertain that the eggs are extremely fresh, beat them well, strain and mix with them the cream, pounded sugar, wine, nutmeg, and as much flour as will make the batter nearly as thick as that for ordinary pancakes. Make the frying-pan hot, wipe it with a clean cloth, pour in sufficient batter to make a thin pancake, and fry it for about 5 minutes. Dish the pancakes piled one above the other, strew sifted sugar between each, and serve.
Time-About 5 minutes.

Rye Batter Cakes
From "The Lady's Receipt-Book; a Useful Companion for Large or Small Families", By Eliza Leslie, 1847

Beat two eggs very light. Mix them, gradually, with a quart of lukewarm milk, and sufficient rye-meal to make a batter about as thick as for buckwheat-cakes. Then stir in a large table-spoonful of the best brewer's yeast; or twice that quantity, if the yeast is home-made. Cover it, and set it to rise in a warm place. If too thin, add more rye-meal. When quite light, and covered on the surface with bubbles, bake it on a griddle, in the manner of buckwheat cakes. Butter them, and eat them warm, at breakfast or tea.

If you cannot obtain good yeast, and wish to have the cakes ready with as much expedition as possible, you may use patent yeast-powders, according to the directions that accompany them. In this case, the cakes must be baked in half an hour after the powders are mixed into the batter.

Yeast-powders, put in at the last, are an improvement to all sorts of batter-cakes that have been previously raised with good *real* yeast; also to cakes made light by eggs. But to depend *entirely* on the powders, without either real yeast, or eggs, is not well; as the cakes, though *eatable,* are generally too tough and leathery to be wholesome. In cities, fresh yeast, from the brewers, can be obtained every day, at a very trifling cost, during the brewing season; which is usually from October till April. At other seasons, it can be procured from the bakers, or made at home; and should always be used in preference to depending solely on yeast-powders. Though they improve the lightness of batter, for which real yeast or beaten eggs have already been used, they will not, of themselves alone, give it a wholesome degree of either lightness or crispness. Too much dependence on yeast-powders is one reason that the buckwheat-cakes of the present day are so inferior to those of former times, when they were always made with real yeast.

Indian batter-cakes may be made as above.

Potato Omelette
From "The Practical Housekeeper; A Cyclopedia of
Domestic Economy", By Elizabeth Fries Ellet, 1857

May be made with a mashed potato or two ounces of potato-flour and four eggs and seasoned with pepper, salt, and a little nutmeg. It should be made thick, and, being rather substantial, a squeeze of lemon will improve it. Fry a light brown.

2. Soups

Bacon and Cabbage Soup
From "A Plain Cookery Book for the Working Classes", By Charles Elme Francatelli, 1852

When it happens that you have a dinner consisting of bacon and cabbages, you invariably throw away the liquor in which they have been boiled, or, at the best, give it to the pigs, if you possess any; this is wrong, for it is easy to turn it to a better account for your own use, by paying attention to the following instructions, viz.:-- Put your piece of bacon on to boil in a pot with two gallons (more or less, according to the number you have to provide for) of water, when it has boiled up, and has been well skimmed, add the cabbages, kale, greens, or sprouts, whichever may be used, well washed and split down, and also some parsnips and carrots; season with pepper, but _no_ salt, as the bacon will season the soup sufficiently; and when the whole has boiled together very gently for about two hours, take up the bacon surrounded with the cabbage, parsnips, and carrots, leaving a small portion of the vegetables in the soup, and pour this into a large bowl containing slices of bread; eat the soup first, and make it a rule that those who eat most soup are entitled to the largest share of bacon.

Baked Soups
From "The Practical Housekeeper; A Cyclopedia of Domestic Economy", By Elizabeth Fries Ellet, 1857

Take a pound of any lean meat and cut it into dice, place in an earthen jar, or pot, that will hold five quarts of liquid. Slice, and add to it, two onions, two carrots, two ounces of rice washed and previously soaked, a pint of whole or split peas, and some pepper and salt to taste; cover all with a gallon of water, tie a cloth over the top of the jar, or close the lid of the pot down very close, and bake.
This is a cheap and useful soup for poor people, and may be much improved by using the liquor that salt beef, or indeed, any meat has been boiled in, instead of water.
Cheap-for the poor-Soak a quart of split peas for a day in cold water, and then put them into a boiler with two gallons and a half of water, and two pounds of cold boiled potatoes, well bruised, a faggot of herbs, salt, pepper, and two onions sliced. Cover it very close, and boil very *gently* for five hours, or until only two gallons of soup remain.
Another-Take two pounds of shin of beef, a quarter of a pound of barley, a half-penny worth of parsley, two onions sliced, salt and pepper to taste, and having cut the meat into dice, and broken the bone, place in a gallon pot and fill up with water;

boil very gently for five hours. Potatoes, celery tops, cabbage, or any vegetable left from the day before may be added.

Barley Soup
From "The Virginia Housewife", By Mary Randolph, 1860

It on three gills of barley, three quarts of water, few onions cut up, six carrots scraped and cut into dice, an equal quantity of turnips cut small; boil it gently two hours, then put in four or five pounds of the rack or neck of mutton, a few slices of lean ham, with pepper and salt; boil it slowly two hours longer and serve it up. Tomatos are an excellent addition to this soup.

Bean Soup
From "Directions for Cookery, in its Various Branches" By Eliza Leslie, 1840

Put two quarts of dried white beans into soak the night before you make the soup, which should be put on as early in the day as possible.
Take five pounds of the lean of fresh beef--the coarse pieces will do. Cut them up, and put them into your soup-pot with the bones belonging to them, (which should be broken to pieces,) and a pound of bacon cut very small. If you have the remains of a piece of beef that has been roasted the day before, and so much under-done that the juices remain in it, you may put it into the pot, and its bones along with it. Season the meat with pepper and salt, and pour on it six quarts of water. As soon as it boils take off the scum, and put in the beans (having first drained them) and a head of celery cut small, or a table-spoonful of pounded celery-seed. Boil it slowly till the meat is done to shreds, and the beans all dissolved. Then strain it through a cullender into the tureen, and put into it small squares of toasted bread with the crust cut off.
Some prefer it with the beans boiled soft, but not quite dissolved. In this case, do not strain it; but take out the meat and bones with a fork before you send it to table.

Bouillabaisse Soup
From "A Plain Cookery Book for the Working Classes", By Charles Elme Francatelli, 1852

Put the following ingredients into a saucepan to boil on the fire:--four onions and six tomatoes, or red love-apples, cut in thin slices, some thyme and winter savory, a little salad-oil, a wine-glassful of vinegar, pepper and salt, and a pint of water to each person. When the soup has boiled fifteen minutes, throw in your fish, cut in pieces or slices, and, as soon as the fish is done, eat the soup with some crusts of bread or toast in it. All kinds of fish suit this purpose.

Bouillon
From "The Practical Housekeeper; A Cyclopedia of Domestic Economy", By Eliza Fries Ellet, 1857

Is the *common soup* of France, and is in use in almost every French family. Put into an earthen stock-pot in the proportion of one pound of beef to one quart of cold water. Place it on the side of the fire, and let it become slowly hot. By so doing the fibre of the meat is enlarged, the gelatine is dissolved, and the savorous parts of the meat are diffused through the broth. When the object is simply to make a good, pure-flavored beef broth, part of the shin or leg will answer the purpose, adding some vegetables, and letting it stew four or five hours; but if the meat is to be eaten, the rump or leg-of-mutton piece should be used.

Broth Made From Bones for Soup
From "A Plain Cookery Book for the Working Classes", By Charles Elme Francatelli, 1852

Fresh bones are always to be purchased from butchers at about a farthing per pound; they must be broken up small, and put into a boiling-pot with a quart of water to every pound of bones; and being placed on the fire, the broth must be well skimmed, seasoned with pepper and salt, a few carrots, onions, turnips, celery, and thyme, and boiled very gently for six hours; it is then to be strained off, and put back into the pot, with any bits of meat or gristle which may have fallen from the bones (the bones left are still worth a farthing per pound, and can be sold to the bone-dealers). Let this broth be thickened with peasemeal or oatmeal, in the proportion of a large table-spoonful to every pint of broth, and stirred over the fire while boiling for twenty-five minutes, by which time the soup will be done. It will be apparent to all good housewives that, with a little trouble and good management, a savoury and substantial meal may thus be prepared for a mere trifle.

Cabbage Soup
From "The Practical Housekeeper; A Cyclopedia of Domestic Economy", By Elizabeth Fries Ellet, 1857

Take four or six pounds of beef, boil with it some black pepper whole for three hours, cut three or four cabbages in quarters, boil them until they are quite tender, turn them into a dish, and serve all together.

Carrot Soup
From "A New System of Domestic Cookery", By Maria Eliza Ketelby Rundell, 1807

Put some beef-bones, with four quarts of the liquor in which a leg of mutton or beef has been boiled, two large onions, a turnip, pepper, and salt, into a sauce-pan, and stew for three hours. Have ready six large carrots scraped and cut thin; strain the soup on them, and stew them till soft enough to pulp through a hair sieve or coarse cloth: then boil the pulp with the soup, which is to be as thick as peas-soup. Use two wooden spoons fo rub the carrots through. Make the soup the day before it is to be used. Add Cayenne. Pulp only the red part of the carrot, and not the yellow.

Catfish Soup
From "Directions for Cookery, in its Various Branches" By Eliza Leslie, 1840

Catfish that have been caught near the middle of the river are much nicer than those that are taken near the shore where they have access to impure food. The small white ones are the best.

Having cut off their heads, skin the fish, and clean them, and cut them in three. To twelve small catfish allow a pound and a half of ham. Cut the ham into small pieces, or slice it very thin, and scald it two or three times in boiling water, lest it be too salt. Chop together a bunch of parsley and some sweet marjoram stripped from the stalks. Put these ingredients into a soup kettle and season them with pepper: the ham will make it salt enough. Add a head of celery cut small, or a large table-spoonful of celery seed tied up in a bit of clear muslin to prevent its dispersing. Pat in two quarts of water, cover the kettle, and let it boil slowly till every thing is sufficiently done, and the fish and ham quite tender. Skim it frequently. Boil in another vessel a quart of rich milk, in which you have melted a quarter of a pound of butter divided into small bits and rolled in flour. Pour it hot to the soup, and stir in at the last the beaten yolks of four eggs. Give it another boil, just to take off the rawness of the eggs, and then put it into a tureen, taking out the bag of celery seed before you send the soup to table, and adding some toasted bread cut into small squares. In making toast for soap, cut the bread thick, and pare off all the crust.

This soup will be found very fine.

Eel soup may be made in the same manner: chicken soup also.

Celery Soup
From "The Book of Household Management", By Isabella Beeton, 1861

9 heads of celery, 1 teaspoonful of salt, nutmeg to taste, 1 lump of sugar, 1/2 pint of strong stock, a pint of cream, and 2 quarts of boiling water.

Cut the celery into small pieces; throw it into the water, seasoned with the nutmeg, salt, and sugar. Boil it till sufficiently tender; pass it through a sieve, add the stock, and simmer it for half an hour. Now put in the cream, bring it to the boiling point, and serve immediately.

Chantilly Soup
From "The Book of Household Management", By Isabella Beeton, 1861

1 quart of young green peas, a small bunch of parsley, 2 young onions, 2 quarts of medium stock No. 105 (see recipe for "Medium Stock").
Boil the peas till quite tender, with the parsley and onions; then rub them through a sieve, and pour the stock to them. Do not let it boil after the peas are added, or you will spoil the colour. Serve very hot.

Chicken Broth
From "A Poetical Cookbook", By Maria J. Moss, 1864

Take the remaining parts of a chicken from which panada has been made, all but the rump; skin, and put them into the water it was first boiled in, with the addition of a little mace, onion, and a few pepper-corns, and simmer it. When of a good flavor, put to it a quarter of an ounce of sweet almond beaten with a spoonful of water; boil it a little while,
and when cold take off the fat.

Chowder
From "Directions for Cookery, in its Various Branches" By Eliza Leslie, 1840

Take a pound or more of salt pork, and having half boiled it, cut it into slips, and with some of them cover the bottom of a pot. Then strew on some sliced onion. Have ready a large fresh cod, or an equal quantity of haddock, tutaug, or any other firm fish. Cut the fish into large pieces, and lay part of it on the pork and onions. Season it with pepper. Then cover it with a layer of biscuit, or crackers that have been previously soaked in milk or water. You may add also a layer of sliced potatoes.
Next proceed with a second layer of pork, onions, fish, &c. and continue as before till the pot is nearly full; finishing with soaked crackers. Pour in about a pint and a half of cold water. Cover it close, set it on hot coals, and let it simmer about an hour. Then skim it, and turn it out into a deep dish. Leave the gravy in the pot till you have thickened it with a piece of butter rolled in flour, and some chopped parsley. Then give it one boil up, and pour it hot into the dish.
Chowder may be made of clams, first cutting off the hard part.

Clam Soup
From "Directions for Cookery, in its Various Branches" By Eliza Leslie, 1840

Having put your clams into a pot of boiling water to make them open easily, take them from the shells, carefully saving the liquor. To the liquor of a quart of opened clams, allow three quarts of water. Mix the water with the liquor of the clams and put it into a large pot with a knuckle of veal, the bone of which should be chopped in four places. When it has simmered slowly for four hours, put in a large bunch of sweet herbs, a beaten nutmeg, a tea-spoonful of mace, and a table-spoonful of whole pepper, but no salt, as the salt of the clam liquor will be sufficient. Stew it slowly an hour longer, and then strain it. When you have returned the liquor to the pot, add a quarter of a pound of butter divided into four and each bit rolled in flour. Then put in the clams, (having cut them, in pieces,) and let it boil fifteen minutes. Send it to table with toasted bread in it cut into dice.

This soup will be greatly improved by the addition of small force-meat balls. Make them of cold minced veal or chicken, mixed with equal quantities of chopped suet and sweet marjoram, and a smaller proportion of hard-boiled egg, grated lemon-peel, and powdered nutmeg. Pound all the ingredients together in a mortar, adding a little pepper and salt. Break in a raw egg or two (in proportion to the quantity) to bind the whole together and prevent it from crumbling to pieces. When thoroughly mixed, make the force-meat into small balls, and let them boil ten minutes in the soup, shortly before you send it to table. If you are obliged to make them of raw veal or raw chicken they must boil longer.

It will be a great improvement to cut up a yam and boil it in the soup.

Oyster soup may be made in this manner.

Cocoa-Nut Soup
From "The Lady's Receipt-Book; a Useful Companion for Large or Small Families", By Eliza Leslie, 1847

Take eight calves' feet (two sets) that have been scalded and scraped, but not skinned; and put them into a soup-kettle with six or seven blades of mace, and the yellow rind of a lemon pared thin. Pour on a gallon of water; cover the kettle, and let it boil very slowly (skimming it well) till the flesh is reduced to rags and has dropped entirely from the bones. Then strain it into a broad white-ware pan, and set it away to get cold. When it has congealed, scrape off the fat and sediment, cut up the cake of jelly, (or stock,) and put it into a clean porcelain or enamelled kettle. Have ready half a pound of very finely grated cocoa-nut. Mix it with a pint of cream. If you cannot obtain cream, take rich unskimmed milk, and add to it three ounces of the best fresh butter divided into three parts, each bit rolled in arrow-root or rice-flour. Mix it, gradually, with the cocoa-nut, and add it to the calves-feet-stock in the

kettle, seasoned with half a grated nutmeg. Set it over the fire, and boil it, slowly, about a quarter of an hour; stirring it well. Then transfer it to a tureen, and serve it up. Have ready small French rolls, or light milk biscuit to eat with it; also powdered sugar in case any of the company should wish to sweeten it.

Cottage Soup
From "The Practical Housekeeper; A Cyclopedia of Domestic Economy", By Elizabeth Fries Ellet, 1857

Take two pounds of lean beef, cut into small pieces, with one-fourth of a pound of bacon, two pounds of meally potatoes, three ounces of rice, carrots, turnips, and onions sliced, or leeks and cabbage. Fry the meat, cabbage, and onions in butter or dripping, the latter being the most savory; and put them into a gallon of water, to stew gently over a slow fire for three hours, putting in the carrots at the same time, but the turnips and rice only time enough to allow of their being well done; and mashing the potatoes, which should be then passed through a colander: season only with pepper and salt: keep the vessel closely covered. It will make five pints of excellent soup at the cost of about one shilling and eight pence.

Crayfish Soup
From "The Book of Household Management", By Isabella Beeton, 1861

50 crayfish, 1/4 lb. of butter, 6 anchovies, the crumb of 1 French roll, a little lobster-spawn, seasoning to taste, 2 quarts of medium stock, No. 105 (see recipe for "Medium Stock"), or fish stock, No. 192 (see recipe for "Fish Stock").
Shell the crayfish, and put the fish between two plates until they are wanted; pound the shells in a mortar, with the butter and anchovies; when well beaten, add a pint of stock, and simmer for 3/4 of an hour. Strain it through a hair sieve, put the remainder of the stock to it, with the crumb of the rolls; give it one boil, and rub it through a tammy, with the lobster-spawn. Put in the fish, but do not let the soup boil, after it has been rubbed through the tammy. If necessary, add seasoning. Time-1-1/2 hour.

Egg Soup
From "The Book of Household Management", By Isabella Beeton, 1861

A tablespoonful of flour, 4 eggs, 2 small blades of finely-pounded mace, 2 quarts of stock No. 105 (see recipe for "Medium Stock").
Beat up the flour smoothly in a teaspoonful of cold stock, and put in the eggs; throw them into boiling stock, stirring all the time. Simmer for 1/4 of an hour. Season and serve with a French roll in the tureen, or fried sippets of bread.

Fish Stock No. 192
From "The Book of Household Management", By Isabella Beeton, 1861

2 lbs. of beef or veal (these can be omitted), any kind of white fish trimmings, of fish which are to be dressed for table, 2 onions, the rind of 1/2 a lemon, a bunch of sweet herbs, 2 carrots, 2 quarts of water.

Cut up the fish, and put it, with the other ingredients, into the water. Simmer for 2 hours; skim the liquor carefully, and strain it. When a richer stock is wanted, fry the vegetables and fish before adding the water.

Time-2 hours.

French Vegetable Soup
From "Miss Beecher's Domestic Receipt Book", By Catharine Esther Beecher, 1850

Take a leg of lamb, of moderate size, and four quarts water. Of potatoes, carrots, cabbage, onions, tomatoes, and turnips take a tea-cup full of each, chopped fine. Salt and black pepper to your taste.

Wash the lamb, and put it into the four quarts of cold water. When the scum rises take it off carefully with a skimmer. After having pared and chopped the vegetables, put them into the soup. Carrots require the most boiling, and should be put in first; onions require the least boiling, and are to be put in the last.

This soup requires about three hours to boil.

Green-Peas Soup
From "A New System of Domestic Cookery", By Maria Eliza Ketelby Rundell, 1807

In shelling the peas, divide the old from the young; put the old ones, with an ounce of butter, a pint of water, the outside leaves of a lettuce or two, two onions, pepper, and salt, to stew till you can pulp the peas; and when you have done so, put to the liquor that stewed them some more water, the hearts and tender stalks of the lettuces, the young peas, a handful of spinach cut small, and salt and pepper to relish properly, and stew till quite soft. If the soup is too thin, or not rich enough, either of these faults may be removed by ounce or two of butter, mixed with a spoonful of rice or wheat-flour, and boiled with it half an hour. Before serving, boil some green mint shred fine in the soup.

When there is plenty of vegetables, no meat is necessary; but if meat be preferred, a pig's foot, or ham-bone, &c. may be boiled with the old peas, which is called the stock. More butter than is mentioned above may be used with advantage, if the soup is required to be very rich.

When peas first come in, or are very young, the stock may be made of the shells washed, and boiled till they will pulp with the above: more thickening will then be wanted.

Hessian Soup
From "The Book of Household Management", By Isabella Beeton, 1861

Half an ox's head, 1 pint of split peas, 3 carrots, 6 turnips, 6 potatoes, 6 onions, 1 head of celery, 1 bunch of savoury herbs, pepper and salt to taste, 2 blades of mace, a little allspice, 4 cloves, the crumb of a French roll, 6 quarts of water.
Clean the head, rub it with salt and water, and soak it for 5 hours in warm water. Simmer it in the water till tender, put it into a pan and let it cool; skim off all the fat; take out the head, and add the vegetables cut up small, and the peas which have been previously
soaked; simmer them without the meat, till they are done enough to pulp through a sieve. Add the seasoning, with pieces of the meat cut up; give one boil, and serve. Time-4 hours.

Maccaroni Soup
From "Directions for Cookery, in its Various Branches" By Eliza Leslie, 1840

This also is made of clear gravy soup. Cut up and boil the maccaroni by itself in a very little water, allowing a quarter of a pound to a quart of soup. The pieces should be about an inch long. Put a small piece of butter with it. It must boil till tender, but not till it breaks. Throw it into the soup shortly before it goes to table, and give it one boil up. Send to table with it a plate or glass of rasped Parmesan or other rich cheese, with a dessert spoon in it, that those who like it may put it into their soup on the plate. While the maccaroni is boiling, take care that it does not get into lumps.

Macaroni Soup (Mrs. F.'s Receipt)
From "Miss Beecher's Domestic Receipt Book", By Catharine Esther Beecher, 1850

Take six pounds of beef, and put it into four quarts of water, with two onions, one carrot, one turnip, and a head of celery. Boil it down three or four hours slowly, till there is about two quarts of water, and let it cool. Next day take off the grease, without shaking the sediment, and pour it off into the kettle, half an hour before dinner (leaving the sediment out), and add salt to suit the taste, a pint of macaroni, broken into inch pieces, and a tablespoonful and a half of tomato catsup.

Medium Stock (No. 105)
From "The Book of Household Management", By Isabella Beeton, 1861

4 lbs. of shin of beef, or 4 lbs. of knuckle of veal, or 2 lbs. of each; any bones,

trimmings of poultry, or fresh meat, 1/2 a lb. of lean bacon or ham, 2 oz. of butter, 2 large onions, each stuck with 3 cloves; 1 turnip, 3 carrots, 1/2 a leek, 1 head of celery, 2 oz. of salt, 1/2 a teaspoonful of whole pepper, 1 large blade of mace, 1 small bunch of savoury herbs, 4 quarts and 1/2 pint of cold water.

Cut up the meat and bacon or ham into pieces about 3 inches square; rub the butter on the bottom of the stewpan; put in 1/2 a pint of water, the meat, and all the other ingredients. Cover the stewpan, and place it on a sharp fire, occasionally stirring its contents. When the bottom of the pan becomes covered with a pale, jelly-like substance, add 4 quarts of cold water, and simmer very gently for 5 hours. As we have said before, do not let it boil quickly. Skim off every particle of grease whilst it is doing, and strain it through a fine hair sieve.

This is the basis of many of the soups afterwards mentioned, and will be found quite strong enough for ordinary purposes.

Time-5-1/2 hours.

Mullagatawny Soup
From "The Book of Household Management", By Isabella Beeton, 1861

2 tablespoonfuls of curry powder, 6 onions, 1 clove of garlic, 1 oz. of pounded almonds, a little lemon-pickle, or mango-juice, to taste; 1 fowl or rabbit, 4 slices of lean bacon; 2 quarts of medium stock, or, if wanted very good, best stock.

Slice and fry the onions of a nice colour; line the stewpan with the bacon; cut up the rabbit or fowl into small joints, and slightly brown them; put in the fried onions, the garlic, and stock, and simmer gently till the meat is tender; skim very carefully, and when the meat is done, rub the curry powder to a smooth batter; add it to the soup with the almonds, which must be first pounded with a little of the stock. Put in seasoning and lemon-pickle or mango-juice to taste, and serve boiled rice with it.

Time-2 hours.

Ochra Soup
From "The Practical Housekeeper; A Cyclopedia of Domestic Economy", By Elizabeth Fries Ellet, 1857

Put on six pounds of fresh beef--allowing a little less than a quart of water to each pound; after it has boiled an hour add two quarts of ochras minced fine as possible. Afterwards a dozen of ripe tomatoes pared and cut up, with two turnips, a few Lima beans, herbs, and other seasoning. The ochras should be dissolved. Strain and serve it with toasted bread cut into slices, put in after it comes out of the pot.

Onion Soup for Six Persons
From "A Plain Cookery Book for the Working Classes", By Charles Elme Francatelli, 1852

Chop fine six onions, and fry them in a gallon saucepan with two ounces of butter or dripping fat, stirring them continuously until they become of a very light colour; then add six ounces of flour or oatmeal, and moisten with three quarts of water; season with pepper and salt, and stir the soup while boiling for twenty minutes, and when done, pour it out into a pan or bowl containing slices of bread.

Plain Green Pea Soup, Without Meat
From "The Great Western Cook Book, or Table Receipts, Adapted to Western Housewifery", By Anna Maria Collins, 1857

Take a quart of green pease, keeping half a pint of the youngest, put them on in boiling water and boil them till they are tender. Then pour off the water, and set it by to make the soup with. Pound the pease to a mash, in a mortar. Boil the young pease separately, to put into the soup when finished. Put into the mashed pease two quarts of the water they were boiled in, stir all well together, and let it boil for about five minutes, and then rub it through a hair sieve.
This will be a thick and fine vegetable soup.

Plum Broth
From "A Plain Cookery Book for the Working Classes", By Charles Elme Francatelli, 1852

Boil one quart of any kind of red plums in three pints of water with a piece of cinnamon and four ounces of brown sugar until the plums are entirely dissolved; then rub the whole through a sieve or colander, and give it to the children to eat with bread.

Potato Soup For Six Persons
From "A Plain Cookery Book for the Working Classes", By Charles Elme Francatelli, 1852

Peel and chop four onions, and put them into a gallon saucepan, with two ounces of dripping fat, or butter, or a bit of fat bacon; add rather better than three quarts of water, and set the whole to boil on the fire for ten minutes; then throw in four

pounds of peeled and sliced-up potatoes, pepper and salt, and with a wooden spoon stir the soup on the
fire for about twenty-five minutes, by which time the potatoes will be done to a pulp, and the soup ready for dinner or breakfast.

Rich Brown Soup
From "Directions for Cookery, in its Various Branches" By Eliza Leslie, 1840

Take six pounds of the lean of fresh beef, cut from the bone. Stick it over with four dozen cloves. Season it with a tea-spoonful of salt, a tea-spoonful of pepper, a tea-spoonful of mace, and a beaten nutmeg. Slice half a dozen onions; fry them in butter; chop them, and spread them over the meat after you have put it into the soup-pot. Pour in five quarts of water, and stew it slowly for five or six hours; skimming it well. When the meat has dissolved into shreds, strain it, and return the liquid to the pot. Then add a tumbler and a half, or six wine glasses of claret or port wine. Simmer it again slowly till dinner time. When the soup is reduced to three quarts, it is done enough. Put it into a tureen, and send it to table.

Soup à-la-sap
From "A New System of Domestic Cookery", By Maria Eliza Ketelby Rundell, 1807

Boil half a pound of grated potatoes, a pound of beef sliced thin, a pint of grey peas, an onion, and three ounces of rice, in six pints of water, to five; strain it through a colander; then pulp the peas to it, and turn it into a sauce-pan again with two heads of celery sliced. Stew it tender, and add pepper and salt; and when you serve, add also fried bread.

Soup De L'Asperge
From "The Practical Housekeeper; A Cyclopedia of Domestic Economy", By Elizabeth Fries Ellet, 1857

Cut into thin slices half a pound of bacon, lay them in the bottom of the stewpan, cut into lumps six pounds of lean beef and roll it well in flour, cover the pan close, shake occasionally until the gravy is all drawn, then add half a pint of old ale and two quarts of water; throw in some whole peppers and a spoonful of salt, stew gently for an hour, skim the fat, and when an hour has elapsed strain off the soup, then put in it some spinach, two cabbage lettuces, the leaves of white beet, a little mint, powdered sweet aroma and sorrel, boil them, then put in the tops of asparagus cut small; when they are tender the soup is done; serve up hot with a French roll in the middle.

Soup Italienne
From "The Practical Housekeeper; A Cyclopedia of Domestic Economy", By Elizabeth Fries Ellet, 1857

Cut the meat from a knuckle of veal, break up the bones and make a broth of them, cut half a pound of ham in slices and lay them at the bottom of a stewpan; upon them the meat from the knuckle of veal, with the slices of four carrots, four turnips, a dozen peppercorns, two blades of mace, a large onion, and a head of celery; cover down close; stew till the gravy is drawn out and the roots are quite tender, pour over them the broth made from the bone of the knuckle until they are covered, add six spoonfuls of rice, stew four hours, work the soup through a sieve, add vermicelli before serving.

Soup Maigre
From "A New System of Domestic Cookery", By Maria Eliza Ketelby Rundell, 1807

Melt half a pound of butter into a stew-pan, shake it round, and throw in six middling onions sliced. Shake the pan well for two or three minutes; then put to it five heads of celery, two handfuls of spinach, two cabbage-lettuces cut small, and some parsley. Shake the pan well for ten minutes; then put in, two quarts of water, some crusts of bread, a tea-spoonful of beaten pepper, three or four blades of mace; and if you have any white beet leaves, add a large handful of them cut small. Boil gently an hour. Just before serving, beat in two yolks of eggs and a large spoonful of vinegar.

Spinach Soup
From "A New System of Domestic Cookery", By Maria Eliza Ketelby Rundell, 1807

Shred two handfuls of spinach, a turnip, two onion, a head of celery, two carrots, and a little thyme and parsley. Put all into a stew-pot, with a bit of butter the size of a walnut, and a pint of broth, or the water in which meat has been boiled; stew till the vegetables are quite tender; work them through a coarse cloth or sieve with a spoon; then to the pulp of the vegetables, and liquor, put a quart of fresh water, pepper, and salt, and boil all together. Have ready some suet-dumplings, the size of a walnut; and before you put the soup into the tureen, put them into it. The suet must not be shred too fine; and take care that it is quite fresh.

Tomato Soup
From "The Practical Housekeeper; A Cyclopedia of Domestic Economy", By Elizabeth Fries Ellet, 1857

Slice two onions and fry them in butter until brown; remove them and fry two dozen tomatoes just sufficient to heat them through, then put them into a stewpan with their gravy and the onions, add a head of celery and a carrot sliced; stew gently for half an hour, add three pints of gravy, stew an hour and a half, pulp the whole of the vegetables through a sieve, season with white pepper, salt, and cayenne, serve with sippets of toasted bread cut in shapes.

Vegetable Soup
From "The Book of Household Management", By Isabella Beeton, 1861

7 oz. of carrot, 10 oz. of parsnip, 10 oz. of potato, cut into thin slices; 1-1/4 oz. of butter, 5 teaspoonfuls of flour, a teaspoonful of made mustard, salt and pepper to taste, the yolks of 2 eggs, rather more than 2 quarts of water.
Boil the vegetables in the water 2-1/2 hours; stir them often, and if the water boils away too quickly, add more, as there should be 2 quarts of soup when done. Mix up in a basin the butter and flour, mustard, salt, and pepper, with a teacupful of cold water; stir in the
soup, and boil 10 minutes. Have ready the yolks of the eggs in the tureen; pour on, stir well, and serve.
Time-3 hours.

Winter Vegetable Soup
From "The Practical Housekeeper; A Cyclopedia of Domestic Economy", By Elizabeth Fries Ellet, 1857

Take carrots, turnips, and the heart of a head of celery, cut into dice, with a dozen button onions; half boil them in salt and water, with a little sugar in it; then throw them into the broth; and, when tender, serve up the soup: or use rice, dried peas and lentils, and pulp them into the soup to thicken it.

3. Main Dishes

Beef

"Last night it commenced snowing and continued all day. Lampe and I were walking around nearly all day. We drew our rations today—enough of blue beef at any rate. We had a lively day of carrying out or rather hauling our provisions to our quarters on our bone wagons."-Capt. Henry A. Chambers, Company C, 4th Regiment, N.C.S.T, February 15, 1862, from his diary.

Beef a-la-Mode
From "A New System of Domestic Cookery", By Maria Eliza Ketelby Rundell, 1807

Choose a piece of thick flank of a line heifer or ox. Cut into long slices some fat bacon, but quite free from yellow; let each bit be near an inch thick: dip them into vinegar, and then into a seasoning ready prepared of salt, black pepper, allspice, and a clove, all in fine powder, with parsley, chives, thyme, savoury, and knotted marjoram, shred as small as possible, and well mixed. With a sharp knife make holes deep enough to let in the larding; then rub the beef over with the seasoning, and bind it up tight with tape. Set it in a well-tinned pot over a fire or rather stove: three or four onions must be fried brown and put to the beef, with two or three carrots, one turnip, a head or two of celery, and a small quantity of water; let it simmer gently ten or twelve hours, or till extremely tender, turning the meat twice. Put the gravy into a pan, remove the fat, keep the beef covered, then put them together, and add a glass of port wine. Take off the tape, and serve with the vegetables; or you may strain them off, and send them up cut into dice for garnish.

Onions roasted, and then stewed with the gravy, are a great improvement. A tea-cupful of vinegar should be stewed with the beef.

Beef Bouilli
From "Directions for Cookery, in its Various Branches" By Eliza Leslie, 1840

Take part of a round of fresh beef (or if you prefer it a piece of the flank or brisket) and rub it with salt. Place skewers in the bottom of the stew-pot, and lay the meat upon them with barely water enough to cover it. To enrich the gravy you may add the necks and other trimmings of whatever poultry you may happen to have; also the root of a tongue, if convenient. Cover the pot, and set it over a quick fire. When it boils and the scum has risen, skim it well, and then diminish the fire so that the meat shall only simmer; or you may set the pot on hot coals. Then put in four or five carrots sliced thin, a head of celery cut up, and four or fire sliced turnips. Add a bunch of sweet herbs, and a small table-spoonful of black pepper-corns tied in a thin muslin rag. Let it stew slowly for four or fire hours, and then add a dozen very small onions roasted and peeled, and a large table-spoonful of capers or nasturtians. You may, if you choose, stick a clove in each onion. Simmer it half an hour longer, then take up the meat, and place-it in a dish, laying the vegetables round it. Skim and strain the gravy; season it with catchup, and made mustard, and serve it up in a boat. Mutton may be cooked in this manner.

Beef-Collops
From "The Book of Household Management", By Isabella Beeton, 1861

2 lbs. of rump-steak, 1/4 lb. of butter, 1 pint of gravy (water may be substituted for this), salt and pepper to taste, 1 shalot finely minced, 1/2 pickled walnut, 1 teaspoonful of capers.
Have the steak cut thin, and divide it in pieces about 3 inches long; beat these with the blade of a knife, and dredge with flour. Put them in a frying-pan with the butter, and let them fry for about 3 minutes; then lay them in a small stewpan, and pour over them the gravy. Add a piece of butter, kneaded with a little flour, put in the seasoning and all the other ingredients, and let the whole simmer, but not boil for 10 minutes. Serve in a hot covered dish.
Time-10 minutes.

Beef With Baked Potatoes
From "A Poetical Cookbook", By Maria J. Moss, 1864

Boil some potatoes, peel, and pound them in a mortar with two small onions; moisten them with milk and an egg beaten up, add a little salt and pepper. Season slices of beef or mutton-chops with salt and pepper, and more onion, if the flavor is

approved. Rub the bottom of a pudding-dish with butter, and put a layer of the mashed potatoes, which
should be as thick as a batter, and then a layer of meat, and so on alternately till the dish is filled, ending with potatoes. Bake it in an oven for an hour.

A Beef Stew
From "The Practical Housekeeper; A Cyclopedia of Domestic Economy", By Elizabeth Fries Ellet, 1857

Take two or three pounds of the rump of beef, cut away all the fat and skin, and cut it into pieces about two or three inches square, put it into a stewpan, and pour upon it a quart of broth, let it boil, sprinkle in a little salt and pepper to taste; when it has boiled very gently, or simmered two hours, shred finely a large lemon, add it to the gravy, and in twenty minutes pour in a flavoring composed of two tablespoonfuls of Harvey's sauce, the juice of the lemon the rind of which has been sliced into the gravy, a spoonful of flour, and a little ketchup; add at pleasure two glasses of Madeira, or one of sherry, or port, a quarter of an hour after the flavoring, and serve.

Chitterlings or Calf's Tripe
From "Directions for Cookery, in its Various Branches" By Eliza Leslie, 1840

See that the chitterlings are very nice and white. Wash them, cut them into pieces, and put them into a stew-pan with pepper and salt to your taste, and about two quarts of water. Boil them two hours or more. In the mean time, peel eight or ten white onions, and throw them whole into a sauce-pan with plenty of water. Boil them slowly till quite soft; then drain them in a cullender, and mash them. Wipe out your sauce-pan, and put in the mashed onions with a piece of butter, two tablespoonfuls of cream or rich milk, some nutmeg, and a very little salt. Sprinkle in a little flour, set the pan on hot coals (keeping it well covered) and give it one boil up. When the chitterlings are quite tender all through, take them up and drain them. Place in the bottom of a dish a slice or two of buttered toast with all the crust cut off. Lay the chitterlings on the toast, and send them to table with the stewed onions in a sauce-boat. When you take the chitterlings on your plate season them with pepper and vinegar.
This, if properly prepared, is a very nice dish.

Broiled Beef-Steaks or Rump Steaks
From "The Book of Household Management", By Isabella Beeton, 1861

Steaks, a piece of butter the size of a walnut, salt to taste, 1 tablespoonful of good mushroom ketchup or Harvey's sauce.

As the success of a good broil so much depends on the state of the fire, see that it is bright and clear, and perfectly free from smoke, and do not add any fresh fuel just before you require to use the gridiron. Sprinkle a little salt over the fire, put on the gridiron for

a few minutes, to get thoroughly hot through; rub it with a piece of fresh, suet, to prevent the meat from sticking, and lay on the steaks, which should be cut of an equal thickness, about 3/4 of an inch, or rather thinner, and level them by beating them as little as possible

with a rolling-pin. Turn them frequently with steak-tongs (if these are not at hand, stick a fork in the edge of the fat, that no gravy escapes), and in from 8 to 10 minutes they will be done. Have ready a very hot dish, into which put the ketchup, and, when liked, a little

minced shalot; dish up the steaks, rub them over with butter, and season with pepper and salt. The exact time for broiling steaks must be determined by taste, whether they are liked underdone or well done; more than from 8 to 10 minutes for a steak 3/4 inch in thickness, we think, would spoil and dry up the juices of the meat. Great expedition is necessary in sending broiled steaks to table; and, to have them in perfection, they should not be cooked till everything else prepared for dinner has been dished up, as their excellence entirely depends on their being served very hot. Garnish with scraped horseradish, or slices of

cucumber. Oyster, tomato, onion, and many other sauces, are frequent accompaniments to rump-steak, but true lovers of this English dish generally reject all additions but pepper and salt.

Time-8 to 10 minutes.

To Broil Beef Steaks
From "Directions for Cookery, in its Various Branches" By Eliza Leslie, 1840

The best beef-steaks are those cut from the ribs or from the inside of the sirloin. All other parts are for this purpose comparatively hard and tough.

They should be cut about three quarters of an inch thick, and, unless the beef is remarkably fine and tender, the steaks will be much improved by beating them on both sides with a steak mallet, or with a rolling-pin. Do not season them till you take them from the fire.

Have ready on your hearth a fine bed of clear bright coals, entirely free from smoke and ashes. Set the gridiron over the coals in a slanting direction, that the meat may not be smoked by the fat dropping into the fire directly under it. When the gridiron is quite hot, rub the bars with suet, sprinkle a little salt over the coals, and lay on the steaks. Turn them frequently with a pair of steak-tongs, or with a knife and fork. A quarter of an hour is generally sufficient time to broil & beef-steak. For those who like them under-done or rare, ten or twelve minutes will be enough.

When the fat blazes and smokes very much as it drips into the fire, quickly remove the gridiron for a moment, till the blaze has subsided. After they are browned, cover the upper side of the steaks with an inverted plate or dish to prevent the flavour from evaporating. Rub a dish with a shalot or small onion, and place it near the gridiron and close to the fire, that it may be well heated. In turning the steak drop the gravy that may be standing on it into this dish, to save it from being lost. When the steaks are done, sprinkle them with a little salt and pepper, and lay them in a hot dish, putting on each a piece of fresh butter. Then, if it is liked, season them with, a very little raw shalot, minced as finely as possible, and moistened with a spoonful of water; and stir a tea-spoonful of catchup into the gravy. Send the steaks to table very hot, in a covered dish. You may serve up with them onion sauce in a small tureen.

Pickles are frequently eaten with beef-steaks.

Mutton chops may be broiled in the same manner.

French Beef
From "The Lady's Receipt-Book; a Useful Companion for Large or Small Families", By Eliza Leslie, 1847

Take a circular piece from the round, (having removed the bone,) and trim it nicely from the fat, skin, &c. Then lard it all over with long slips of fat pork or bacon. The place from whence the bone was taken must be filled with a force-meat, made of minced suet; grated bread-crumbs; sweet-marjoram rubbed fine; and grated lemon-peel; add a little salt and pepper, and mix in the beaten yolk of an egg to bind together the other ingredients. Tie a twine or tape closely round the outside of the beef, to keep it compact, and in shape. Put it into a broad earthen jar with a cover; or into an iron bake-oven. Add some whole pepper; a large onion stuck over with a dozen cloves; a bunch of sweet herbs; three bay-leaves; a quarter of a pound of butter, divided into small bits, (each piece rolled in flour,) and half a pint of claret, or port-wine. Bake or stew it thus in its own liquor, for five, six, or seven hours, (in proportion to its size,) for it must be thoroughly done, quite tender, and brown all through the inside. Serve it up hot with the gravy round it. It is also very good when cold.

A fillet of veal may be cooked in this manner.

Calf's Heart, A Nice Dish
From "The Virginia Housewife", By Mary Randolph, 1860

Take the heart and liver from the harslet, and cut off the windpipe, boil the lights very tender, and cut them in small pieces--take as much of the water they were boiled in as will be sufficient for gravy; add to it a large spoonful of white wine, one of lemon pickle, some grated nutmeg, pepper and salt, with a large spoonful of butter, mixed with one of white flour; let it boil a few minutes, and put in the minced lights, set it by till the heart and liver are ready, cut the ventricle out of the heart, wash it well, lard it all over with narrow slips of middling, fill the cavity with good forcemeat, put it in a pan on the broad end, that the stuffing may not come out; bake it a nice brown, slice the liver an inch thick and broil it, make the mince hot, set the heart upright in the middle of the dish, pour it around, lay the broiled liver on, and garnish with bunches of fried parsley; it should be served up extremely hot.

To Fry Calf's Liver
From "Directions for Cookery, in its Various Branches" By Eliza Leslie, 1840

Cut the liver into thin slices. Season it with pepper, salt, chopped sweet herbs, and parsley. Dredge it with flour, and fry it brown in lard or dripping. See that it is thoroughly done before you send it to table. Serve it up with its own gravy.
Some slices of cold boiled ham fried with it will be found an improvement.
You may dress a calf's heart in the same manner.

To Stuff and Roast A Calf's Liver
From "The Virginia Housewife", By Mary Randolph, 1860

Take a fresh calf's liver, and having made a hole in it with a large knife run in lengthways, but not quite through, have ready a forced meat, or stuffing made of part of the liver parboiled, fat of bacon minced very fine, and sweet herbs powdered; add to these some grated bread and spice finely powdered, with pepper and salt. With this stuffing fill the hole in the liver, which must be larded with fat bacon, and then roasted, flouring it well, and basting with butter till it is enough. This is to be served up hot, with gravy sauce having a little wine in it.

The English Dish of Beefsteak and Onions
From "The Practical Housekeeper; A Cyclopedia of Domestic Economy", By Elizabeth Fries Ellet, 1857

Pound the steak, season, and fry it in a saute or fryingpan; then dredge flour over it, and add, by degrees, a cup of boiling water with more seasoning. Drain the onions, which must have been boiled, cut them up, and put them into the pan, having taken out the steak; add a lump of butter and a little more flour; stir them to prevent scorching; and when the onions are well browned, put in the steak, and place the whole over the fire till heated thoroughly. In serving, heap the onions upon the steak.

Fried Steaks
From "The Complete Cook", By J. M. Sanderson, 1864

Cut them rather thinner than for broiling; put some butter, or, what is much cheaper and quite as good, some clarified dripping or suet, into an iron frying-pan, and when it is quite hot put in the steaks, and keep turning them until they are done enough. The sauce for steaks, chops, cutlets, &c., is made as follows:--Take the chops, steaks or cutlets, out of the frying pan; for a pound of meat, keep a table-spoonful of the fat in the pan, or put in an ounce of butter; put to it as much flour as will make it a paste; rub it well together over the fire till they are a little brown; then add as much boiling water as will reduce it to the thickness of good cream, and a table-spoonful of mushroom or walnut catsup, or pickle, or browning; let it boil together a few minutes, and pour it through a sieve to the steaks, &c. To the above is sometimes added a sliced onion, or a minced eschalot, with a table-spoonful of port wine, or a little eschalot wine. Garnish with scraped horse-radish, or pickled walnut, gherkins, &c. Some beef-eaters like chopped eschalots in one saucer, and horse-radish grated in vinegar in another. Broiled mushrooms are favourite relishes to beef-steaks.

Beef À La Braise
From "A Poetical Cookbook", By Maria J. Moss, 1864

Bone a rump of beef, lard it very thickly with salt pork seasoned with pepper, salt, cloves, mace, and allspice, and season the beef with pepper and salt; put some slices of bacon into the bottom of the pan, with some whole black pepper, a little allspice, one or two bay leaves, two onions, a clove of garlic, and a bunch of sweet herbs. Put in the beef, and lay over it some slices of bacon, two quarts of weak stock, and half a pint of white wine. Cover it closely, and let it stew between six and seven hours. Sauce for the beef is made of part of the liquor it has been stewed in, strained, and thickened with a little flour and butter, adding some green onions cut small, and pickled mushrooms. Pour it over the beef.

Beef Steaks, A La Francaise
From "The Practical Housekeeper; A Cyclopedia of Domestic Economy", By Elizabeth Fries Ellet, 1857

Take a fine steak and dip it into cold spring water, let it drain a few minutes, lay it in a dish and pour over it sufficient clarified butter hot, and cover it; let it remain twelve hours, then remove the butter, and roll the steak with the rolling-pin a dozen times rather hardly, let it lie in front of a clear fire ten minutes, turning it once or twice, put it into a fryingpan. with water half an inch in depth, and let it fry until it browns.

Mince some parsley very fine, chop an eschalot as fine as can be, and season them with cayenne, salt, and a little white pepper; work them with a lump of fresh butter, and when the steak is brown take it from the pan, rub it well with the mixture on both sides, and return it to the pan until done enough; dish it, thicken the gravy in the pan with a little butter rolled in flour if it requires it, and pour it over the steak and serve.

Beef Steaks A La Parisienne
From "The Practical Housekeeper; A Cyclopedia of Domestic Economy", By Elizabeth Fries Ellet, 1857

Cut thin steaks from the finest and tenderest part of the rump, sprinkle pounded salt, a little cayenne and white pepper combined, over them; lay them in a pan with an ounce of fresh butter, cut in pieces; work half a teaspoonful of flour with three ounces of fresh butter, as much parsley minced exceedingly fine as would lie on a shilling, roll it, and cut in large dice, lay it in a dish, squeeze the half of a lemon over the butter, and when the steaks are done lay them upon the butter; have ready a quantity of raw peeled potatoes, cut in thin slices, and washed in milk and water ready, fry them in the butter and gravy left by the steak, and lay them round the dish; they will be done when they are a rich brown.

To Fry Beefsteaks
From "The Great Western Cook Book, or Table Receipts, Adapted to Western Housewifery", By Anna Maria Collins, 1857

Cut the steak rather thin. Put some lard into an iron frying pan, and, when it is hot, lay in the steaks, and keep turning them till they are done enough.

Fried Steaks and Onions
From "A Plain Cookery Book for the Working Classes", By Charles Elme Francatelli, 1852

Season the steaks with pepper and salt, and when done brown on both sides, without being overdone, place them in a dish before the fire while you fry some sliced onions in the fat which remains in the pan; as soon as the onions are done, and laid upon the steaks, shake a spoonful of flour in the pan, add a gill of water and a few drops of vinegar; give this gravy a boil up on the fire, and pour it over the steaks, etc.

Beef Steaks With Mushrooms
From "The Lady's Receipt-Book; a Useful Companion for Large or Small Families", By Eliza Leslie, 1847

Take four pounds of the best sirloin steaks, cut thin. Season them with black pepper, and a very little salt. Put four table-spoonfuls of butter into a frying-pan, and set it over the fire. When it is quite hot, put in the steaks and let them brown. Have ready a quart of mushrooms, stemmed and skinned, and moistened with a pint of water, seasoned with a little pepper and salt, and thickened slightly with a good dredging of flour. Pour it over the steaks in the frying-pan, and then let them cook till thoroughly done.

Venison steaks will be found excellent dressed in this manner, but the venison must be fresh.

Beef Steaks Rolled and Roasted
From "The Practical Housekeeper; A Cyclopedia of Domestic Economy", By Elizabeth Fries Ellet, 1857

Cut handsome steaks from the rump, and if not sufficiently tender let them be well beaten; make a rich stuffing of equal parts of ham and veal well peppered; stew it for a short time, and pound it in a mortar with bread steeped in milk, a lump of butter, and the yolk of two or three eggs; spread this forcemeat over the steaks, roll them up and tie them tightly, roast them before a clear fire. They will occupy an hour and twenty minutes to an hour and a half roasting; baste well with butter while roasting, and serve with brown gravy.

Fried Rump-Steak
From "The Book of Household Management", By Isabella Beeton, 1861

Steaks, butter or clarified dripping.
Although broiling is a far superior method of cooking steaks to frying them, yet, when the cook is not very expert, the latter mode may be adopted; and, when properly done, the dish may really look very inviting, and the flavour be good. The steaks should be cut rather

thinner than for broiling, and with a small quantity of fat to each. Put some butter or clarified dripping into a frying-pan; let it get quite hot, then lay in the steaks. Turn them frequently until done, which will be in about 8 minutes, or rather more, should the steaks be very thick. Serve on a very hot dish, in which put a small piece of butter and a tablespoonful of ketchup, and season with pepper and salt. They should be sent to table quickly, as, when cold, the steaks are entirely spoiled. Time-8 minutes for a medium-sized steak, rather longer for a very thick one.

Beef-Steaks with Fried Potatoes, or Biftek Aux Pommes-De-Terre (a la mode Francaise)
From "The Book of Household Management", By Isabella Beeton, 1861

2 lbs. of steak, 8 potatoes, 1/4 lb. of butter, salt and pepper to taste, 1 teaspoonful of minced herbs.

Put the butter into a frying or _sauté_ pan, set it over the fire, and let it get very hot; peel, and cut the potatoes into long thin slices; put them into the hot butter, and fry them till of a nice brown colour. Now broil the steaks over a bright clear fire, turning them frequently, that every part may be equally done: as they should not be thick, 5 minutes will broil them. Put the herbs and seasoning in the butter the potatoes were fried in, pour it under the steak, and place the fried potatoes round, as a garnish. To have this dish in perfection,
a portion of the fillet of the sirloin should be used, as the meat is generally so much more tender than that of the rump, and the steaks should be cut about 1/3 of an inch in thickness.
Time-5 minutes to broil the steaks, and about the same time to fry
the potatoes.

Italian Beef-Steaks
From "A New System of Domestic Cookery", By Maria Eliza Ketelby Rundell, 1807

Cut a fine large steak from a rump that has been well hung, or it will do from any *tender* part: beat it, and season with pepper, salt and onion; lay it in an iron stew-pan that has a cover to fit quite close, and set it by the side of the fire without water. Take care it does not burn, but it must have a strong heat: in two or three hours it will be quite tender, and then serve with its own gravy.

Jerked Beef
From "The Complete Cook", By J. M. Sanderson, 1864

Jerked beef is made by cutting it into thin pieces, or slices, and dipping them into sea or salt water, and then drying them quickly in the sun. In the West Indies, where they can scarcely cure meat in the ordinary way on account of the excessive heat, they adopt the above method of preserving beef. <u>*Author's Note*</u>: *The recipe for "Jerked Beef" is included in this book simply for historical education. It is NOT recommended as a safe way to Jerk beef at home, as, for the most part, the North American climate is not sufficiently hot enough to complete the process, as it is in the West Indies!*

Larded Calf's Liver
From "Directions for Cookery, in its Various Branches" By Eliza Leslie, 1840

Take a calf's liver and wash it well. Cut into long slips the fat of some bacon or salt pork, and insert it all through the surface of the liver by means of a larding-pin. Put the liver into a pot with a table-spoonful of lard, a little water, and a few tomatas, or some tomata catchup; adding one large or two small onions minced fine, and some sweet marjoram leaves rubbed very fine. The sweet marjoram will crumble more easily if you first dry it before the fire on a plate.

Having put in all these ingredients, set the pot on hot coals in the corner of the fire-place, and keep it stewing, regularly and slowly, for four hours. Send the liver to table with the gravy round it.

Mock Hare
From "The Complete Cook", By J. M. Sanderson, 1864

The inside lean of a sirloin of beef may be dressed so as to resemble hare, and is by many people greatly preferred to it. Make a good stuffing. If possible, get the inside meat of the whole length of sirloin, or even of two, lay the stuffing on half the length, turn the other end over and sew up the two sides with a strong twine, that will easily draw out when done; roast it nicely, taking care to baste it well, and serve with sauces and garnishes the same as hare; or, it may be partly roasted and then stewed, in rich thickened gravy with force meat balls, and sauce.

Beef-Steak Pie
From "The Book of Household Management", By Isabella Beeton, 1861

3 lbs. of rump-steak, seasoning to taste of salt, cayenne, and black pepper, crust, water, the yolk of an egg.

Have the steaks cut from a rump that has hung a few days, that they may be tender, and be particular that every portion is perfectly sweet. Cut the steaks into pieces about 3 inches long and 2 wide, allowing a small piece of fat to each piece of lean, and arrange the meat in layers in a pie-dish. Between each layer sprinkle a seasoning of salt, pepper, and, when liked, a few grains of cayenne. Fill the dish sufficiently with meat to support the crust, and to give it a nice raised appearance when baked, and not to look flat and hollow. Pour in sufficient water to half fill the dish, and border it with paste (see Pastry); brush it over with a little water, and put on the cover; slightly press down the edges with the thumb, and trim off close to the dish. Ornament the pie with leaves, or pieces of paste cut in any shape that fancy may direct, brush it over with the beaten yolk of an egg; make a hole in the top of the crust, and bake in a hot oven for about 1-1/2 hour.

Beef Ragout
From "A Poetical Cookbook", By Maria J. Moss, 1864

Take a rump of beef, cut the meat from the bone, flour and fry it, pour over it a little boiling water, about a pint of small-beer, add a carrot or two, an onion stuck with cloves, some whole pepper, salt, a piece of lemon-peel, a bunch of sweet herbs; let it stew an hour, then add some good gravy; when the meat is tender take it out and strain the sauce;
thicken it with a little flour; add a little celery ready boiled, a little ketchup, put in the meat; just simmer it up.

Roast Beef
From "Miss Beecher's Domestic Receipt Book", By Catharine Esther Beecher, 1850

The sirloin, and the first and second cuts of the rack, are the best roasting pieces. Rub it with salt; set the bony side to the fire to heat awhile, then turn it, and have a strong fire; and if thick, allow fifteen minutes to the pound; if thin, allow a little less. If fresh killed, or if it is very cold, allow a little more time. Half an hour before it is done, pour off the gravy, thicken it with brown flour, and season it with salt and pepper. It is the fashion to serve roast beef with no other gravy than the juice of the meat.

To Stew a Rump of Beef
From "A New System of Domestic Cookery", By Maria Eliza Ketelby Rundell, 1807

Wash it well; and season it high with pepper, Cayenne, salt, allspice, three cl and a blade of mace, all in fine-powder. Bind it up tight, and lay it into a pr will just hold it. Fry three large onions sliced, and put them to it, with thre two turnips, a shalot, four cloves, a blade of mace, and some celery. Cover the meat with good beef-broth, or weak gravy. Simmer it as gently as possible for several hours, till quite tender. Clear off the fat: and add to the gravy half a pint of port wine, a glass of vinegar, and a large spoonful of ketchup; simmer half an hour, and serve in a deep dish. Half a pint of table-beer may be added. The herbs to be used should be burnet, tarragon, parsley, thyme, basil, savoury, marjoram, pennyroyal, knotted marjoram, and some chives if you can get them, but observe to proportion the quantities to the pungency of the several sorts; let there be a good handful altogether.

Garnish with carrots, turnips, or truffles and morels, or pickles of different colours, cut small, and laid in little heaps separate; chopped parsley, chives, beet-root, &c. If, when clone, the gravy is too much to fill the dish, take only a part to season for serving, but the less water the better; and to increase the richness, add a few beef-bones and shanks of mutton in stewing.

A spoonful or two of made mustard is a great improvement to the gravy.

Rump *roasted* is excellent; but in the country it is generally sold whole with the edgebone, or cut across instead of lengthways as in London, where one piece is for boiling, and the rump for stewing or roasting. This must be attended to, the whole being too large to dress together.

Beef Steaks
From "Miss Beecher's Domestic Receipt Book", By Catharine Esther Beecher, 1850

Those from the sirloin are best, those from the shoulder clod and round are not so good, but cheaper. Meat, if tough, is made more tender by pounding, if it is done very thoroughly, so as to break the fibres. Cut the steaks from half an inch to an inch thick. Broil on hot coals, and the quicker it is done the better. Ten or twelve minutes is enough time. Turn it four or five times, and when done put on butter, salt, and if you like pepper, and on both sides. Do not let your butter be turned to oil before putting it on. It is best to have beef tongs to turn beef, as pricking it lets out the juices. Often turning prevents the surface from hardening and cooks it more equally.

To Broil Beefsteaks
From "The Great Western Cook Book, or Table Receipts, Adapted to Western Housewifery", By Anna Maria Collins, 1857

Try to have your steaks cut of an even thickness throughout, and throw a little salt and pepper on them. Do not beat them, unless you suspect they will not be tender. Have a clear, brisk fire, make the gridiron hot, and set it slanting, to prevent the fat from dripping into the fire and making it smoke. Turn it once; it will be done in fifteen or twenty minutes. Rub some butter over it, and send it up, garnished with pickles and finely-scraped horseradish.

Rump of Beef Stew
From "The Practical Housekeeper; A Cyclopedia of Domestic Economy", By Elizabeth Fries Ellet, 1857

Half roast it; then put it into a pot with three pints of water, a pound of slice bacon, a bunch of sweet herbs, two wine-glasses of vinegar, and a bottle of cider or small wine; stick cloves into a couple of large onions, add a few sage-leaves, and cover the beef closely, adding more water should there not be suffficient gravy from the meat. Let it simmer for three hours; then strain the gravy. Boil or bake some button onions, and lay them round the beef; cover it also with forcemeat balls, fried ornaments of paste, and mushrooms, if in season; add to the gravy a glass of port wine, a spoonful of soy and Oude sauce; boil down a part to a glaze, and put it on the beef: thicken the remainder if necessary, and pour it round, garnishing the dish with pickles.

Stewed Rump Another Way
From "A New System of Domestic Cookery", By Maria Eliza Ketelby Rundell, 1807

Half-roast it; then put it into a large pot with three pints of water, one of small-beer, one of port wine, some salt, three or four spoonfuls of vinegar, two of ketchup, a bunch of sweet herbs of various kinds (such as burnet, tarragon, parsley, thyme, basil, savoury, pennyroyal, marjoram, knotted marjoram, and a leaf or two of sago), some onions, cloves, and Cayenne; cover it close, and simmer till quite tender: two or three hours will do it When done lay it into a deep dish, set it over hot water, and cover it close. Skim the gravy; put in a few pickled-mushrooms, truffles, morels, and oysters if agreeable, but it is very good without; thicken the gravy with flour and tatter, and heat it with the above, and pour over the beef. Forcemeat-balls of veal, anchovies, bacon, suet, herbs, spice, bread, and eggs, to bind, are a great improvement.

Beef, or Veal Stewed with Apples (very good)
From "Miss Beecher's Domestic Receipt Book", By Catharine Esther Beecher, 1850

Rub a stew-pan with butter, cut the meat in thin slices, and put in, with pepper, salt, and apple sliced fine; some would add a little onion. Cover it tight, and stew till tender.

To Stew Cold Corned Beef
From "The Lady's Receipt-Book; a Useful Companion for Large or Small Families", By Eliza Leslie, 1847

Cut about four pounds of lean from a cold round of beef, that tastes but little of the salt. Lay it in a stew-pan, with a quarter of a peck of tomatoes quartered, and the same quantity of ochras sliced; also, two small onions peeled and sliced, and two ounces of fresh butter rolled in flour. Add a tea-spoonful of whole pepper-corns, (*no salt,*) and four or five blades of mace. Place it over a steady but moderate fire. Cover it closely, and let it stew three or four hours. The vegetables should be entirely dissolved. Serve it up hot.

This is an excellent way of using up the remains of a cold round of beef at the season of tomatoes and ochras, particularly when the meat has been rather under-boiled the first day of cooking it.

A few pounds of the lean of a *fresh* round of beef, will be still better cooked in this manner, increasing the quantity of ochras and tomatoes, and stewing it six hours. Cold fillet of veal is very good stewed with tomatoes, ochras, and an onion or two. Also, the thick or upper part of a cold leg of mutton; or of pork, either fresh or corned.

Salt Beef
From "A Poetical Cookbook", By Maria J. Moss, 1864

Make a pickle of rock salt and cold water strong enough to bear an egg, let a little salt remain in the bottom of the tub; two quarts of molasses and a quarter pound of saltpetre is sufficient for a cwt. of beef. It is fit for use in ten days. Boil the beef slowly until the bones come out easily, then wrap it in a towel, and put a heavy weight on it till cold.

Scotch Kail
From "The Practical Housekeeper; A Cyclopedia of Domestic Economy", By Elizabeth Fries Ellet, 1857

Is chiefly made of mutton, either fresh or salted; beef is only used when mutton cannot conveniently be had. Three or four pounds of meat should be put into a gallon of cold water, along with a moderate quantity of pearl-barley, with leeks or onions, and allowed to stew until tender; if salted, put the meat into water over night, changing it once before boiling. Then have ready the hearts of two cabbages cut small, or greens, if cabbages are not in season; put them into the broth, which must be allowed to boil up uncovered until reduced to two quarts. It should only be seasoned with pepper and salt; but will be much improved by the addition of a couple of onions fried in butter; indeed, both carrots and turnips are also sometimes used, but their addition deprives the soup of the title of "Kail," which is derived from the greens which are usually employed.

The meat is served with the soup, and, in like manner as the *olla* of the Spaniards, or the *pot au feu* of the French, is the standing household dish among the middle classes of Scotland.

Pork

"Artillerymen, having tender consciences and no muskets, seldom, if ever, shot stray pigs; but they did sometimes, as an act of friendship, wholly disinterested, point out to the infantry a pig which seemed to need shooting, and by way of dividing the danger and responsibility of the act, accept privately a choice part of the deceased."-Pvt. Carlton McCarthy, Second company Richmond Howitzers, Cutshaw's Battalion from *Detailed Minutiae Of Soldier Life In The Army Of Northern Virginia*

"I & one of the boys taken some flour & bacon & went out the other night to get cooked for the company. We got to a man's house between 11 & 12 o'clock. We called him up & told him we wanted to get his negro to cook for us. He said it was all right & in place of charging for it, he had 2 shoulders of bacon & about 30 pounds of flour cooked besides what we [had] taken & give to us. He said if everyone on his place had to stay up & cook until the next night, it was nothing to what we had to go through. He was one of the cleverest men I ever saw." - Corporal Burr J. Caldwell, Co. D, 22nd Mississippi Infantry, July 22, 1864, near LaGrange, Georgia. Letter to his wife Sarah (Sallie)

To Make Black Puddings
From "A New System of Domestic Cookery", By Maria Eliza Ketelby Rundell, 1807

The blood must be stirred with salt till cold. Put a quart of it, or rather more, to a quart of whole grits, to soak one night; and soak the crumb of a quartern loaf in rather more than two quarts of new milk made hot. In the mean time prepare the guts by washing, turning, and scraping with salt and water, and changing the water several times. Chop fine a little winter-savoury and thyme, a good quantity of penny-royal, pepper, and salt, a few cloves, some allspice, ginger, and nutmeg: mix these with three pounds of beef-suet, and six eggs well beaten and strained; and then beat the bread, grits, &c. all up with the seasoning: when well mixed, have ready some hogs' fat cut into large bits; and as you fill the skins, put it in at proper distances. Tie in links, only half filled; and boil in a large kettle, pricking them as they swell or they will burst. When boiled, lay them between clean cloths till cold, and hang them up in the kitchen. When to be used, scald them a few minutes in water, wipe and put them into a Dutch oven.

If there are not skins enough, put the stuffing into basons, and boil it covered with floured cloths; and slice and fry it when used.

Another way.-Soak all night a quart of bruised grits in as much boiling-hot milk as will swell them and leave half a pint of liquid. Chop a good quantity of pennyroyal, some savoury, and thyme; salt, pepper, and allspice, finely powdered. Mix the above with a quart of the blood, prepared as before directed; then half fill the skins, after they have been cleaned thoroughly, and put as much of the leaf (that is, the inward fat) of the pig as will make it pretty rich. Boil as before directed. A small quantity of leeks finely shred and well mixed, is a great improvement.

Another way.-Boil a quart of half-grits in as much milk as will swell them to the utmost; then drain them and add a quart of blood, a pint of rich cream, a pound of suet, some mace, nutmeg, allspice, and four cloves, all in fine powder; two pounds of the hog's leaf cut into dice, two leeks, a handful of parsley, ten leaves of sage, a large handful of penny-royal, and a sprig of thyme and knotted marjoram, all minced fine; eight eggs well
beaten, half a pound of bread-crumbs that have been scalded with a pint of milk, pepper, and salt. Half fill the skins; which must first be cleaned with the greatest care, turned several times, and soaked in several waters and last in rose-water. Tie the skins in links, boil and prick them with a clean fork to prevent their bursting. Cover them with a clean cloth till cold.

Broiled Rashers of Bacon (a Breakfast Dish)
From "The Book of Household Management", By Isabella Beeton, 1861

Before purchasing bacon, ascertain that it is perfectly free from rust, which may easily be detected by its yellow colour; and for broiling, the streaked part of the thick flank, is generally the most esteemed. Cut it into _thin_ slices, take off the rind, and broil over a nice clear fire; turn it 2 or 3 times, and serve very hot. Should there be any cold bacon left from the previous day, it answers very well for breakfast, cut into slices, and broiled or fried.

Time-3 or 4 minutes.

To Cure Hams

From "A New System of Domestic Cookery", By Maria Eliza Ketelby Rundell, 1807

Hang them a day or two; then sprinkle them with a little salt, and drain them another day; pound an ounce and a half of saltpetre, the same quantity of bay-salt, half an ounce of sal-prunel, and a pound of the coarsest sugar. Mix these well; and rub them into each ham every day for four days, and turn it. If a small one, turn it every day for three weeks; if a large one, a week longer; but don't rub after four days. Before you dry it, drain and cover with bran. Smoke it ten days.

Another way.--Choose the leg of a hog that is fat and well-fed; hang it as above; if large, put to it a pound of bay-salt, four ounces of salt-petre, a pound of the coarsest sugar, and a handful of common salt, all in fine powder, and rub it thoroughly. Lay the rind downwards, and cover the fleshy part with the salts. Baste it as often as you can with the pickle; the more the better. Keep it four weeks, turning it every day. Drain it, and throw bran over it; then hang it in a chimney where wood is burnt, and turn it sometimes for ten days.

Another way.--Hang the ham, and sprinkle it with salt as above; then rub it every day with the following, in fine powder: half a pound of common salt, the same quantity of bay-salt, two ounces of saltpetre, and two ounces of black pepper, mixed with a pound and a half of treacle. Turn it twice a day in the pickle, for three weeks. Lay it into a pail of water for one night, wipe it quite dry, and smoke it two or three weeks.

Another way, that gives a high flavour.--When the weather will permit, hang the ham three days; mix an ounce of saltpetre with a quarter of a pound of bay-salt, the same quantity of common salt, and also of coarse sugar, and a quart of strong beer; boil them together, and pour them immediately upon the ham; turn it twice a day in the pickle for three weeks. An ounce of black pepper, and the same quantity of allspice, in fine powder, added to the above, will give still more flavour. Cover it with bran when wiped: and smoke it from three to four weeks, as you approve; the latter will make it harder and give it more of the flavour of Westphalia. Sew hams in hessings (that is, coarse wrappers), if to be smoked where there is a strong fire.

<u>A method of giving a still higher flavour.</u>--Sprinkle the ham with salt, after it has hung two or three days; let it drain; make a pickle of a quart of strong beer, half a pound of treacle, an ounce of coriander seeds, two ounces of juniper-berries, an ounce of pepper, the same quantity of allspice, an ounce of saltpetre, half an ounce of sal-prunel, a handful of common salt, and a head of shalot, all pounded or cut fine. Boil these all together a few minutes, and pour them over the ham: this quantity is for one of ten pounds. Rub and turn it every day, for a fortnight; then sew it up in a thin linen bag, and smoke it three weeks. Take care to drain it from the pickle, and rub it in bran, before drying.

To Bake A Ham
From "The Book of Household Management", By Isabella Beeton, 1861

Ham; a common crust.
As a ham for baking should be well soaked, let it remain in water for at least 12 hours. Wipe it dry, trim away any rusty places underneath, and cover it with a common crust, taking care that this is of sufficient thickness all over to keep the gravy in. Place it in a
moderately-heated oven, and bake for nearly 4 hours. Take off the crust, and skin, and cover with raspings, the same as for boiled ham, and garnish the knuckle with a paper frill. This method of cooking a ham is, by many persons, considered far superior to boiling it, as it cuts fuller of gravy and has a finer flavour, besides keeping a much longer time good.
Time-A medium-sized ham, 4 hours.

To Stuff A Ham
From "The Virginia Housewife", By Mary Randolph, 1860

Take a well smoked ham, wash it very clean, make incisions all over the top two inches deep, stuff them quite full with parsley chopped small and some pepper, boil the ham sufficiently; do not take off the skin. It must be eaten cold.

Economical Dish
From "The Practical Housekeeper; A Cyclopedia of Domestic Economy", By Elizabeth Fries Ellet, 1857

Cut some pretty fat ham or bacon into slices, and fry of a nice brown; lay them aside to keep warm; then mix equal quantities of potatoes and cabbage, bruised well together, and fry them iia the fat left from the ham. Place the mixture at the bottom, and lay the slices of bacon on the top. Cauliflower or broccoli, substituted for cabbage is truly delicious, and, to any one possess-ing a garden, quite easily procured—as those newly blown will do. The dish must be well seasoned with pepper.

A French Ham Pie
From "The Lady's Receipt-Book; a Useful Companion for Large or Small Families", By Eliza Leslie, 1847

Having soaked and boiled a small ham, and taken out the bone, trim the ham nicely so as to make it a good shape; and of the bone and trimmings make a rich gravy, by stewing them in a sauce-pan with a little water; carefully skimming off the fat. Make a sufficient quantity of force-meat, out of cold roast chicken or veal, minced suet, grated bread-crumbs, butter, pepper, chopped sweet-marjoram or tarragon; and grated lemon-peel, adding the lemon-juice, and some beaten egg. Mix the ingredients thoroughly. You may add some chopped oysters.

Having made a standing crust, allowing to two pounds of flour half a pound of butter, and a pound of minced suet, wetted to a paste with boiling water, put in the ham, (moistening it with the gravy,) and fill in all the vacancies with the force-meat, having a layer of force-meat at the bottom and top. Then put on the lid, pinching the edges together so as to close them well. Brush the paste all over with beaten yolk of egg; then put on the ornamental flowers and leaves that have been cut out of the dough. Bake it three or four hours. It may be eaten warm, but is generally preferred cold. It keeps well, if carefully secluded from the air.

A Fillet of Pork to Resemble Veal
From "The Practical Housekeeper; A Cyclopedia of Domestic Economy", By Elizabeth Fries Ellet, 1857

The fillet should be cut from the leg of a very large pig; remove the bone and fill the orifice with veal stuffing; roast it until it is more than half done, then take some thin broth and put it in the stewpan, put in the pork, stew until it is thoroughly done, then thicken the gravy, and send it to table with force-meat balls and lemon cut in slices.

To Melt Lard
From "The Practical Housekeeper; A Cyclopedia of Domestic Economy", By Elizabeth Fries Ellet, 1857

Take the inner fat of a newly killed pig and strip off the skin completely and carefully, slice it and put it into a jar, a sprig of rosemary may be placed with it, and set the jar in a pan of boiling water; let it melt, and when perfectly fluid pour it into dry clean jars, and cover them closely; it may be kept some time in a dry place, and when used may be mixed with butter for pastry, for frying fish, and many other purposes in cooking.

Liver Pudding
From "The Practical Housekeeper; A Cyclopedia of Domestic Economy", By Elizabeth Fries Ellet, 1857

Boil pigs' livers, mince, and season them with pepper, salt, and chopped sweet marjoram and sage, adding cloves. Put them in skins, prick them, and boil slowly an hour or so. Keep them, in covered jars, to eat cold in slices, or to fry in larger pieces. Boiled pigs' feet may be mixed with the livers.

Tongue Pie
From "The Lady's Receipt-Book; a Useful Companion for Large or Small Families", By Eliza Leslie, 1847

Is made as above (see recipe for "A French Ham Pie"); only substituting a smoked tongue for the ham. The tongue must be nicely trimmed and peeled, and the root minced fine, and mixed with the veal or chicken force-meat.
Either of these pies may be made and baked in deep dishes, and with paste made in the usual way of butter and flour, wetted with a little cold water.

A Leg of Pork Roasted
From "The Practical Housekeeper; A Cyclopedia of Domestic Economy", By Elizabeth Fries Ellet, 1857

The pork should be young and dairy-fed; score the skin with a sharp penknife, a little fresh butter is sometimes rubbed over the skin to make it brown, and crisp without blistering. Chop some sage that has been scalded, very fine, add to it an onion parboiled, mix breadcrumbs and a small portion of apple chopped very fine, mix all together, season with pepper and salt, make an incision, separating the skin from the fat in the under and fillet end of the leg, and place the stuffing there; the time of roasting will depend upon the size of the leg; serve up with apple sauce.

To Roast A Loin of Pork
From "Directions for Cookery, in its Various Branches" By Eliza Leslie, 1840

Score the skin in narrow strips, and rub it all over with a mixture of powdered sage leaves, pepper and salt. Have ready a force-meat or stuffing of minced onions and sage, mixed with a little grated bread and beaten yolk of egg, and seasoned with pepper and salt. Make deep incisions between the ribs and fill them with this stuffing. Put it on the spit before a clear fire and moisten it with butter or sweet oil, rubbed lightly over it. It will require three hours to roast.

Having skimmed the gravy well, thicken it with a little flour, and serve it up in a boat. Have ready some apple-sauce to eat with the pork. Also mashed turnips and mashed potatoes.

You may roast in the same manner, a shoulder, spare-rib, or chine of pork; seasoning it with sage and onion.

Pig's Feet Fried
From "The Lady's Receipt-Book; a Useful Companion for Large or Small Families", By Eliza Leslie, 1847

Pig's feet are frequently used for jelly, instead of calves' feet. They are very good for this purpose, but a larger number is required (from eight to ten or twelve) to make the jelly sufficiently firm. After they have been boiled for jelly, extract the bones, and put the meat into a deep dish; cover it with some good cider-vinegar, seasoned with sugar and a little salt and cayenne. Then cover the dish, and set it away for the night. Next morning, take out the meat, and having drained it well from the vinegar, put it into a frying-pan in which some lard has just come to a boil, and fry it for a breakfast dish.

Spare Rib
From "The Complete Cook", By J. M. Sanderson, 1864

When you put it down to roast, dust on some flour, and baste it with a little butter; dry a dozen sage leaves, rub them through a hair sieve, put them into the top of a pepper box, and about a quarter of an hour before the meat is done baste it with butter; dust the pulverised sage, or savoury powder, in, or sprinkle it with duck stuffing; some people prefer it plain.

To Roast a Spare Rib
From "Miss Beecher's Domestic Receipt Book", By Catharine Esther Beecher, 1850

Rub with salt, pepper, and powdered sage. Put the bone side to warm slowly. Dredge on a little flour, and put a little salted water and butter into the dripping-pan, and baste with it. If large, it requires three hours; if small, only one to cook it. Pork must be cooked slowly and very thoroughly.

To Roast a Sucking Pig
From "A New System of Domestic Cookery", By Maria Eliza Ketelby Rundell, 1807

If you can get it when just killed, this is of great advantage. Let it be scalded, which the dealers usually do; then put some sage, crumbs of bread, salt, and pepper, into the belly, and sew it up. Observe to skewer the legs back, or the under part will not crisp.

Lay it to a brisk fire till thoroughly dry; then have ready some butter in a dry cloth, and rub the pig with it in every part. Dredge as much flour over as will possibly lie, and do not touch it again till ready to serve; then scrape off the flour very carefully with a blunt knife, rub it well with the buttered cloth, and take off the head while at the fire; take out the brains, and mix them with the gravy that comes from the pig. Then take it up; and without withdrawing the spit, cut it down the back and belly, lay it into the dish, and chop the sage and bread quickly as fine as you can, and mix them with a large quantity of line melted butter that has very little flour. Put the sauce into the dish after the pig has been split down the back, and garnished with the ears and the two jaws; take off the upper part of the head down to the snout.

In Devonshire it is served whole, if very small; the head only being cut off, to garnish as above.

To Stew Pork
From "Directions for Cookery, in its Various Branches" By Eliza Leslie, 1840

Take a nice piece of the fillet or leg of fresh pork; rub it with a little salt, and score the skin. Put it into a pot with sufficient water to cover it, and stew it gently for two hours or more, in proportion to its size. Then put into the same pot a dozen or more sweet potatoes, scraped, split, and cut in pieces. Let the whole stew gently together for an hour and a half, or till all is thoroughly done, skimming it frequently. Serve up all together in a large dish.

This stew will be found very good. For sweet potatoes you may substitute white ones mixed with sliced turnips, or parsnips scraped or split.

Pork Cheese (an Excellent Breakfast Dish)
From "The Book of Household Management", By Isabella Beeton, 1861

2 lbs. of cold roast pork, pepper and salt to taste, 1 dessertspoonful of minced parsley, 4 leaves of sage, a very small bunch of savoury herbs, 2 blades of pounded mace, a little nutmeg, ½ teaspoonful of minced lemon-peel; good strong gravy, sufficient to fill the mould.

Cut, but do not chop, the pork into fine pieces, and allow ¼ lb. of fat to each pound of lean. Season with pepper and salt; pound well the spices, and chop finely the parsley, sage, herbs, and lemon-peel, and mix the whole nicely together. Put it into a mould, fill
up with good strong well-flavoured gravy, and bake rather more than one hour. When cold, turn it out of the mould.

Pork Chops Grilled or Broiled
From "A Plain Cookery Book for the Working Classes", By Charles Elme Francatelli, 1852

Score the rind of each chop by cutting through the rind at distances of half-an-inch apart; season the chops with pepper and salt, and place them on a clean gridiron over a clear fire to broil; the chops must be turned over every two minutes until they are done; this will take about fifteen minutes. The chops are then to be eaten plain, or, if convenient, with brown gravy, made as shown in No. 17 (see recipe for "Brown Gravy").

Pork Chops
From "The Complete Cook", By J. M. Sanderson, 1864

Take care that they are trimmed very neatly; they should be about half an inch thick; put a frying-pan on the fire, with a bit of butter; as soon as it is hot, put in your chops, turning them often till brown all over, and done; take one upon a plate and try it; if done, season it with a little finely minced onion, powdered sage, and pepper and salt. Sauce, sage and onions, or Robert sauce.

Pork Cutlets
From "The Book of Household Management", By Isabella Beeton, 1861

The remains of cold roast loin of pork, 1 oz. of butter, 2 onions, 1 dessertspoonful of flour, 1/2 pint of gravy, pepper and salt to taste, 1 teaspoonful of vinegar and mustard.
Cut the pork into nice-sized cutlets, trim off most of the fat, and chop the onions. Put the butter into a stewpan, lay in the cutlets and chopped onions, and fry a light brown; then add the remaining ingredients, simmer gently for 5 or 7 minutes, and serve.
Time-5 to 7 minutes.

Pork Cutlets
From "Directions for Cookery, in its Various Branches" By Eliza Leslie, 1840

Cut them from the leg, and remove the skin; trim them and beat them, and sprinkle on salt and pepper. Prepare some beaten egg in a pan; and on a flat dish a mixture of bread-crumbs, minced onion, and sage. Put some lard or drippings into a frying-pan over the fire; and when it boils, put in the cutlets; having dipped every one first in the egg, and then in the seasoning. Fry them twenty or thirty minutes, turning them often. After you have taken them out of the frying-pan, skim the gravy, dredge in a little flour, give it one boil, and then pour it on the dish round the cutlets.

Have apple-sauce to eat with them.

Pork cutlets prepared in this manner may be stewed instead of being fried. Add to them a little water, and stew them slowly till thoroughly done, keeping them closely covered except when you remove the lid to skim them.

Pork Cutlets or Chops
From "The Book of Household Management", By Isabella Beeton, 1861

Loin of pork, pepper and salt to taste.

Cut the cutlets from a delicate loin of pork, bone and trim them neatly, and cut away the greater portion of the fat. Season them with pepper; place the gridiron on the fire; when quite hot, lay on the chops and broil them for about 1/4 hour, turning them 3 or 4 times; and be particular that they are thoroughly done, but not dry. Dish them, sprinkle over a little fine salt, and serve plain, or with tomato sauce, sauce piquante, or pickled gherkins, a few of which should be laid round the dish as a garnish.

Time-About 1/4 hour.

Pork Steaks
From "Directions for Cookery, in its Various Branches" By Eliza Leslie, 1840

Pork steaks or chops should be taken from the neck, or the loin. Cut them about half an inch thick, remove the skin, trim them neatly, and beat them. Season them with pepper, salt, and powdered sage-leaves or sweet marjoram, and broil them over a clear fire till quite done all through, turning them once. They require much longer broiling than beef-steaks of mutton chops. When you think they are nearly done, take up one on a plate and try it. If it is the least red inside, return it to the gridiron. Have ready a gravy made of the trimmings, or any coarse pieces of pork stewed in a little water with chopped onions and sage, and skimmed carefully. When all the essence is extracted, take out the bits of meat, &c., and serve up the gravy in a boat to eat with the steaks.

They should be accompanied with apple-sauce.

Sausages
From "A New System of Domestic Cookery", By Maria Eliza Ketelby Rundell, 1807

Chop fat and lean of pork together; season it with sage, pepper, and salt, and you may add two or three berries of allspice: half fill hog's guts that have been soaked and made extremely clean: or the meat may be kept in a very small pan, closely covered; and so rolled and dusted with a very little flour before it is fried. Serve on stewed red cabbage; or mash potatoes put in a form, brown with salamander, and garnish with the above; they must be pricked with a fork before they are dressed, or they will burst.

An Excellent Sausage to Eat Cold
From "A New System of Domestic Cookery", By Maria Eliza Ketelby Rundell, 1807

Season fat and lean pork with some salt, saltpetre, black pepper, and allspice, all in fine powder, and rub into the meat: the sixth day cut it small; and mix with it some shred shalot or garlick, as fine as possible. Have ready an ox-gut that has been scoured, salted, and soaked well, and fill it with the above stuffing; tie up the ends, and hang it to smoke as you would hams, but first wrap it in a fold or two of old muslin. It must be high-dried. Some eat it without boiling, but others like it boiled first. The skin should be tied in different places, so as to make each link about eight or nine inches long.

Tongue Toast
From "The Lady's Receipt-Book; a Useful Companion for Large or Small Families", By Eliza Leslie, 1847

Take a cold smoked tongue that has been well boiled; and grate it with a coarse grater, or mince it fine. Mix it with cream, and beaten yolk of egg; and give it a simmer over the fire. Having first cut off all the crust, toast very nicely some slices of bread; and then butter them rather slightly. Lay them in a flat dish that has been heated before the fire; and cover each slice of toast thickly with the tongue-mixture, spread on hot; and send them to table covered. This is a nice breakfast or supper dish.

For tongue, you may substitute cold ham finely minced.

Chicken and Fowl

"The chickens and biscuits you sent us were perfectly sound and still tasted of home though they had been on the way more than a week." –Pvt. James A. Durrett, Co. E, 18th Alabama Infantry, Nov. 12, 1863 in the Chattanooga Valley, Tennessee. Letter to his mother. He was shot through the head and died April 3, 1865 at Spanish Fort, Mobile Alabama

Chicken Croquets and Rissoles
From "Directions for Cookery, in its Various Branches" By Eliza Leslie, 1840

Take some cold chicken, and having; cut the flesh from the bones, mince it small with a little suet and parsley; adding sweet marjoram and grated lemon-peel. Season it with pepper, salt and nutmeg, and having mixed the whole very well pound it to a paste in a marble mortar, putting in a little at a time, and moistening it frequently with yolk of egg that has been previously beaten. Then divide it into equal portions and having floured your hands, make it up in the shape of pears, sticking the head of a clove into the bottom of each to represent the blossom end, and the stalk of a clove into the top to look like the stem. Dip them into beaten yolk of egg, and then into bread-crumbs grated finely and sifted. Fry them in butter, and when you take them out of the pan, fry some parsley in it. Having drained the parsley, cover the bottom of a dish with it, and lay the croquets upon it. Send it to table as a side dish.
Croquets maybe made of cold sweet-breads, or of cold veal mixed with ham or tongue.

Rissoles are made of the same ingredients, well mixed, and beaten smooth in a mortar. Make a fine paste, roll it out, and cut it into round cakes. Then lay some of the mixture on one half of the cake, and fold over the other upon it, in the shape of a half-moon. Close and crimp the edges nicely, and fry the rissoles in butter. They should be of a light brown on both sides. Drain them and send them to table dry.

Chicken or Fowl Patties
From "The Book of Household Management", By Isabella Beeton, 1861

The remains of cold roast chicken or fowl; to every 1/4 lb. of meat allow 2 oz. of ham, 3 tablespoonfuls of cream, 2 tablespoonfuls of veal gravy, 1/2 teaspoonful of minced lemon-peel; cayenne, salt, and pepper to taste; 1 tablespoonful of lemon-juice, 1 oz. of butter rolled in flour; puff paste.

Mince very small the white meat from a cold roast fowl, after removing all the skin; weigh it, and to every 1/4 lb. of meat allow the above proportion of minced ham. Put these into a stewpan with the remaining ingredients, stir over the fire for 10 minutes or 1/4 hour,

taking care that the mixture does not burn. Roll out some puff paste about 1/4 inch in thickness; line the patty-pans with this, put upon each a small piece of bread, and cover with another layer of paste; brush over with the yolk of an egg, and bake in a brisk oven for about 1/4 hour. When done, cut a round piece out of the top, and, with a small spoon, take out the bread (be particular in not breaking the outside border of the crust), and fill the patties with the mixture.

Time-1/4 hour to prepare the meat; not quite 1/4 hour to bake the crust.

Chicken Gumbo
From "The Lady's Receipt-Book; a Useful Companion for Large or Small Families", By Eliza Leslie, 1847

Cut up a young fowl as if for a fricassee. Put into a stew-pan a large table-spoonful of fresh butter, mixed with a tea-spoonful of flour, and an onion finely minced. Brown them over the fire, and then add a quart of water, and the pieces of chicken, with a large quarter of a peck of ochras, (first sliced thin, and then chopped,) and a salt-spoon of salt. Cover the pan, and let the whole stew together till the ochras are entirely dissolved, and the fowl thoroughly done. If it is a very young chicken, do not put it in at first; as half an hour will be sufficient to cook it. Serve it up hot in a deep dish.

A cold fowl may be used for this purpose.

You may add to the ochras an equal quantity of tomatoes cut small. If you use tomatoes, no water will be necessary, as their juice will supply a sufficient liquid.

Chickens Stewed Whole
From "The Lady's Receipt-Book; a Useful Companion for Large or Small Families", By Eliza Leslie, 1847

Having trussed a pair of fine fat young fowls or chickens, (with the liver under one wing, and the gizzard under the other,) fill the inside with large oysters, secured from falling out, by fastening tape round the bodies of the fowls. Put them into a tin butter-kettle with a close cover. Set the kettle into a larger pot or sauce-pan of boiling water, (which must not reach quite to the top of the kettle,) and place it over the fire. Keep it boiling till the fowls are well done, which they should be in about an hour after they begin to simmer. Occasionally take off the lid to remove the scum; and be sure to put it on again closely. As the water in the outside pot boils away, replenish it with more *hot* water from a tea-kettle that is kept boiling hard. When the fowls are stewed quite tender, remove them from the fire; take from them all the gravy that is about them, and put it into a small sauce-pan, covering closely the kettle in which they were stewed, and leaving the fowls in it to keep warm. Then add to the gravy two table-spoonfuls of butter rolled in flour; two table-spoonfuls of chopped oysters; the yolks of three hard-boiled eggs minced fine; half a grated nutmeg; four blades of mace; and a small tea-cup of cream. Boil this gravy about five minutes. Put the fowls on a dish, and send them to table, accompanied by the gravy in a sauce-boat. This is an excellent way of cooking chickens.

Curried Fowl
From "The Book of Household Management", By Isabella Beeton, 1861

1 fowl, 2 oz. of butter, 3 onions sliced, 1 pint of white veal gravy, 1 tablespoonful of curry-powder, 1 tablespoonful of flour, 1 apple, 4 tablespoonfuls of cream, 1 tablespoonful of
lemon-juice.
Put the butter into a stewpan, with the onions sliced, the fowl cut into small joints, and the apple peeled, cored, and minced. Fry of a pale brown, add the stock, and stew gently for 20 minutes; rub down the curry-powder and flour with a little of the gravy, quite smoothly, and stir this to the other ingredients; simmer for rather more than ½ hour, and just before serving, add the above proportion of hot cream and lemon-juice. Serve with boiled rice, which may either be heaped lightly on a dish by itself, or put round the curry as a border.
Time-50 minutes.

Fricasseed Chickens
From "Directions for Cookery, in its Various Branches" By Eliza Leslie, 1840

Having cut up your chickens, lay them in cold water till all the blood is drawn out. Then wipe the pieces, season them with pepper and salt, and dredge them with flour. Fry them in lard or butter; they should be of a fine brown on both sides. When they are quite done, take them, out of the frying-pan, cover them up, and set them by the fire to keep warm. Skim the gravy in the frying-pan and pour into it half a pint of cream; season it with a little nutmeg, pepper and salt, and thicken it with, a small bit of butter rolled in flour. Give it a boil, and then pour it round the chickens, which must he kept hot. Put some lard into the pan, and fry some parsley in It to lay on the pieces of chicken; it must be done green and crisp. To make a white fricassee of chickens, skin them, cut them in pieces, and having soaked out the blood, season them with salt, pepper, nutmeg and mace, and strew over them some sweet marjoram shred fine. Put them into a stew-pan, and pour over them half a pint of cream, or rich unskimmed milk. Add some butter rolled in Hour, and (if you choose) some small force-meat balls. Set the stew-pan over hot coals. Keep it closely covered, and stew or simmer it gently till the chicken is quite tender, but do not allow it to boil. You may improve it by a few small slices of cold ham.

Fried Fowls
From "The Book of Household Management", By Isabella Beeton, 1861

The remains of cold roast fowls, vinegar, salt and cayenne to taste, 3 or 4 minced shalots. For the batter,--1/2 lb. of flour, 1/2 pint of hot water, 2 oz. of butter, the whites of 2 eggs.
Cut the fowl into nice joints; steep them for an hour in a little vinegar, with salt, cayenne, and minced shalots. Make the batter by mixing the flour and water smoothly together; melt in it the butter, and add the whites of egg beaten to a froth; take out the pieces of fowl, dip them in the batter, and fry, in boiling lard, a nice brown. Pile them high in the dish, and garnish with fried parsley or rolled bacon. When approved, a sauce or gravy may be served with them.
Time-10 minutes to fry the fowl.

French Chicken Cutlets
From "The Book of Household Management", By Isabella Beeton, 1861

The remains of cold roast or boiled fowl, fried bread, clarified butter, the yolk of 1 egg, bread crumbs, ½ teaspoonful of finely-minced lemon-peel; salt, cayenne, and mace to
taste. For sauce,--1 oz. of butter, 2 minced shalots, a few slices of carrot, a small bunch of savoury herbs, including parsley, 1 blade of pounded mace, 6 peppercorns, 1/4 pint of gravy.

Cut the fowls into as many nice cutlets as possible; take a corresponding number of sippets about the same size, all cut one shape; fry them a pale brown, put them before the fire, then dip the cutlets into clarified butter mixed with the yolk of an egg, cover with bread crumbs seasoned in the above proportion, with lemon-peel, mace, salt, and cayenne; fry them for about 5 minutes, put each piece on one of the sippets, pile them high in the dish, and serve with the following sauce, which should be made ready for the cutlets. Put the butter into a
stewpan, add the shalots, carrot, herbs, mace, and peppercorns; fry for 10 minutes or rather longer; pour in 1/2 pint of good gravy, made of the chicken bones, stew gently for 20 minutes, strain it, and serve.
Time-5 minutes to fry the cutlets; 35 minutes to make the gravy.

French Chicken Pie
From "The Lady's Receipt-Book; a Useful Companion for Large or Small Families", By Eliza Leslie, 1847

Parboil a pair of full-grown, but fat and tender chickens. Then take the giblets, and put them into a small sauce-pan with as much of the water in which the chickens were parboiled as will cover them well, and stew them for gravy; add a bunch of sweet herbs and a few blades of mace. When the chickens are cold, dissect them as if for carving. Line a deep dish with thick puff-paste, and put in the pieces of chicken. Take a nice thin slice of cold ham, or two slices of smoked tongue, and pound them one at a time in a marble mortar, pounding also the livers of the chickens, and the yolks of half a dozen hard-boiled eggs. Make this force-meat into balls, and intersperse them among the pieces of chicken. Add some bits of fresh butter rolled in flour, and then (having removed the giblets) pour on the gravy. Cover the pie with a lid of puff-paste, rolled out thick; and notch the edges handsomely; placing a knot or ornament of paste on the centre of the top. Set it directly into a well-heated oven, and bake it brown. It should be eaten warm.
This pie will be greatly improved by a pint of mushrooms, cut into pieces. Also by a small tea-cup of cream.
Any pie of poultry, pigeons, or game may be made in this manner.

Fowl A La Hollandaise
From "A Poetical Cookbook", By Maria J. Moss, 1864

Make a forcemeat of grated bread, half its quantity of minced suet, an onion, or a few oysters and some boiled parsley, season with pepper, salt, and grated lemon-peel, and an egg beaten up to bind it. Bone the breast of a good sized young fowl, put in the forcemeat, cover the fowl with a piece of white paper buttered, and roast it half an hour; make a thick batter of flour, milk, and eggs, take off the paper, and pour some of the batter over the fowl; as soon as it becomes dry, add more, and do this till it is all crusted over and a nice brown color, serve it with melted butter and lemon pickle, or a thickened brown gravy.

Poulet A La Marengo
From "The Book of Household Management", By Isabella Beeton, 1861

1 large fowl, 4 tablespoonfuls of salad oil, 1 tablespoonful of flour, 1 pint of stock No. 105 see recipe for "Medium Stock No. 105"), or water, about 20 mushroom-buttons, salt and pepper to taste, 1 teaspoonful of powdered sugar, a very small piece of garlic.

Cut the fowl into 8 or 10 pieces; put them with the oil into a stewpan, and brown them over a moderate fire; dredge in the above proportion of flour; when that is browned, pour in the stock or water; let it simmer very slowly for rather more than 1/2 hour, and skim off
the fat as it rises to the top; add the mushrooms; season with salt, pepper, garlic, and sugar; take out the fowl, which arrange pyramidically on the dish, with the inferior joints at the bottom. Reduce the sauce by boiling it quickly over the fire, keeping it stirred
until sufficiently thick to adhere to the back of a spoon; pour over the
fowl, and serve.
Time-Altogether 50 minutes.

Chicken Pudding, A Favourite Virginia Dish
From "The Virginia Housewife", By Mary Randolph, 1860

Beat ten eggs very light, add to them a quart of rich milk, with a quarter of a pound of butter melted, and some pepper and salt; stir in as much flour as will make a thin good batter; take four young chickens, and after cleaning them nicely, cut off the legs, wings, &c. put them all in a sauce pan, with some salt and water, and a bundle of thyme and parsley, boil them till nearly done, then take the chicken from the water and put it in the batter pour it in a dish, and bake it; send nice white gravy in a boat.

To Pull Chickens
From "A New System of Domestic Cookery", By Maria Eliza Ketelby Rundell, 1807

Take off the skin; and pull the flesh off the bone of a cold fowl, in as large pieces as you can: dredge it with flour, and fry it of a nice brown in butter. Drain the butter from it; and then simmer the flesh in a good gravy well-seasoned, and thickened with a little flour and butler. Add the juice of half a lemon.

<u>Another way.</u>-Cut off the legs, and the whole back, of a dressed chicken; if underdone the better. Pull all the white part into little flakes free from skin; toss it up with a little cream thickened with a piece of butter mixed with flour, half a blade of mace in powder, white pepper, salt, and a squeeze of lemon. Cut off the neck-end of the chicken; and broil the back and sidesmen in one piece, and the two legs seasoned. Put the hash in the middle, with the back on it; and the two legs at the end.

Rice Chicken Pie
From "Miss Beecher's Domestic Receipt Book", By Catharine Esther Beecher, 1850

Line a pudding dish with slices of broiled ham, cut up a boiled chicken, and nearly fill the dish, filling in with gravy or melted butter; add minced onions if you like, or a little curry powder, which is better. Then pile boiled rice to fill all interstices, and cover the top quite thick. Bake it for half or three quarters of an hour.

Roast Chickens
From "Miss Beecher's Domestic Receipt Book", By Catharine Esther Beecher, 1850

Wash them clean outside and inside, stuff them as directed for turkeys, baste them with butter, lard, or drippings, and roast them about an hour. Chickens should be cooked thoroughly. Stew the inwards till tender, and till there is but little water, chop them and mix in gravy from the dripping-pan, thicken with brown flour, and season with salt, pepper, and butter. Cranberry, or new-made apple sauce, is good with them.

Fish

"I have been here about two weeks and have been enjoying the oysters & fish very much as it is the first opportunity I have had of getting any of late." –Dr. Charles Abram Rutledge, Assistant Surgeon, Confederate States Army, Savannah, Georgia, March 14, 1863. Letter to his sister, Henrietta

"Last night as we were going to bed Charley Hafner came fr. River & brot us a nice shad and a string of Perch that Mr. Jas. sent, & this morning, we had a nice mess for breakfast. we drew also a day's ration fish-fresh herring-1/4 lb. & had a mess for dinner & some left."- Pvt. Samuel Pickens, 5th Alabama Infantry, Company D, April 15, 1863. Diary entry. During the course of the war, he was wounded once and captured twice.

Anchovy Toast
From "The Lady's Receipt-Book; a Useful Companion for Large or Small Families", By Eliza Leslie, 1847

Cut four slices of bread and toast them; having first pared off the crust. Butter the toast on both sides. Wash, scrape, and chop ten anchovies and put them thickly between the slices of toast. Beat the yolks of four eggs, and then mix them with half a pint of cream. Put the mixture into a sauce-pan, and set it over the fire to simmer till thick; but do not allow it to boil. Stir it well, lest it should curdle. When it is *near* boiling, take it off, and pour it hot over the toast.
Tongue toast may be made in this way.

Baked Carp
From "A New System of Domestic Cookery", By Maria Eliza Ketelby Rundell, 1807

Clean a large carp; put a stuffing as for soals, dressed in the Portuguese way. Sew it up; brush it all over with yolk of egg, and put plenty of crumbs; then drop oiled butter to baste them; place the carp in a deep earthen dish, a pint of stock (or, if fast-day, fish-stock) a few sliced onions, some bay-leaves, a faggot of herbs, (such as basil, thyme, parsley, and both sorts of marjoram) half a pint of port wine, and six anchovies. Cover over the pan, and bake it an hour. Let it be done before it is wanted. Pour the liquor from it, and keep the fish hot while you heat up the liquor with a good piece of butter rolled in flour, a tea-spoonful of mustard, a little Cayenne, and a spoonful of soy. Serve the fish on the dish, garnished with lemon, and parsley, and horse-radish, and put the gravy into the sauce-tureen.

To Stew Carp
From "The Virginia Housewife", By Mary Randolph, 1860

Gut and scale your fish, wash and dry them well with a clean cloth, dredge them with flour, fry them in lard until they are a light brown, and then put them in a stew pan with half a pint of water, and half a pint of red wine, a meat spoonful of lemon pickle, the same of walnut catsup, a little mushroom powder and cayenne to your taste, a large onion stuck with cloves, and a slick of horse-radish; cover your pan close up to keep in the steam; let them stew gently over a stove fire, till the gravy is reduced to just enough to cover your fish in the dish; then take the fish out, and put them on the dish you intend for the table, set the gravy on the fire, and thicken it with flour, and a large lump of butter; boil it a little, and strain it over your fish; garnish them with pickled mushrooms and scraped horse-radish, and send them to the table.

Baked Fish
From "A Plain Cookery Book for the Working Classes", By Charles Elme Francatelli, 1852

Wash and wipe the fish, and lay it, heads and tails, in a baking-dish, the bottom of which has been spread all over with a little butter or dripping, add a little vinegar and water, and, when procurable, some mushroom ketchup. Season with chopped onions and parsley, shake plenty of raspings of bread all over the top of the fish, and bake it in your oven, or send it to the baker's.

Chowder
From "Directions for Cookery, in its Various Branches" By Eliza Leslie, 1840

Take a pound or more of salt pork, and having half boiled it, cut it into slips, and with some of them cover the bottom of a pot. Then strew on some sliced onion. Have ready a large fresh cod, or an equal quantity of haddock, tutaug, or any other firm fish. Cut the fish into large pieces, and lay part of it on the pork and onions. Season it with pepper. Then cover it with a layer of biscuit, or crackers that have been previously soaked in milk or water. You may add also a layer of sliced potatoes.

Next proceed with a second layer of pork, onions, fish, &c. and continue as before till the pot is nearly full; finishing with soaked crackers. Pour in about a pint and a half of cold water. Cover it close, set it on hot coals, and let it simmer about an hour. Then skim it, and turn it out into a deep dish. Leave the gravy in the pot till you have thickened it with a piece of butter rolled in flour, and some chopped parsley. Then give it one boil up, and pour it hot into the dish.

Chowder may be made of clams, first cutting off the hard part.

Clam Pie
From "The Lady's Receipt-Book; a Useful Companion for Large or Small Families", By Eliza Leslie, 1847

Take a sufficient number of clams to fill a large pie-dish when opened. Make a nice paste in the proportion of a pound of fresh butter to two quarts of flour. Paste for shell-fish, or meat, or chicken pies should be rolled out double the thickness of that intended for fruit pies. Line the sides and bottom of your pie-dish with paste. Then cover the bottom with a thin beef-steak, divested of bone and fat. Put in the clams, and season them with mace, nutmeg, and a few whole pepper-corns. No salt. Add a spoonful of butter rolled in flour, and some hard-boiled yolks of eggs crumbled fine. Then put in enough of the clam-liquor to make sufficient gravy. Put on the lid of the pie, (which like the bottom crust should be rolled out thick,) notch it handsomely, and bake it well. It should be eaten warm.

Cod's Head and Shoulders
From "The Book of Household Management", By Isabella Beeton, 1861

Sufficient water to cover the fish; 5 oz. of salt to each gallon of water.

Cleanse the fish thoroughly, and rub a little salt over the thick part and inside of the fish, 1 or 2 hours before dressing it, as this very much improves the flavour. Lay it in the fish-kettle, with sufficient cold water to cover it. Be very particular not to pour the water on the fish, as it is liable to break it, and only keep it just simmering. If the water should boil away, add a little by pouring it in at the side of the kettle, and not on the fish. Add salt in the above proportion, and bring it gradually to a boil. Skim very carefully, draw it to the side of the fire, and let it gently simmer till done. Take it out and drain it; serve on a hot napkin, and garnish with cut lemon, horseradish, the roe and liver.

Time-According to size, 1/2 an hour, more or less.

Note-Oyster sauce and plain melted butter should be served with this.

Halibut Cutlets
From "Directions for Cookery, in its Various Branches" By Eliza Leslie, 1840

Cut your halibut into steaks or cutlets about an inch thick. Wipe them with a dry cloth, and season them with salt and cayenne pepper. Have ready a pan of yolk of egg well beaten, and a large flat dish of grated bread crumbs.

Put some fresh lard or clarified beef dripping into a frying pan, and hold it over a clear fire till it boils. Dip your cutlets into the beaten egg, and then into the bread crumbs. Fry them of a light brown. Serve them up hot, with the gravy in the bottom of the dish.

Salmon or any large fish may be fried in the same manner.

Halibut cutlets are very fine cut quite thin and fried in the best sweet oil, omitting the egg and bread crumbs.

To Fry Fish
From "Miss Beecher's Domestic Receipt Book", By Catharine Esther Beecher, 1850

Fry some slices of salt pork, say a slice for each pound, and when brown take them up, and add lard enough to cover the fish. Skim it well, and have it hot, then dip the fish in flour, without salting it, and fry a light brown. Then take the fish up, and add to the gravy a little flour paste, pepper, salt; also wine, catsup, and spices, if you like. Put the fish and pork on a dish, and, after one boil, pour this gravy over the whole.

Fish are good dipped first in egg and then in Indian meal, or cracker crumbs and egg, previous to frying.

To Fry Fish
From "A Plain Cookery Book for the Working Classes", By Charles Elme Francatelli, 1852

For this purpose you must have some kind of fat. Either lard, butter, or dripping fat, would be excellent; but they must be bought, and cost a little money. True; but then, if you can afford yourselves a bit of meat occasionally, by dint of good thrift you should save the fat from the boiled meat, or the dripping from your baked meats, and thus furnish yourselves with fat for frying your fish twice a-week; and let me tell you that by introducing fish as an occasional part of your daily food, your health, as well as your pockets, would feel the benefit of such a system of economy. Suppose, then, that you have bought some cheap kind
of fish, such as herrings, large flounders, plaice, small soles, or any other small or flat fish. First of all, let the fish be washed and wiped dry, and rubbed all over with a little flour. Next, put about two ounces of fat, free from water, in a frying-pan on the fire, and, as soon as it is hot, put the fish in to fry, one or two at a time, according to their size, as, unless they have room enough in the frying-pan they do not fry well; this must be carefully attended to, and when the fish is a little browned on one side, turn it over with a tin fish-slice, that it may be fried on the other side also; and, as soon as done, place the fried fish on a dish and then fry the others. When all your fish are fried, with what fat remains in the pan fry some onions, and place them round the fish, and, by way of adding an extra relish to your meal, just throw a few table-spoonfuls of vinegar, some pepper and salt, into the frying-pan, give it a boil up, and pour this round the fish.

Lobster
From "The Cook's Oracle; and Housekeeper's Manual", By William Kitchiner, 1830

Buy these alive; the lobster merchants sometimes keep them till they are starved, before they boil them; they are then watery, have not half their flavour, and like other persons that die of a consumption, have lost the calf of their legs.

Choose those that (as an old cook says, are "heavy and lively," and) are full of motion, which is the index of their freshness.

Those of the middle size are the best. Never take them when the shell is incrusted, which is a sign they are old. The male lobster is preferred to eat, and the female (on account of the eggs) to make sauce of. The hen lobster is distinguished by having a broader tail than the male, and less claws.

Set on a pot, with water salted in the proportion of a table-spoonful of salt to a quart of water; when the water boils, put it in, and keep it boiling briskly from half an hour to an hour, according to its size; wipe all the scum off it, and rub the shell with a very little butter or sweet oil; break off the great claws, crack them carefully in each joint, so that they may not be shattered, and yet come to pieces easily; cut the tail down the middle, and send up the body whole.

Boiled Lobster
From "A Poetical Cookbook", By Maria J. Moss, 1864

Those of the middle size are best. The male lobster is preferred to eat, and the female to make sauce of. Set on a pot with water, salted in proportion of a tablespoonful of salt to a quart of water. When the water boils, put it in, and keep it boiling briskly from half an hour to an hour, according to its size; wipe all the scum off it, and rub the shell with a little butter or sweet oil, break off the great claws, crack them carefully in each joint, so that they may not be shattered, and yet come to pieces easily, cut the tail down the middle, and send the body whole.

A Matelote of Fish (English)
From "The Practical Housekeeper; A Cyclopedia of Domestic Economy", By Elizabeth Fries Ellet, 1857

Take carp or tench, or both, together with an eel and any small fish; cut them into pieces, and put them along with a quantity of button-onions into a stewpan containing just wine or gravy enough of any sort to cover them, and let them stew very gently until nearly done; then have ready a couple of minced truffles and a good handful of shrimps to mix into the sauce, which may be made of either white or red wine; the *red* may be made the more savory, but the *white wine* will be found the most delicate: it should be thickened with yolk of egg, and the dish garnished with sippets of fried bread.

Soused Mackerel
From "A Plain Cookery Book for the Working Classes", By Charles Elme Francatelli, 1852

When mackerel are to be bought at six for a shilling, this kind of fish forms a cheap dinner. On such occasions, the mackerel must be placed heads and tails in an earthen dish or pan, seasoned with chopped onions, black pepper, a pinch of allspice, and salt; add sufficient vinegar and water in equal proportions to cover the fish. Bake in your own oven, if you possess one, or send them to the baker's. Note-Herrings, sprats, or any other cheap fish, are soused in the same manner.

To Stew Fish White
From "A Poetical Cookbook", By Maria J. Moss, 1864

Let your fish be cleaned and salted; save your melts or kows. Cut three onions and parsley root, boil them in a pint of water; cut your fish in pieces to suit; take some clever sized pieces, cut them from the bone, chop them fine, mix with them the melts, crumbs of bread, a little ginger, one egg well beaten, leeks, green parsley, all made fine; take some bread, and make them in small balls; lay your fish in your stewpan, layer of fish and layer of onions; sprinkle with ginger, pour cold water over to cover your fish; let it boil till done, then lay your fish nicely on a dish. To make the sauce, take the juice of a large lemon and yolk of an egg, well beaten together, teaspoonful of flour; mix it gradually with half a pint of the water the fish was done in, then with all your water put in your balls; let it boil very quick; when done throw the balls and gravy over your fish.

Another Way To Stew Fish: Boil six onions in water till tender, strain, and cut them in slices. Put your fish, cut in slices, in a stewpan with a quart of water, salt, pepper, ginger and mace to suit taste; let it boil fifteen minutes; add the onions, and forcemeat balls made of chopped fish, grated bread, chopped onion, parsley, marjoram, mace, pepper, ginger and salt, and five eggs beat up with a spoon into balls, and drop them into the pan of
fish when boiling; cover close for ten minutes, take it off the fire, and then add six eggs with the juice of five lemons; stir the gravy very slowly, add chopped parsley, and let it all simmer on a slow fire, keeping the pan in motion until it just boils, when it must be taken off quickly, or the sauce will break. A little butter or sweet oil added to the balls is an improvement. If you meet with good success in the cooking of this receipt, you will often have stewed fish.

Fried Oysters
From "Directions for Cookery, in its Various Branches" By Eliza Leslie, 1840

Get the largest and finest oysters. After they are taken from the shell wipe each of them quite dry with a cloth. Then beat up in a pan yolk of egg and milk, (in the proportion of two yolks to half a jill or a wine glass of milk,) and grate some stale broad grated very fine in a large flat dish. Cut up at least half a pound of fresh butter in the frying-pan, and hold it over the fire till it is boiling hot. Dip the oysters all over lightly in the mixture of egg and milk, and then roll them up and down in the grated bread, making as many crumbs stick to them as you can.

Put them into the frying-pan of hot butter, and keep it over a hot fire. Fry them brown, turning them that they may be equally browned on both sides. If properly done they will be crisp, and not greasy.

Serve them, dry in a hot dish, and do not pour over them the butter that may be left in the pan when they are fried.

Oysters are very good taken out of the shells and broiled on a gridiron.

Oyster Loaves
From "A Poetical Cookbook", By Maria J. Moss, 1864

Cut off the tops of some small French rolls, take out the crumb, fry them brown and crisp with clarified butter, then fry some breadcrumbs; stew the requisite quantity of oysters, bearded and cut in two, in their liquor, with a little white wine, some gravy, and seasoned with grated lemon-peel, powdered mace, pepper and salt; add a bit of butter, fill the rolls with oysters, and serve them with the fried breadcrumbs in a dish.

Oyster Pie
From "Directions for Cookery, in its Various Branches" By Eliza Leslie, 1840

Make a puff-paste, in the proportion of a pound and a half of fresh butter to two pounds of sifted flour. Roll it out rather thick, into two sheets. Butter a deep dish, and line the bottom and sides of it with paste. Fill it up with crusts of bread for the purpose of supporting the lid while it is baking, as the oysters will be too much done if they are cooked in the pie. Cover it with the other sheet of paste, having first buttered the flat rim of the dish. Notch the edges of the pie handsomely, or ornament them with leaves of paste which you may form with tin cutters made for the purpose. Make a little slit in the middle of the lid, and stick firmly into it a paste tulip or other flower. Put the dish into a moderate oven, and while the paste is baking prepare the oysters, which should he large and fresh. Put them into a stew-pan with half their liquor thickened with yolk of egg boiled hard and grated, enriched with pieces of butter rolled in bread crumbs, and seasoned with mace and nutmeg. Stew the oysters five minutes. When the paste is baked, carefully take off the lid, remove the pieces of bread, and put in the oysters and gravy. Replace the lid, and send the pie to table warm.

To Stew Oysters
From "The Great Western Cook Book, or Table Receipts, Adapted to Western Housewifery", By Anna Maria Collins, 1857

Take a quart of oysters, lay them out of the liquor, into cold water, take the liquor and strain it through a sieve, add an equal quantity of water, put it in a saucepan, then a tea-spoonful of black pepper, an ounce of sweet butter, then lay the oysters in, let them simmer a few minutes, have ready a deep dish with some nice slices of toasted bread, then pour the oysters over them.

Perch Stewed With Wine
From "The Book of Household Management", By Isabella Beeton, 1861

Equal quantities of stock No. 105 and sherry, 1 bay-leaf, 1 clove of garlic, a small bunch of parsley, 2 cloves, salt to taste; thickening of butter and flour, pepper, grated nutmeg, ½ teaspoonful of anchovy sauce.
Scale the fish and take out the gills, and clean them thoroughly; lay them in a stewpan with sufficient stock and sherry just to cover them. Put in the bay-leaf, garlic, parsley, cloves, and salt, and simmer till tender. When done, take out the fish, strain the liquor, add a thickening of butter and flour, the pepper, nutmeg, and the anchovy sauce, and stir it over the fire until somewhat reduced, when pour over the fish, and serve.
Time-About 20 minutes.

Perch With Wine
From "A Poetical Cookbook", By Maria J. Moss, 1864

Having scalded and taken out the gills, put the perch into a stew-pan, with equal quantities of stock and white wine, a bay leaf, a clove of garlic, a bunch of parsley, and scallions, two cloves, and some salt.
When done, take out the fish, strain off the liquor, the dregs of which mix with some butter and a little flour; beat these up, set them on the fire, stewing till quite done, adding pepper, grated nutmeg, and a ball of anchovy butter. Drain the perch well, and dish them with the above sauce (To make the sauce, take the juice of a large lemon and yolk of an egg, well beaten together, teaspoonful of flour; mix it

gradually with half a pint of the water the fish was done in, then with all your water put in your balls; let it boil very quick; when done throw the balls and gravy over your fish.)

To Bake Pike
From "A New System of Domestic Cookery", By Maria Eliza Ketelby Rundell, 1807

Scale it, and open as near the throat as you can, then stuff it with the following: grated bread, herbs, anchovies, oysters, suet, salt, pepper, mace, half a pint of cream, four yolks of eggs; mix all over the fire till it thickens, then put it into the fish, and sew it up; butter should be put over it in little bits; bake it. Serve sauce of gravy, butter, and anchovy, *Note:* if in helping a pike, the back and belly are slit up, and each slice gently drawn downwards, there will be fewer bones given.

Baked Salmon-Trout
From "The Lady's Receipt-Book; a Useful Companion for Large or Small Families", By Eliza Leslie, 1847

Having cleaned the fish, and laid it two hours in weak salt and water, dry it in a cloth, and then rub both the inside and outside with a seasoning of cayenne pepper, powdered mace, nutmeg, and a little salt mixed well together. Then lay it in a deep baking pan, turn the tail round into the mouth, and stick bits of fresh butter thickly over the fish. Put it into an oven, bake it well; basting it frequently with the liquid that will soon surround it. When you suppose it to be nearly done, try it by sticking down to the back-bone a thin-bladed knife. When you find that the flesh separates immediately from the bone, it is done sufficiently. Serve it up with lobster-sauce.
Any large fresh fish may be baked in this way.

Baked Salmon
From "The Lady's Receipt-Book; a Useful Companion for Large or Small Families", By Eliza Leslie, 1847

A small salmon may be baked whole. Stuff it with forcemeat made of bread-crumbs; chopped oysters, or minced lobster; butter; cayenne; a little salt, and powdered mace,--all mixed well, and moistened with beaten yolk of egg. Bend the salmon round, and put the tail into the mouth, fastening it with a skewer. Put it into a large deep dish; lay bits of butter on it at small intervals; and set it into the oven. While baking, look at it occasionally, and baste it with the butter. When one side is well browned, turn it carefully in the dish, and add more butter. Bake it till the other side is well browned. Then transfer it to another dish with the gravy that is about it, and send it to table.
If you bake salmon in slices, reserve the forcemeat for the outside. Dip each slice

first in beaten yolk of egg, and then in the forcemeat, till it is well coated. If in one large piece, cover it in the same manner thickly with the seasoning.

The usual sauce for baked salmon is melted butter, flavoured with the juice of a lemon, and a glass of port wine, stirred in just before the butter is taken from the fire. Serve it up in a sauce-boat.

Salmon Baked In Slices
From "Directions for Cookery, in its Various Branches" By Eliza Leslie, 1840

Take out the bone and cut the flesh into slices. Season them with cayenne and salt. Melt two ounces of butter that has been rolled in flour, in a half pint of water, and mix with it two large glasses of port wine, two table-spoonfuls of catchup, and two anchovies. This allowance is for a small quantity of salmon. For a large dish you must proportion the ingredients accordingly. Let the anchovies remain in the liquid till they are dissolved. Then strain it and pour it over the slices of salmon. Tie a sheet of buttered paper over the dish, and put it into the oven. You may bake trout or carp in the same manner.

Roasted Salmon
From "The Lady's Receipt-Book; a Useful Companion for Large or Small Families", By Eliza Leslie, 1847

Take a large piece of fine fresh salmon, cut from the middle of the fish, well cleaned and carefully scaled. Wipe it dry in a clean coarse cloth. Then dredge it with flour, put it on the spit, and place it before a clear bright fire. Baste it with fresh butter, and roast it well; seeing that it is thoroughly done to the bone. Serve it up plain; garnishing the dish with slices of lemon, as many persons like a little lemon-juice with salmon. This mode of cooking salmon will be found excellent. A small one or a salmon-trout may be roasted whole.

To Roast Shad-(Sea-Shore Receipt)
From "The Practical Housekeeper; A Cyclopedia of Domestic Economy", By Elizabeth Fries Ellet, 1857

Split your fish down the back after he is cleansed and washed; nail the halves on shingles or shortboard; stick them erect in the sand round a large fire; as soon as they are well browned, serve on whatever you have; eat with cold butter, black pepper, salt, and a good appetite. (This is a delicious way of cooking this fish.)

To Bake Smelts
From "The Book of Household Management", By Isabella Beeton, 1861

12 smelts, bread crumbs, 1/4 lb. of fresh butter, 2 blades of pounded mace; salt and cayenne to taste.

Wash, and dry the fish thoroughly in a cloth, and arrange them nicely in a flat baking-dish. Cover them with fine bread crumbs, and place little pieces of butter all over them. Season and bake for 15 minutes. Just before serving, add a squeeze of lemon-juice, and garnish with fried parsley and cut lemon.

Time-1/4 hour.

To Fry Smelts
From "A New System of Domestic Cookery", By Maria Eliza Ketelby Rundell, 1807

They should not be washed more than is necessary to clean them. Dry them in a cloth; then lightly flour them, but shake it off. Dip them into plenty of egg, then into bread-crumbs grated fine, and plunge them into a good pan of *boiling* lard; let them continue gently boiling, and a few minutes will make them a bright yellow-brown. Take cave not to take off the light roughness of the crumbs, or their beauty will be lost.

To Fry Trout
From "Directions for Cookery, in its Various Branches" By Eliza Leslie, 1840

Having cleaned the fish, and cut off the fins, dredge them with flour. Have ready some beaten yolk of egg, and in a separate dish some grated bread crumbs. Dip each fish into the egg, and then strew them with bread crumbs. Put some butter or fresh beef-dripping into a frying-pan, and hold it over the fire till it is boiling hot; then, (having skimmed it,) put in the fish and fry them.

Prepare some melted butter with a spoonful of mushroom-catchup and a spoonful of lemon-pickle stirred into it. Send it to table in a sauce-boat to eat with the fish. You may fry carp and flounders in the same manner.

Stewed Trout
From "The Book of Household Management", By Isabella Beeton, 1861

2 middling-sized trout, 1/2 onion cut in thin slices, a little parsley, 2 cloves, 1 blade of mace, 2 bay-leaves, a little thyme, salt and pepper to taste, 1 pint of medium stock No. 105, 1 glass
of port wine, thickening of butter and flour.

Wash the fish very clean, and wipe it quite dry. Lay it in a stewpan, with all the ingredients but the butter and flour, and simmer gently for 1/2 hour, or rather

more, should not the fish be quite done. Take it out, strain the gravy, add the thickening, and stir it over a
sharp fire for 5 minutes; pour it over the trout, and serve.
Time-According to size, 1/2 hour or more.

4. Side Dishes and Salads

"What was lacking in company was made up for by the excellence of old Colonel Chesnut's ancient Madeira and champagne. If everything in the Confederacy were only as truly good as the old Colonel's wine cellars! Then we had a salad and jelly cake." -Mary Boykin Chesnut, October 27, 1863. "A Diary From Dixie", describing a party for "Young" Wade Hampton.

"On one march, from Petersburg to Appomattox, no rations were issued to Cutshaw's battalion of artillery for one entire week, and the men subsisted on the corn intended for the battery horses, raw bacon captured from the enemy, and the water of springs, creeks and rivers. No doubt there were other commands suffering the same privations."-Pvt. Carlton McCarthy, Second company Richmond Howitzers, Cutshaw's Battalion from *Detailed Minutiae Of Soldier Life In The Army Of Northern Virginia*

Asparagus Loaves
From "The Lady's Receipt-Book; a Useful Companion for Large or Small Families", By Eliza Leslie, 1847

Having scraped the stalks of three bundles of fine, large asparagus, (laying it, as you proceed, in a pan of cold water,) tie it up again in bunches, put them into a pot with a great deal of boiling water, and a little salt, and boil them about twenty minutes, or till quite tender. Then take out the asparagus, and drain it. Cut off the green tops of two-thirds of the asparagus, and on the remainder leave about two inches of the white stalk; this remaining asparagus must be kept warm. Put the tops into a stew-pan with a pint of cream, or rich milk, sufficient to cover them well; adding three table-spoonfuls of fresh butter, rolled in flour, half a grated nutmeg, and the well-beaten yolks of three eggs. Set the stew-pan over hot coals, and stir the mixture till it comes to a boil. Then immediately remove it. Have ready some tall fresh rolls or penny loaves; cut the tops carefully off, in a nice circular or oval piece, and then scoop out the inside of the rolls, and fill them with the stewed asparagus while it is hot. Make small holes very nicely in the tops or lids. Fit the lids again on the rolls, and stick in the holes (of which you must make as many as you can) the remaining asparagus, that has had the bit of stalk left on for this purpose. Send them to table warm, as side-dishes.

Asparagus Pudding
From "The Book of Household Management", By Isabella Beeton, 1861

1/2 pint of asparagus peas, 4 eggs, 2 tablespoonfuls of flour, 1 tablespoonful of *very finely* minced ham, 1 oz. of butter, pepper and salt to taste, milk.

Cut up the nice green tender parts of asparagus, about the size of peas; put them into a basin with the eggs, which should be well beaten, and the flour, ham, butter, pepper, and salt. Mix all these ingredients well together, and moisten with sufficient milk to make the pudding of the consistency of thick batter; put it into a pint buttered mould, tie it down tightly with a floured cloth, place it in *boiling water*, and let it boil for 2 hours; turn it out of the mould on to a hot dish, and pour plain melted butter *round*, but not over, the pudding. Green peas pudding may be made in exactly the same manner, substituting peas for the asparagus.

Baked Beans-Yankee Fashion
From "The Great Western Cook Book, or Table Receipts, Adapted to Western Housewifery", By Anna Maria Collins, 1857

Take three pints of white beans, put them in cold water over night, take them out in the morning, wash and rub them well, then put them in a pot, and boil them until tender; then put them in an earthen dish. Cut a neat piece of pork, place it on the top of the beans; bake them slowly until well browned. This is a fine dish for a snowy day.

Baked Potatoes
From "The Great Western Cook Book, or Table Receipts, Adapted to Western Housewifery", By Anna Maria Collins, 1857

Prepare them as the foregoing; make it into a round shape in a baking dish; egg the top with yolk of egg, and brown very slightly. Take them out of the oven, make a little hole as large as an egg in the top, and fill it with melted butter.

Baked Tomatoes
From "The Great Western Cook Book, or Table Receipts, Adapted to Western Housewifery", By Anna Maria Collins, 1857

Scald your tomatoes, peel off the skins, lay them in a pan, sprinkle them with pepper and salt, then put a layer of bread-crumbs and butter, then, again, tomatoes, until your pan is full. One hour in a quick stove will bake it perfectly. Some love onions in this dish.

Beet Roots
From "A New System of Domestic Cookery", By Maria Eliza Ketelby Rundell, 1807

Make a very pleasant addition to winter-salad; of which they may agreeably form a full half, instead of being only used to ornament it. This root is cooling, and very wholesome.
It is extremely good boiled, and sliced with a small quantity of onion; or stewed with whole onions, large or small, as follows:
Boil the beet tender with the skin on; slice it into a stew-pan with a little broth, and a spoonful of vinegar: simmer till the gravy is tinged with the colour; then put it into a small dish, and make a round of the button-onions, first boiled till tender; take off the skin just before serving, and mind they are quite hot, and clear.
Or roast three large onions, and peel off the outer skins till they look clear; and serve the beet-root stewed, round them.
If beet-root is in the least broken before dressed, it parts with its colour, and looks ill.

Boiled Cauliflowers

From "The Book of Household Management", By Isabella Beeton, 1861

To each 1/2 gallon of water allow 1 heaped tablespoonful of salt.
Choose cauliflowers that are close and white; trim off the decayed outside leaves, and cut the stalk off flat at the bottom. Open the flower a little in places to remove the insects, which generally are found about the stalk, and let the cauliflowers lie in salt and water for an hour previous to dressing them, with their heads downwards: this will effectually draw out all the vermin. Then put them into fast-boiling water, with the addition of salt in the above proportion, and let them boil briskly over a good fire, keeping the saucepan uncovered. The water should be well skimmed; and, when the cauliflowers are tender, take them up with a slice; let them drain, and, if large enough, place them upright in the dish. Serve with plain melted butter, a little of which may be poured over the flower.
Time-Small cauliflower, 12 to 15 minutes, large one, 20 to 25 minutes, after the water boils.

Brain Balls
From "The Complete Cook", By J. M. Sanderson, 1864

Take a calf's brains, or two or three lambs', scald them for ten minutes, quite free from every bit of vein and skin, beat up with seasoning the same as egg balls, adding a tea spoonful of chopped sage; rub a tea-cup full of bread crumbs, three tea spoonfuls of flour, and a raw egg with them. Make them up into balls, rub each ball with bread, fry them with butter or lard; serve as a garnish to calf's head, or as a separate side dish.

Buttered Parsnips
From "A Plain Cookery Book for the Working Classes", By Charles Elme Francatelli, 1852

Scrape or peel the parsnips, and boil them in hot water till they are done quite tender, then drain off all the water, add a bit of butter, some chopped parsley, pepper and salt; shake them together on the fire until all is well mixed.

Buttered Swedish Turnips
From "A Plain Cookery Book for the Working Classes", By Charles Elme Francatelli, 1852

Swedish turnips are mostly given as food to cattle; true, but there is no good reason why they should not be considered as excellent food for man, for they are sweeter, and yield more substance than the ordinary turnips; let them be peeled, boiled in plenty of water, and when done, mashed with a little milk, butter, pepper, and salt.

Cabbage
From "Directions for Cookery, in its Various Branches" By Eliza Leslie, 1840

All vegetables of the cabbage kind should be carefully washed, and examined in case of insects lurking among the leaves. To prepare a cabbage for boiling, remove the outer leaves, and pare and trim the stalk, cutting it close and short. If the cabbage is large, quarter it; if small, cut it in half; and let it stand for a while in a deep part of cold water with the large end downwards. Put it into a pot with plenty of water, (having first tied it together to keep it whole while boiling,) and, taking off the scum, boil it two hours, or till the stalk is quite tender. When done, drain and squeeze it well. Before you send it to table introduce a little fresh butter between the leaves; or have melted butter in a boat. If it has been boiled with meat add no butter to it.

A young cabbage will boil in an hour or an hour and a half.

Cabbage
From "The Great Western Cook Book, or Table Receipts, Adapted to Western Housewifery", By Anna Maria Collins, 1857

Is best boiled with middling or side of bacon, never fill the pot up with cold water after it has commenced boiling; a tea-spoonful of saleratus improves boiled cabbage, when they are old. Always dish the cabbage first, and after you skin the bacon lay it on top.

Corn bread is a necessary appendage to bacon and cabbage.

To Dress Carrots In The German Way
From "The Book of Household Management", By Isabella Beeton, 1861

8 large carrots, 3 oz. of butter, salt to taste, a very little grated nutmeg, 1 tablespoonful of finely-minced parsley, 1 dessertspoonful of minced onion, rather more than 1 pint of weak stock or broth, 1 tablespoonful of flour.

Wash and scrape the carrots, and cut them into rings of about 1/4 inch in thickness. Put the butter into a stewpan; when it is melted, lay in the carrots, with salt, nutmeg, parsley, and onion in the above proportions. Toss the stewpan over the fire for a few minutes, and when the carrots are well saturated with the butter, pour in the stock, and simmer gently until they are nearly tender. Then put into another stewpan a small piece of butter; dredge in about a tablespoonful of flour; stir this over the fire, and when of a nice brown colour, add the liquor that the carrots have been boiling in; let this just boil up, pour it over the carrots in the other stewpan, and let them finish simmering until quite tender. Serve very hot. This vegetable, dressed as above, is a favourite accompaniment of roast pork, sausages, &c. &c.

Time-About 3/4 hour.

Cauliflower Dressed Like Macaroni
From "The Practical Housekeeper; A Cyclopedia of
Domestic Economy", By Elizabeth Fries Ellet, 1857

Boil a cauliflower in milk and water, with a little butter, half an hour, skimming well; when tender, drain, and divide it small; put a quarter of a pound of butter, half as much grated cheese, half a gill of milk, in a pan to boil up, and put in the sprigs of cauliflower-- stew five minutes; then put it into a dish, grate over it as much more cheese, and brown it with a shovel.

To dress Cauliflowers, separate the green part, and cut the flower close to the bottom from the stalk; let it soak an hour in clear cold water, and then lay it in boiling milk and water, or water alone, observing to skim it well. When the flower or stalk feels tender, it is done enough, and should be instantly taken up. Drain it for a minute, and serve it up in a dish by itself, with plain melted butter in a sauce-tureen.

Cauliflower Maccaroni
From "The Lady's Receipt-Book; a Useful Companion for Large or Small
Families", By Eliza Leslie, 1847

Having removed the outside leaves, and cut off the stalk, wash the cauliflower, and examine it thoroughly to see if there are any insects about it. Next lay it for an hour in a pan of cold water. Then put it into a pot of boiling milk and water that has had a little fresh butter melted in it. Whatever scum may float on the top of the water must be removed before the cauliflower goes in. Boil it, steadily, half an hour, or till it is quite tender. Then take it out, drain it, and cut it into short sprigs. Have ready three ounces of rich, but not strong cheese, grated fine. Put into a stew-pan a quarter of a pound of fresh butter; nearly half of the grated cheese; two large tablespoonfuls of cream or rich milk; and a very little salt and cayenne. Toss or shake it over the fire, till it is well mixed, and has come to a boil. Then add the tufts of cauliflower; and let the whole stew together about five minutes. When done, put it into a deep dish; strew over the top the remaining half of the grated cheese, and brown it with a salamander or a red hot shovel held above the surface.

This will be found very superior to real maccaroni.

Cauliflowers With Parmesan Cheese
From "The Book of Household Management", By Isabella Beeton, 1861

2 or 3 cauliflowers, rather more than 1/2 pint of white sauce No. 378 (see recipe for "Melted Butter"), 2 tablespoonfuls of grated Parmesan cheese, 2 oz. of fresh butter, 3 tablespoonfuls of bread crumbs.

Cleanse and boil the cauliflowers by recipe No. 1104 (see recipe for "Boiled Cauliflowers from The Book of Household Management"), and drain them and dish them with the flowers standing upright. Have ready the above proportion of white sauce; pour sufficient of it over the cauliflowers just to cover the top; sprinkle over this some rasped Parmesan cheese and bread crumbs, and drop on these the butter, which should be melted, but not oiled. Brown with a salamander, or before the fire, and pour round, but not over, the flowers the remainder of the sauce, with which should be mixed a small quantity of grated Parmesan cheese.
Time-Altogether, 1/2 hour.

Cauliflower in White Sauce
From "A New System of Domestic Cookery", By Maria Eliza Ketelby Rundell, 1807

Half-boil it; then cut it into handsome pieces, and lay them in a stew-pan with a little broth, a bit of mace, a little salt, and a dust of white pepper; simmer half an hour; then put a little cream, butter, and flour: shake; and simmer a few minutes, and serve.

Cold Slaw
From "Directions for Cookery, in its Various Branches" By Eliza Leslie, 1840

Take a nice fresh cabbage, wash and drain it, and cut off all the stalk. Shave down the head into very small slips, with a cabbage cutter, or a very sharp knife. It must be done evenly and nicely. Put it into a deep china dish, and prepare for it the following dressing. Melt in a sauce-pan a quarter of a pound of butter, with half a pint of water, a large table-spoonful of vinegar, a salt-spoon of salt, and a little cayenne. Give this a boil up, and pour it hot upon the cabbage.
Send it to table as soon as it is cold.

Cucumbers A La Poulette
From "The Book of Household Management", By Isabella Beeton, 1861

2 or 3 cucumbers, salt and vinegar, 2 oz. of butter, flour, 1/2 pint of broth, 1 teaspoonful of minced parsley, a lump of sugar, the yolks of 2 eggs, salt and pepper to taste.
Pare and cut the cucumbers into slices of an equal thickness, and let them remain in a pickle of salt and vinegar for 1/2 hour; then drain them in a cloth, and put them into a stewpan with the butter. Fry them over a brisk fire, but do not brown them, and then dredge over them a little flour; add the broth, skim off all the fat, which will rise to the surface, and boil gently until the gravy is somewhat reduced;

but the cucumber should not be broken. Stir in the yolks of the eggs, add the parsley, sugar, and a seasoning of pepper and salt; bring the whole to the point of boiling, and serve.

Time-Altogether, 1 hour.

Cucumbers Stewed
From "The Cook's Oracle; and Housekeeper's Manual", By William Kitchiner, 1830

Peel and cut cucumbers in quarters, take out the seeds, and lay them on a cloth to drain off the water: when they are dry, flour and fry them in fresh butter; let the butter be quite hot before you put in the cucumbers; fry them till they are brown, then take them out with an
egg-slice, and lay them on a sieve to drain the fat from them (some cooks fry sliced onions, or some small button onions, with them, till they are a delicate light-brown colour, drain them from the fat, and then put them into a stew-pan with as much gravy as will cover them): stew slowly till they are tender; take out the cucumbers with a slice, thicken the gravy with flour and butter, give it a boil up, season it with pepper and salt, and put in the cucumbers; as soon as they are warm, they are ready.

Egg Balls
From "The Complete Cook", By J. M. Sanderson, 1864

Boil four eggs for ten minutes and put them into cold water; when they are cold beat the yolks in a mortar with the yolk of a raw egg, some chopped parsley, a teaspoonful of flour, a pinch or two of salt, and a little black pepper, or cayenne; rub them well together, roll them into small balls, and boil them two minutes.

Egg Plant
From "The Virginia Housewife", By Mary Randolph, 1860

The purple ones are best; get them young and fresh; pull out the stem, and parboil them to take off the bitter taste; cut them in slices an inch thick, but do not peel them; dip them in the yelk of an egg, and cover them with grated bread, a little salt and pepper--when this has dried, cover the other side the same way--fry them a nice brown. They are very delicious, tasting much like soft crabs. The egg plant may be dressed in another manner: scrape the rind and parboil them; cut a slit from one end to the other, take out the seeds, fill the space with a rich forcemeat, and stew them in well seasoned gravy, or bake them, and serve up with gravy in the dish.

French Spinach
From "The Lady's Receipt-Book; a Useful Companion for Large or Small Families", By Eliza Leslie, 1847

Having picked them from the stalks, wash the leaves carefully in two or three cold waters, till they are quite free from grit. Put the spinach into a sauce-pan of hot water, in which a very small portion of salt has been boiled. There must be sufficient water to allow the spinach to float. Stir it frequently, that all the leaves may be equally done. Let it boil for a quarter of an hour. Then take it out, lay it in a sieve, and drain it well; pressing it thoroughly with your hands. Next chop it as fine as possible. For a large dish of spinach, put two ounces of butter into a stew-pan; dredge in a table-spoonful of flour and four or five table-spoonfuls of rich cream, mixed with a tea-spoonful of powdered loaf-sugar. Mix all well, and when they have come to a boil, add, gradually, the spinach. Stew it about ten minutes, (stirring it frequently,) till the superfluous moisture is all absorbed. Then serve it up very hot, garnishing it all round with leaves of puff-paste, that have been handsomely formed with a tin cutter, and are fresh from the oven.

Fricassee of Parsnips
From "A New System of Domestic Cookery", By Maria Eliza Ketelby Rundell, 1807

Boil in milk till they are soft. Then cut them lengthways into bits two or three inches long; and simmer in a white sauce, made of two spoonfuls of broth, a bit of mace, half a cupful of cream, a bit of butter, and some. flour, pepper, and salt.

Fried Artichokes
From "The Book of Household Management", By Isabella Beeton, 1861

5 or 6 artichokes, salt and water: for the batter,—1/4 lb. of flour, a little salt, the yolk of 1 egg, milk.Trim and boil the artichokes by recipe No. 1080, and rub them over with lemon-juice, to keep them white. When they are quite tender, take them up, remove the chokes, and divide the bottoms; dip each piece into batter, fry them in hot lard or dripping, and garnish the dish with crisped parsley. Serve with plain melted butter.
Time-20 minutes to boil the artichokes, 5 to 7 minutes to fry them.

Fried Cauliflower
From "The Lady's Receipt-Book; a Useful Companion for Large or Small Families", By Eliza Leslie, 1847

Having laid a fine cauliflower in cold water for an hour, put it into a pot of boiling water that has been slightly salted, (milk and water will be still better,) and boil it twenty-five minutes, or till the large stalk is perfectly tender. Then divide it,

equally, into small tufts, and spread it on a dish to cool. Prepare a sufficient quantity of batter made in the proportion of a table-spoonful of flour, and two table-spoonfuls of milk to each egg. Beat the eggs very light; then stir into them the flour and milk alternately; a spoonful of flour, and two spoonfuls of milk at a time. When the cauliflower is cold, have ready some fresh butter in a frying-pan over a clear fire. When it has come to a boil and has done bubbling, dip each tuft of cauliflower twice into the pan of batter, and fry them a light brown. Send them to table hot.
Broccoli may be fried in this manner.

Fried Celery
From "The Lady's Receipt-Book; a Useful Companion for Large or Small Families", By Eliza Leslie, 1847

Take fine large celery; cut it into pieces three or four inches in length, and boil it tender; having seasoned the water with a very little salt. Then drain the pieces well, and lay them, separately, to cool on a large dish. Make a batter in the proportion of three well-beaten eggs stirred into a pint of rich milk, alternately with half a pint of grated bread-crumbs, or of sifted flour. Beat the batter very hard after it is all mixed. Put into a hot frying-pan, a sufficiency of fresh lard; melt it over the fire, and when it comes to a boil, dip each piece of celery *twice* into the batter, put them into the pan, and fry them a light brown. When done, lay them to drain on an inverted sieve with a broad pan placed beneath it. Then dish the fried celery, and send it to table hot.
Parsnips, and salsify (or oyster plant) may be fried in butter according to the above directions.
Also the tops of asparagus cut off from the stalk; and the white part or blossom of cauliflower.
Cold sweet potatoes are very nice, peeled, cut into long slips, and fried in this way.

How To Fry Potatoes
From "A Plain Cookery Book for the Working Classes", By Charles Elme Francatelli, 1852

Peel, split, and cut the potatoes into slices of equal thickness, say the thickness of two penny pieces; and as they are cut out of hand, let them be dropped into a pan of cold water. When about to fry the potatoes, first drain them on a clean cloth, and dab them all over, in order to absorb all moisture; while this has been going on, you will have made some kind of fat (entirely free from water or gravy, such as lard, for instance) very hot in a frying-pan, and into this drop your prepared potatoes, only a good handful at a time; as, if you attempt to fry too many at once, instead of being crisp, as they should be, the potatoes will fry flabby, and consequently will be unappetising. As soon as the first lot is fried in a satisfactory manner, drain them from the fat with a skimmer, or spoon, and then fry the remainder; and when all are fried, shake a little salt over them.

Greens
From "Miss Beecher's Domestic Receipt Book", By Catharine Esther Beecher, 1850

Beet tops, turnip tops, spinach, cabbage sprouts, dandelions, cowslips, all these boil in salted water till they are tender, then drain in a colander, pressing hard. Chop them a little, and warm them in a sauce-pan, with a little butter.
Lay them on buttered toast, and if you like, garnish them with hard-boiled egg, cut in slices. If not fresh, soak them half an hour in salt and water.

Green Corn Pudding
From "The Practical Housekeeper; A Cyclopedia of Domestic Economy", By Elizabeth Fries Ellet, 1857

Twelve ears of green corn, grated a quart of milk, four ounces butter, the same of sugar, four eggs beaten light. Bake in a buttered dish, and eat with butter and sugar sauce. The corn may be previously boiled, when the pudding will bake more quickly.

Green Peas A La Francaise
From "The Book of Household Management", By Isabella Beeton, 1861

2 quarts of green peas, 3 oz. of fresh butter, a bunch of parsley, 6 green onions, flour, a small lump of sugar, 1/2 teaspoonful of salt, a teaspoonful of flour.
Shell sufficient fresh-gathered peas to fill 2 quarts; put them into cold water, with the above proportion of butter, and stir them about until they are well covered with the butter; drain them in a colander, and put them in a stewpan, with the parsley and onions; dredge over them a little flour, stir the peas well, and moisten them with boiling water; boil them quickly over a large fire for 20 minutes, or until there is no liquor remaining. Dip a small lump of sugar into some water, that it may soon melt; put it with the peas, to which add 1/2 teaspoonful of salt. Take a piece of butter the size of a walnut, work it together with a teaspoonful of flour; and add this

to the peas, which should be boiling when it is put in. Keep shaking the stewpan, and, when the peas are nicely thickened, dress them high in the dish, and serve. Time-Altogether, 3/4 hour.

Lettuce Peas
From "The Lady's Receipt-Book; a Useful Companion for Large or Small Families", By Eliza Leslie, 1847

Having washed four lettuces, and stripped off the outside leaves, take their hearts, and (having chopped them well) put them into a stew-pan with two quarts of young green peas, freshly shelled; a lump or two of loaf-sugar; and three or four leaves of green mint minced as finely as possible. Then put in a slice of cold ham, and a quarter of a pound of butter divided into four bits and rolled in flour; and two table-spoonfuls of water. Add a little black pepper, and let the whole stew for about twenty-five minutes, or till the peas are thoroughly done. Then take out the ham, and add to the stew half a pint of cream. Let it continue stewing five minutes longer. Then send it to table.

Macaroni As Usually Served
From "A New System of Domestic Cookery", By Maria Eliza Ketelby Rundell, 1807

Boil it in milk, or a weak veal broth, pretty well flavoured with salt. When tender, put it into a dish without the liquor, and among it put some bits of butter and grated cheese, and over the top grate more, and a little more butter. Set the dish into a Dutch oven a quarter of an hour, but do not let the top become hard.
Another way-Wash it well, and simmer in half milk, and half broth of veal or mutton, till it is tender. To a spoonful of this liquor, put the yolk of an egg beaten in a spoonful of cream; just make it hot to thicken, but not boil; put it over the macaroni, and then grate fine old cheese all over, and bits of butter. Brown with the salamander.
Another-Wash the macaroni, then simmer it in a little broth, with a little pounded mace and salt. When quite tender, take it out of the liquor, lay it in a dish, grate a good deal of cheese over, then cover that with bread grated fine. Warm some butter without oiling, and pour it from a boat through a little earthen colander all over the crumbs, then put the dish in a Dutch oven, to roast the cheese, and brown the bread of a fine colour. The bread, should be in separated crumbs, and, look light.

Macaroni Gratin
From "A Poetical Cookbook", By Maria J. Moss, 1864

Lay fried bread pretty closely round a dish; boil your macaroni in the usual way, and pour it into the dish; smooth it all over, and strew breadcrumbs on it, then a pretty thick layer of grated Parmesan cheese; drop a little melted butter on it, and put it in the oven to brown.

Onion Custard
From "The Lady's Receipt-Book; a Useful Companion for Large or Small Families", By Eliza Leslie, 1847

Peel and slice some mild onions, (ten or twelve, in proportion to their size,) and fry them in fresh butter; draining them well when you take them up. Then mince them as fine as possible. Beat four eggs very light, and stir them gradually into a pint of milk, in turn with the minced onions. Season the whole with plenty of grated nutmeg, and stir it very hard. Then put it into a deep, white dish, and bake it about a quarter of an hour. Send it to table as a side dish to be eaten with meat or poultry. It is a French preparation of onions, and will be found very fine.

Peas and Bacon
From "A Plain Cookery Book for the Working Classes", By Charles Elme Francatelli, 1852

Shave off any brown rancid part from the bacon, and put it on to boil in plenty of cold water; when it is nearly done put in the peas with a good bunch of mint, and let all boil together until the peas are done soft; then dish up the peas round the bacon.

Boiled Salad
From "The Cook's Oracle; and Housekeeper's Manual", By William Kitchiner, 1830

This is best compounded of boiled or baked onions (if Portugal the better), some baked beet-root, cauliflower, or broccoli, and boiled celery and French beans, or any of these articles, with the common salad dressing; added to this, to give it an enticing appearance, and to give some of the crispness and freshness so pleasant in salad, a small quantity of raw endive, or lettuce and chervil, or burnet, strewed on the top: this is by far more wholesome than the raw salad, and is much eaten when put on the table.

Potato Salad
From "The Book of Household Management", By Isabella Beeton, 1861

10 or 12 cold boiled potatoes, 4 tablespoonfuls of tarragon or plain vinegar, 6 tablespoonfuls of salad-oil, pepper and salt to taste, 1 teaspoonful of minced parsley.
Cut the potatoes into slices about 1/2 inch in thickness; put these into a salad-bowl with oil and vinegar in the above proportion; season with pepper, salt, and a teaspoonful of minced parsley; stir the salad well, that all the ingredients may be thoroughly incorporated, and it is ready to serve. This should be made two or three hours before it is wanted for table. Anchovies, olives, or pickles may be added to this salad, as also slices of cold beef, fowl, or turkey.

To Roast Onions
From "Directions for Cookery, in its Various Branches" By Eliza Leslie, 1840

Onions are best when parboiled before roasting. Take large onions, place them on a hot hearth and roast them before the fire in their skins, turning them as they require it. Then peel them, send them to table whole, and eat them with butter and salt.

Russian or Swedish Turnips
From "Directions for Cookery, in its Various Branches" By Eliza Leslie, 1840

This turnip (the Ruta Baga) is very large and of a reddish yellow colour; they are generally much liked. Take off a thick paring, cut the turnips into large pieces, or thick slices, and lay them awhile in cold water. Then boil them gently about two hours, or till they are quite soft. When done, drain, squeeze and mash them, and season them with pepper and salt, and a very little butter. Take care not to set them in a part of the table where the sun comes, as it will spoil the taste.
Russian turnips should always be mashed.

Squashes
From "Miss Beecher's Domestic Receipt Book", By Catharine Esther Beecher, 1850

Summer squashes boil whole, when very young. When older, quarter them, and take out the seeds. Put them into boiling salted water; when done, squeeze out the water by wringing in a cloth, and add butter and salt to your taste.

The neck part of the winter squash is the best; cut it into slices, peel it, boil it in salted water till tender, then drain off the water, and serve it without mashing, or, if preferred, wring it and season with butter and salt. What is left over is excellent *fried* for next day's breakfast or dinner. It must be in slices, and not mashed. Save the water in which they are boiled, to make yeast or brown bread, for which it is excellent.

To Make Sour Kraut
From "The Great Western Cook Book, or Table Receipts, Adapted to Western Housewifery", By Anna Maria Collins, 1857

Take a strong wooden vessel that will not leak, and large enough to hold sufficient for the consumption of a family during the winter. Take off the green leaves from the cabbage heads, and chop the cabbage into small pieces, pressing them closely, and between every two or three layers of cabbage, scatter an handful of salt, until the cask is full. Then cover it, and place a heavy weight in it, and let it stand in a warm place four or five days. Then remove the cask to a cool situation, and keep it always covered up. Anise-seed, strewed among the layers in the course of preparation, communicates to it a peculiar and agreeable flavor.

It requires two hours to boil.

Spinach
From "Directions for Cookery, in its Various Branches" By Eliza Leslie, 1840

Spinach requires close examination and picking, as insects are frequently found among it, and it is often gritty. Wash it through three or four waters. Then drain it, and put it on in boiling water. Ten minutes is generally sufficient time to boil spinach. Be careful to remove the scum. When it is quite tender, take it up, and drain and squeeze it well. Chop it fine, and put it into a sauce-pan with a piece of butter and a little pepper and salt. Set it on hot coals, and let it stew five minutes, stirring it all the time.

To Stew Celery
From "The Practical Housekeeper; A Cyclopedia of Domestic Economy", By Elizabeth Fries Ellet, 1857

Wash the heads, and strip off their outer leaves; either halve or leave them whole, according to their size, and cut them into length of four inches. Put into a stewpan with a cup of broth or weak white gravy; stew till tender; then add two spoonfuls of cream, a little flour and butter, seasoned with pepper, salt, nutmeg, and a little pounded white sugar; and simmer all together.

Stewed Eggplant
From "Directions for Cookery, in its Various Branches" By Eliza Leslie, 1840

The purple egg plants are better than the white ones. Put them whole into a pot with plenty of water, and simmer them till quite tender. Then take them out, drain them, and (having peeled off the skins) cut them up, and mash them smooth in a deep dish. Mix with them some grated bread, some powdered sweet marjoram, and a large piece of butter, adding a few pounded cloves. Grate a layer of bread over the top, and put the dish into the oven and brown it. You must send it to table in the same dish.
Eggplant is sometimes eaten at dinner, but generally at breakfast.

Stewed Green Peas
From "The Book of Household Management", By Isabella Beeton, 1861

1 quart of peas, 1 Lettuce, 1 onion, 2 oz. of butter, pepper and salt to taste, 1 egg, 1/2 teaspoonful of powdered sugar.
Shell the peas, and cut the onion and lettuce into slices; put these into a stewpan, with the butter, pepper, and salt, but with no more water than that which hangs round the lettuce from washing. Stew the whole very gently for rather more than 1 hour; then stir to it a well-beaten egg, and about 1/2 teaspoonful of powdered sugar. When the peas, &c., are nicely thickened, serve but, after the egg is added, do not allow them to boil.
Time-1-1/4 hour.

Stewed Red Cabbage
From "The Book of Household Management", By Isabella Beeton, 1861

1 red cabbage, a small slice of ham, 1/2 oz. of fresh butter, 1 pint of weak stock or broth, 1 gill of vinegar, salt and pepper to taste, 1 tablespoonful of pounded sugar.
Cut the cabbage into very thin slices, put it into a stewpan, with the ham cut in dice, the butter, 1/2 pint of stock, and the vinegar; cover the pan closely, and let it stew for 1 hour. When it is very tender, add the remainder of the stock, a seasoning of salt and pepper, and the pounded sugar; mix all well together, stir over the fire until nearly all the liquor is dried away, and serve. Fried sausages are usually sent to table with this dish: they should be laid round and on the cabbage, as a garnish.
Time-Rather more than 1 hour.

Succotash
From "The Practical Housekeeper; A Cyclopedia of Domestic Economy", By Elizabeth Fries Ellet, 1857

Is made by boiling young lima beans with green corn cut from the cob. A slice of fat pork may be boiled with it, and the mixture must have a lump of butter stirred in before serving. The beans should be boiled before the corn is added, as they take longer to cook.

Succotash, á La Tecumsah
From "The Great Western Cook Book, or Table Receipts, Adapted to Western Housewifery", By Anna Maria Collins, 1857

Boil the beans from half to three-quarters of an hour, in water, a little salt. Cut off the corn from the cobs, boil the cobs with the beans, be sure and not cut *too* close to the cob. When the beans have boiled three-quarters of an hour, take out the cobs and put the corn in; let it, then, boil fifteen minutes, if the corn is tender, if not, twenty. Have more corn than beans. When it is boiled sufficiently, take a lump of butter as large as you think will be in proportion with the vegetables, roll it well in flour, put it in the pot with the beans, with black pepper enough to season it well. This is a real Western dish, and is very easily made.

Turnips
From "A Poetical Cookbook", By Maria J. Moss, 1864

Wash, peel, and boil them till tender, in water with a little salt; serve them with melted butter. Or they may be stewed in a pint of milk, thickened with a bit of butter rolled in flour, and seasoned with salt and pepper, and served with the sauce.

Warm Slaw
From "Directions for Cookery, in its Various Branches" By Eliza Leslie, 1840

Cut the cabbage into shavings as for cold slaw; (red cabbage is best) and put it into a deep earthen dish. Cover it closely, and set it on the top of a stove, or in a slack oven for half an hour till it is warm all through; but do not let it get so heated as to boil. Then make a mixture as for cold slaw, of a quarter of a pound of butter, half a pint of water, a little salt and cayenne, and add to it a clove of garlic minced fine. Boil this mixture in a sauce-pan, and pour it hot over the warm cabbage. Send it to table immediately.
This is a French method of dressing cabbage.

5. Wild Game

"Well, Pless, I would like to see you very much and go a possum hunting with you for I have not been a possum hunting since I have been out. I want you to have my pup well trained by the time I get back so we can rake in a few of the fattest of them." - Pvt. George Washington Brummett, Jr., Co. I, 9th Arkansas Infantry, Jan. 22, 1862, Bowling Green, Kentucky. Letter to his brother, Pleasy. Pvt. Brummett was captured in Jefferson County, Arkansas on February 1, 1864 and sent to prison at Rock Island Barracks in Illinois in May 1864 where. He died September 20, 1864 from Erysipelas while languishing in prison. He is buried in the post cemetery, grave #1516.

"I had most as good luck the other day shooting Yankees, as I have had sometimes shooting squirrels around Father's plantation...."-Pvt. I. I. Miller, 2nd South Carolina Infantry, July 21, 1861. Letter to his friend, Ladson Fraser.

"Before the war shut him in General Preston sent to the lakes for his salmon, to Mississippi for his venison, to the mountains for his mutton and grouse. It is good enough, the best dish at all these houses, what the Spanish call the "hearty welcome." -Mary Boykin Chesnut, May 24, 1862. "A Diary From Dixie".

"Shortly before the evacuation of Petersburg, a country boy went hunting. He killed and brought to camp a muskrat. It was skinned, cleaned, buried a day or two, disinterred and eaten with great relish. It was splendid."-Pvt. Carlton McCarthy, Second company Richmond Howitzers, Cutshaw's Battalion from *Detailed Minutiae Of Soldier Life In The Army Of Northern Virginia.*

A Nice Way of Cooking Game
From "The Lady's Receipt-Book; a Useful Companion for Large or Small Families", By Eliza Leslie, 1847

Pheasants, partridges, quails, grouse, plovers, &c,. are excellent stuffed with chesnuts: boiled, peeled, and mashed or pounded. Cover the birds with very thin slices of cold ham; then enclose them in vine-leaves tied on securely so as to keep in the gravy. Lay them in a deep dish, and bake them in a close oven that has nothing else in it, (for instance an iron dutch oven,) that the game may imbibe no other flavour. When done, remove the ham and the vine leaves, and dish the birds with the gravy that is about them.

Pheasants are unfit to eat after the first snow, as they then, for want of other food, are apt to feed on wild laurel berries, which give their flesh a disagreeably bitter taste, and are said to have sometimes produced deleterious effects on persons who have eaten it.

To Boil Ducks With Onion Sauce
From "The Virginia Housewife", By Mary Randolph, 1860

Scald and draw your ducks, put them in warm water for a few minutes, then take them out and put them in an earthen pot; pour over them a pint of boiling milk, and let them lie in it two or three hours; when you take them out, dredge them well with flour, and put them in a copper of cold water; put on the cover, let them boil slowly twenty minutes, then take them out, and smother them with onion sauce.

To Make Onion Sauce
From "The Virginia Housewife", By Mary Randolph, 1860

Boil eight or ten large onions, change the water two or three times while they are boiling; when enough, chop them on a board to keep them a good colour, put them in a sauce pan with a quarter of a pound of butter and two spoonsful of thick cream; boil it a little, and pour it over the ducks.

Hashed Duck
From "The Book of Household Management", By Isabella Beeton, 1861

The remains of cold roast duck, rather more than 1 pint of weak stock or water, 1 onion, 1 oz. of butter, thickening of butter and flour, salt and cayenne to taste, 1/2 teaspoonful of minced lemon-peel, 1 dessertspoonful of lemon-juice, 1/2 glass of port wine.

Cut the duck into nice joints, and put the trimmings into a stewpan; slice and fry the onion in a little butter; add these to the trimmings, pour in the above proportion of weak stock or water, and stew gently for 1 hour. Strain the liquor, thicken it with butter and flour, season with salt and cayenne, and add the remaining ingredients; boil it up and skim well; lay in the pieces of duck, and let them get thoroughly hot through by the side of the fire, but do not allow them to boil: they should soak in the gravy for about 1/2 hour. Garnish with sippets of toasted bread. The hash may be made richer by using a stronger and more highly-flavoured gravy; a little spice or pounded mace may also be added, when their flavour is liked.

Time:1-1/2 hour.

To Ragout A Duck Whole
From "The Book of Household Management", By Isabella Beeton, 1861

1 large duck, pepper and salt to taste, good beef gravy, 2 onions sliced, 4 sage-leaves, a few leaves of lemon thyme, thickening of butter and flour.

After having emptied and singed the duck, season it inside with pepper and salt, and truss it. Roast it before a clear fire for about 20 minutes, and let it acquire a nice brown colour. Put it into a stewpan with sufficient well-seasoned beef gravy to cover it; slice and fry the onions, and add these, with the sage-leaves and lemon thyme, both of which should be finely minced, to the stock. Simmer gently until the duck is tender; strain, skim, and thicken the gravy with a little butter and flour; boil it up, pour over the duck, and serve. When in season, about, 1-1/2 pint of young green peas, boiled separately, and put in the ragoût, very much improve this dish.

Time-20 minutes to roast the duck; 20 minutes to stew it.

Roast Ducks
From "Miss Beecher's Domestic Receipt Book", By Catharine Esther Beecher, 1850

Wash the ducks, and stuff them with a dressing made with mashed potatoes, wet with milk, and chopped onions, sage, pepper, salt, and a little butter, to suit your taste. Reserve the inwards to make the gravy, as is directed for turkeys, except it should be seasoned with sage and chopped onions. They will cook in about an hour. Ducks are to be cooked rare. Baste them with salt water, and before taking up, dredge on a little flour and let it brown.

Green peas and stewed cranberries are good accompaniments.

Canvass-back ducks are cooked without stuffing.

Wild ducks must be soaked in salt and water the night previous, to remove the fishy taste, and then in the morning put in fresh water, which should be changed once or twice.

Salmis of Wild Duck
From "A Poetical Cookbook", By Maria J. Moss, 1864

Cut off the best parts of a couple of roasted wild ducks, and put the rest of the meat into a mortar, with six shallots, a little parsley, some pepper, and a bay leaf; pound all these ingredients well, and then put into a saucepan, with four ladlesful of stock, half a glass of white wine, the same of broth, and a little grated nutmeg; reduce these to half, strain them, and having laid the pieces on a dish, cover them with the above; keep the whole hot, not boiling, until wanted for table.

To Stew Canvas-Back Ducks
From "The Lady's Receipt-Book; a Useful Companion for Large or Small Families", By Eliza Leslie, 1847

Put the giblets into a sauce-pan with the yellow rind of a lemon pared thin, a very little water, and a piece of butter rolled in flour, and a very little salt and cayenne. Let them stew gently to make a gravy; keeping the sauce-pan covered. In the mean time, half roast the ducks, saving the gravy that falls from them. Then cut them up; put them into a large stew-pan, with the gravy (having first skimmed off the fat) and merely water enough to keep them from burning. Set the pan over a moderate fire, and let them stew gently till done. Towards the last (having removed the giblets) pour over the ducks the gravy from the small sauce-pan, and stir in a large glass of port wine, and a glass of currant jelly. Send them to table as hot as possible.

Any ducks may be stewed as above. The common wild-ducks, teal, &c., should always be parboiled with a large carrot in the body to extract the fishy or sedgy taste. On tasting this carrot before it is thrown away, it will be found to have imbibed strongly that disagreeable flavour.

To Stew Ducks
From "A New System of Domestic Cookery", By Maria Eliza Ketelby Rundell, 1807

Half-roast a duck; put it into a stew-pan with a pint of beef-gravy, a few leaves of sage and mint cut small, pepper and salt, and a small bit of onion shred as fine as possible. Simmer a quarter of an hour, and skim clean: then add near a quart of green peas. Cover close, and simmer near half an hour longer. Put in a piece of butter and a little flour, and give it one boil; then serve in one dish.

Stewed Wild Ducks
From "The Lady's Receipt-Book; a Useful Companion for Large or Small Families", By Eliza Leslie, 1847

Having rubbed them slightly with salt, and parboiled them for about twenty minutes with a large carrot (cut to pieces) in each, to take off the sedgy or fishy taste, remove the carrots, cut up the ducks, and put them into a stew-pan with just sufficient water to cover them, and some bits of butter rolled slightly in flour. Cover the pan closely; and let the ducks stew for a quarter of an hour or more. Have ready a mixture in the proportion of a wine-glass of sherry or madeira; the grated yellow rind and the juice of a large lemon or orange, and one large table-spoonful of powdered loaf-sugar. Pour this over the ducks, and let them stew in it about five minutes longer. Then serve them up in a deep dish with the gravy about them. Eat the stewed duck on hot plates with heaters under them.
Cold roast duck that has been under-done is very fine stewed as above.
Venison also, and wild geese.

To Boil Fowl with Rice
From "A New System of Domestic Cookery", By Maria Eliza Ketelby Rundell, 1807

Stew the foul very slowly in some clear mutton-broth well skimmed; and seasoned with onion, mace, pepper, and salt. About half an hour before it is ready, put in 3 quarter of a pint of rice well washed and soaked. Simmer till tender; then strain it from the broth, and put the rice on a sieve before the fire. Keep the fowl hot, lay it in the middle of the dish, and the rice round it without (he broth. The broth will be very nice to eat as such, but the less liquor (the fowl is done with the better. Gravy, or parsley and butter, for sauce.

To Braise (Fowl)
From "A New System of Domestic Cookery", By Maria Eliza Ketelby Rundell, 1807

Is to put meat into a stew-pan covered, with fat bacon: then add six or eight onions, a faggot of herbs, carrots if to be brown, celery, any bones, or trimmings of meat or fowls, and some stock (which you will find among Soups and Gravies). The bacon must be covered with a paper, and the lid of the pan must be put down close. Set it on a slow stove; and according to what it is, it will require two or three hours. The meat is then to be taken out; and the gravy very nicely skimmed, and set on to boil very quick till it is thick. The meat is to be kept hot; and if larded, put into the oven for a few minutes: and then put the jelly over it, which is called glazing, and is used for ham, tongue, and many made dishes. White wine is added to some glazing. The glaze should be of a beautiful clear yellow brown, and it is best to put it on with a nice brush.

Davenport Fowls
From "A New System of Domestic Cookery", By Maria Eliza Ketelby Rundell, 1807

Hang young fowls a night: take the livers, hearts; and tenderest parts of the gizzards, shred very small, with half a handful of young clary, an anchovy to each fowl, an onion, and the yolks of four eggs boiled hard, with pepper, salt, and mace, to your taste. Stuff the fowls with this, and sew up the vents and necks quite close, that the water may not get in. Boil them in salt and water till almost done: then drain them, and put them into a stew-pun with butter enough to brown them. Serve them with line melted butter, and a spoonful of ketchup, of either sort in the dish.

Fowl and Oysters
From "The Lady's Receipt-Book; a Useful Companion for Large or Small Families", By Eliza Leslie, 1847

Take a fine fat young fowl, and having trussed it for boiling, fill the body and crop with oysters, seasoned with a few blades of mace; tying it round with twine to keep them in. Put the fowl into a tall strait-sided jar, and cover it closely. Then place the jar in a kettle of water; set it over the fire, and let it boil at least an hour and a half after the water has come to a hard boil. When it is done, take out the fowl, and keep it hot while you prepare the gravy, of which you will find a quantity in the jar. Transfer this gravy to a sauce-pan; enrich it with the beaten yolks of two eggs, mixed with three table-spoonfuls of cream; and add a large table-spoonful of fresh butter rolled in flour. If you cannot get cream, you must have a double portion of butter. Set this sauce over the fire; stirring it well; and when it comes to a boil, add twenty oysters chopped small. In five minutes take it off; put it into a sauce-boat, and serve it up with the fowl, which cooked in this manner will be found excellent. Clams may be substituted for oysters; but they should be removed from the fowl before it is sent to table. Their flavour being drawn out into the gravy, the clams themselves will be found tough, tasteless, and not proper to be eaten.

Game Soup
From "The Complete Cook", By J. M. Sanderson, 1864

In the game season it is easy to make very good soup at a little expense, by taking all the meat off the breasts of any cold birds that have been left on the preceding day, and pound it in a mortar; beat to pieces the legs and bones, and boil in some broth for an hour; boil six turnips, and mash them and strain them through a tamis cloth, with the meat that has been pounded in a mortar; strain your broth and put a little of it at a time into the tamis to help you to strain all of it through. Put your soup kettle near the fire, but do not let it boil. When ready to dish your dinner, have six yolks or eggs mixed with half a pint of cream, then strain it through a sieve; put your soup on the fire, and as it is coming to boil, put in the eggs, and stir it well with a wooden spoon. Do not let it boil, or it will curdle.

Baked Goose
From "A Plain Cookery Book for the Working Classes", By Charles Elme Francatelli, 1852

Pluck and pick out all the stubble feathers thoroughly clean, draw the goose, cut off the head and neck, and also the feet and wings, which must be scalded to enable you to remove the pinion feathers from the wings and the rough skin from the feet; split and scrape the inside of the gizzard, and carefully cut out the gall from the liver. These giblets well stewed, as shown in No. 62, will serve to make a pie for another day's dinner. Next stuff the goose in manner following, viz.:--First put six potatoes to bake in the oven, or even in a Dutch oven; and, while they are being baked, chop six onions with four apples and twelve sage leaves, and fry these in a saucepan with two ounces of butter, pepper and salt; when the whole is slightly fried, mix it with the pulp of the six baked potatoes, and use this very nice stuffing to fill the inside of the goose. The goose being stuffed, place it upon an iron trivet in a baking dish containing peeled potatoes and a few apples; add half-a-pint of water, pepper and salt, shake some flour over the goose, and bake it for about an hour and a-half.

Roast Goose
From "Miss Beecher's Domestic Receipt Book", By Catharine Esther Beecher, 1850

A goose should be roasted in the same manner as a turkey. It is better to make the stuffing of mashed potatoes, seasoned with salt, pepper, sage, and onions, to the taste. Apple sauce is good to serve with it. Allow fifteen minutes to a pound, for a goslin, and twenty or more for an older one. Goose should be cooked rare.

Hare, Rabbit, or Partridge Soup
From "The Complete Cook", By J. M. Sanderson, 1864

When hares and rabbits and other game are too tough to eat (in the ordinary way of cooking,) they will make very good soup. Cut off the legs and shoulders of a hare, divide the body crossways, and stew very gently in three quarts of water, with one carrot, about one ounce of onions, two blades of pounded mace, four cloves, twenty-four black peppers, and a bundle of sweet herbs; stew it till the hare is tender. Most cooks add to the above two slices of ham or bacon, and a bay leaf, but the hare makes sufficiently savoury soup without this addition. The time this will take depends upon the age and time it has been kept before it is dressed; as a general rule, about three hours. Make a dozen and a half of force meat balls, as big as nutmegs. When hare is tender, take the meat off the back and upper joints of the legs; cut it into mouthfuls, and put on one side; cut the rest of the meat off the legs, shoulders, &c., mince it and pound it in a mortar with an ounce of butter, and two or three table-spoonfuls of flour moistened with a little soup; rub this through a hair sieve, and put it into the soup to thicken it; let it simmer for half an hour longer, skim it well, and put it through the tamis in the pan again; put the meat in, a glass of port or claret wine, with a table-spoonful of currant jelly to each quart of soup. Season it with salt; put in the force meat balls, and when all is hot, the soup is ready.

Jugged Hare
From "The Complete Cook", By J. M. Sanderson, 1864

Wash it very nicely, cut it up in pieces proper to help at table, and put them into a jugging pot, or into a stone jar, just sufficiently large to hold it well; put in some sweet herbs, a roll or two of rind of a lemon, and a fine large onion with five cloves stuck in it; and if you wish to preserve the flavour of the hare, a quarter of a pint of water; if you are for a ragoût, a quarter of a pint of claret or port wine, and the juice of a lemon. Tie the jar down closely with a bladder, so that no steam can escape; put a little hay in the bottom of the saucepan, in which place the jar; let the water boil for about three hours, according to the age and size of the hare (take care it is not over-done, which is the general fault in all made dishes,) keeping it boiling all the time, and fill up the pot as it boils away. When quite tender, strain off gravy from fat, thicken it with flour, and give it a boil up; lay the hare in a soup dish, and pour the gravy to it. You may make a pudding the same as for roast hare, and boil it in a cloth, and when you dish your hare, cut it in slices, or make force meat balls of it for garnish. For sauce, currant jelly. Or a much easier and quicker way of proceeding is the following: Prepare the hare as for jugging; put it into a stew-pan with a few sweet herbs, half a dozen cloves, the same of allspice and black pepper, two large onions, and a roll of lemon peel; cover it with water; when it boils, skim it clean, and let it simmer gently till tender (about two hours;) then take it up with a slice, set it by a fire to keep hot while you thicken the gravy; take three ounces of butter and some flour, rub together, put in the gravy, stir it well, and let it boil about ten minutes; strain it through a sieve over the hare, and it is ready.minutes; strain it through a sieve over the hare, and it is ready.

Roasted Hare

From "A Poetical Cookbook", By Maria J. Moss, 1864

Cut the skin from a hare that has been well soaked, put it on the spit, and rub it well with Madeira, pricking it in various places that it may imbibe plenty of wine; cover it entirely with a paste, and roast it. When done, take away the paste, rub it quickly over with egg, sprinkle breadcrumbs, and baste it gently with butter (still keeping it turning before the fire), until a crust is formed over it, and it is of a nice brown color; dish it over some espagnole with Madeira wine boiled in it; two or three cloves may be stuck into the knuckles, if you think proper.

To Roast Hare
From "A New System of Domestic Cookery", By Maria Eliza Ketelby Rundell, 1807

After it is skinned, let it be extremely well washed, and then soaked an hour or two in water: and if old, lard it; which will make it tender, as also will letting it lie in vinegar.

If however it is put into vinegar, it should be exceedingly well washed in water afterwards. Put a large relishing stuffing into the belly, and then sew it up. Baste it well with milk till half-done, and afterwards with butter. If the blood has settled in the neck, soaking the part in warm water, and putting it to the fire warm, will remove it; especially if yon also nick the skin here and there with a small knife, to let it out. The hare should be kept at a distance from the fire at first. Serve with a fine froth, rich gravy, melted butter, and currant-jelly-sauce; the gravy in the dish. For stuffing use the liver, an anchovy, some fat bacon, a little suet, herbs, pepper, salt, nutmeg, a little onion, crumbs of bread, and an egg to bind it all.

The ears must be nicely cleaned and singed. They are reckoned a dainty.

Partridges In Pears
From "The Lady's Receipt-Book; a Useful Companion for Large or Small Families", By Eliza Leslie, 1847

Cut off the necks of the partridges close to the breast. Truss them very tight and round, and rub over them a little salt and cayenne pepper mixed. Cut off one of the legs, and leave the other on. Make a rich paste of flour, butter, and beaten yolk of egg, with as little water as possible. Roll it out thin and evenly, and put a portion of it nicely round each partridge, pressing it on closely with your hand, and forming it into the shape of a large pear. Leave one leg sticking out at the top to resemble the stem. Set them in a pan; and bake them in a dutch oven. In the mean time, make in a small sauce-pan, a rich brown gravy of the livers, and other trimmings of the partridges, and some drippings of roast veal or roasted poultry. It will be better still if you reserve one or two small partridges to cut up, and stew for the gravy. Season it with a little salt and cayenne. When it has boiled long enough to be very thick

and rich, take it off, strain it, and put the liquid into a clean sauce-pan. Add the juice of a large orange or lemon, made very sweet with powdered white sugar. Set it over the fire; and when it comes to a boil, stir in the beaten yolks of two eggs. Let it boil two or three minutes longer; then take it off, and keep it hot till the partridges and their paste are thoroughly well-baked. When done, stand up the partridges in a deep dish, and serve up the gravy in a sauce-boat. Ornament the partridge-pears by sticking some orange or lemon leaves into the end that represents the stalk. This is a nice and handsome side dish, of French origin.
Pigeons and quails may be dressed in this manner.

To Stew Pigeons
From "A New System of Domestic Cookery", By Maria Eliza Ketelby Rundell, 1807

Take care that they are quite fresh, and carefully cropped, drawn, and washed; then soak them half an hour. In the mean time cut a hard white cabbage in slices (as if for pickling) into water: drain it, and then boil it in milk and water: drain it again, and lay some of it at the bottom of a stew-pan. Put the pigeons upon it, but first season them well with pepper and salt; and cover them with the remainder of the cabbage. Add a little broth, and stew gently till the pigeons are tender; then put among them two or three spoonfuls of cream, and a piece of butter and flour, for thickening. After a boil or two, serve the birds in the. middle, and the cabbage placed round them.

Another way.--Stew the birds in a good brown gravy, either stuffed or not; and seasoned high with spice and mushrooms fresh, or a little ketchup.

Pheasant Cutlets
From "The Book of Household Management", By Isabella Beeton, 1861

2 or 3 pheasants, egg and bread crumbs, cayenne and salt to taste, brown gravy. Procure 3 young pheasants that have been hung a few days; pluck, draw, and wipe them inside; cut them into joints; remove the bones from the best of these; and the backbones, trimmings, &c., put into a stewpan, with a little stock, herbs, vegetables, seasoning, &c.,
to make the gravy. Flatten and trim the cutlets of a good shape, egg and bread crumb them, broil them over a clear fire, pile them high in the dish, and pour under them the gravy made from the bones, which should be strained, flavoured, and thickened. One of the small bones should be stuck on the point of each cutlet. Time-10 minutes.

To Roast Pheasants
From "A Poetical Cookbook", By Maria J. Moss, 1864

Chop some fine raw oysters, omitting the head part, mix them with salt and nutmeg, and add some beaten yolk of egg to bind the other ingredients. Cut some very thin slices of cold ham or bacon, and cover the birds with them, then wrap them in sheets of paper well buttered, put them on the spit, and roast them before a clear fire.

To Cook Pigeons
From "Miss Beecher's Domestic Receipt Book", By Catharine Esther Beecher, 1850

Pigeons are good stuffed and roasted, or baked. They are better stewed thus:--Stuff them like turkeys, put them in a pot, breast downwards, and cover them with salted water an inch above the top, and simmer them two hours if tender, and three if tough. When nearly done, stir in a bit of butter the size of a goose egg, for every dozen pigeons. Take them up and add a little flour paste to the gravy, with salt and pepper, and pour some of it over them, and put the rest in a gravy dish.

Pigeons
From "The Complete Cook", By J. M. Sanderson, 1864

Clean them well, and pepper and salt them; broil them over a clear slow fire; turn them often, and put a little butter on them; when they are done, pour over them either stewed or pickled mushrooms, or catsup and melted butter. Garnish with fried bread crumbs, or sippets. Or, when the pigeons are trussed for broiling, flat them with a cleaver, taking care not to break the skin of the backs or breast; season them with pepper and salt, a little bit of butter, and a tea spoonful of water, and tie them close at both ends; so, when they are brought to table, they bring their sauce with them Egg and dredge them well with grated bread (mixed with spice and sweet herbs), lay them on the gridiron, and turn them frequently; if your fire is not very clear, lay them on a sheet of paper well buttered, to keep them from getting smoked. They are much better broiled whole.

Boiled Rabbit
From "The Book of Household Management", By Isabella Beeton, 1861

Rabbit; water.

For boiling, choose rabbits with smooth and sharp claws, as that denotes they are young: should these be blunt and rugged, the ears dry and tough, the animal is old. After emptying and skinning it, wash it well in cold water, and let it soak for about 1/4 hour in warm water, to draw out the blood. Bring the head round to the side, and fasten it there by means of a skewer run through that and the body. Put the rabbit into sufficient hot water to cover it, let it boil very gently until tender, which will be in from 1/2 to 3/4 hour, according to its size and age. Dish it, and smother it either with onion, mushroom, or liver sauce, or parsley-and-butter; the former is, however, generally preferred to any of the last-named sauces. When liver-sauce is preferred, the liver should be boiled for a few minutes, and minced very finely, or rubbed through a sieve before it is added to the sauce.

Time-A very young rabbit, 1/2 hour; a large one, 3/4 hour; an old one, 1 hour or longer.

Fricaseed Rabbits
From "A Poetical Cookbook", By Maria J. Moss, 1864

Take two fine white rabbits, and cut them in pieces; blanch them in boiling water, and skim them for one minute; stir a few trimmings of mushrooms in a stewpan over the fire, with a bit of butter, till it begins to fry, then stir in a spoonful of flour; mix into the flour, a

little at a time, nearly a quart of good consommé, which set on the fire, and when it boils put the rabbits in, and let them boil gently till done; then put them in another stewpan, and reduce the sauce till nearly as thick as paste; mix in about half a pint of good boiling cream, and when it becomes the thickness of bechamelle sauce in general, squeeze it through the tammy to the rabbits; make it very hot, put in a few mushrooms, the yolk of an egg, a little cream, and then serve it to table.

A Boned Turkey
From "The Lady's Receipt-Book; a Useful Companion for Large or Small Families", By Eliza Leslie, 1847

For this purpose you must have a fine, large, tender turkey; and after it is drawn, and washed, and wiped dry, lay it on a clean table, and take a very sharp knife, with a narrow blade and point. Begin at the neck; then go round to the shoulders and wings, and carefully separate the flesh from the bone, scraping it down as you proceed. Next loosen the flesh from the breast, and back, and body; and then from the thighs. It requires care and patience to do it nicely, and to avoid tearing or breaking the skin. The knife should always penetrate quite to the bone; scraping loose the flesh rather than cutting it. When all the flesh has been completely loosened, take the turkey by the neck, give it a pull, and the whole skeleton will come out entire from the flesh, as easily as you draw your hand out of a glove. The flesh will then fall down, a flat and shapeless mass. With a small needle and thread, carefully sew up any holes that have accidentally been torn in the skin.

Have ready a large quantity of stuffing, made as follows:--Take three sixpenny loaves of stale bread; grate the crumb; and put the crusts in water to soak. When quite soft, break them up small into the pan of grated bread-crumbs, and mix in a pound of fresh butter, cut into little pieces. Take two large bunches of sweet-marjoram; the same of sweet-basil; and one bunch of parsley. Mince the parsley very fine, and rub to a powder the leaves of the marjoram and basil. You should have two large, heaping table-spoonfuls of each. Chop, also, two very small onions or shalots, and mix them with the herbs. Pound to powder a quarter of an ounce of mace; a quarter of an ounce of cloves; and two large nutmegs. Mix the spices together, and add a tea-spoonful of salt and a teaspoonful of ground black pepper. Then mix the herbs, spice, &c., thoroughly into the bread-crumbs; and add, by degrees, four beaten eggs to bind the whole together.

Take up a handful of this filling; squeeze it hard, and proceed to stuff the turkey with it,--beginning at the wings; next do the body; and then the thighs. Stuff it very hard, and as you proceed, form the turkey into its natural shape, by filling out, properly, the wings, breast, body, &c. When all the stuffing is in, sew up the body, and skewer the turkey into the usual shape in which they are trussed; so that, if skilfully done, it will look almost as if it had not been boned. Tie it round with tape, and bake it three hours or more; basting it occasionally with fresh butter. Make a gravy of the giblets, chopped, and stewed slowly in a little water. When done, add to it the gravy that is in the dish about the turkey, (having first skimmed off the fat,) and enrich it with a glass of white wine, and two beaten yolks of eggs, stirred in just before you take it from the fire.

If the turkey is to be eaten cold at the supper-table, drop table-spoonfuls of currant or cranberry jelly all over it at small distances, and in the dish round it.

A very handsome way of serving it up cold is, after making a sufficiency of nice clear calves'-foot jelly, (seasoned, as usual, with wine, lemon, cinnamon, &c.,) to lay the turkey in the dish in which it is to go to table, and setting it under the jelly-bag, let the jelly drip upon it, so as to form a transparent coating all over it; smoothing the jelly evenly with the back of a spoon, as it congeals on the turkey. Apple jelly may be substituted.

Large fowls may be boned and stuffed in the above manner: also a young roasting pig.

Venison
From "A Poetical Cookbook", By Maria J. Moss, 1864

The haunch of buck will take about three hours and three quarters roasting. Put a coarse paste of brown flour and water, and a paper over that, to cover all the fat;

baste it well with dripping, and keep it at a distance, to get hot at the bones by degrees. When near done, remove the covering, and baste it with butter, and froth it up before you serve. Gravy for it should be put in a boat, and not in the dish (unless there be none in the venison), and made thus: cut off the fat from two or three pounds of a loin of old mutton, and set it in steaks on a gridiron for a few minutes, just to brown one side; put them in a saucepan with a quart of water, cover quite close for an hour, and gently simmer it; then uncover, and stew till the gravy be reduced to a pint. Season only with salt.

Stewed Venison
From "The Book of Household Management", By Isabella Beeton, 1861

A shoulder of venison, a few slices of mutton fat, 2 glasses of port wine, pepper and allspice to taste, 1-1/2 pint of weak stock or gravy, 1/2 teaspoonful of whole pepper, 1/2 teaspoonful of whole allspice.

Hang the venison till tender; take out the bone, flatten the meat with a rolling-pin, and place over it a few slices of mutton fat, which have been previously soaked for 2 or 3 hours in port wine; sprinkle these with a little fine allspice and pepper, roll the meat up, and bind and tie it securely. Put it into a stewpan with the bone and the above proportion of weak stock or gravy, whole allspice, black pepper, and port wine; cover the lid down closely, and simmer, very gently, from 3-1/2 to 4 hours. When quite tender, take off the tape, and dish the meat; strain the gravy over it, and send it to table with red-currant jelly. Unless the joint is very fat, the above is the best mode of cooking it.

Time-3-1/2 to 4 hours.

Venison Pasty
From "A Poetical Cookbook", By Maria J. Moss, 1864

Cut a neck or breast into small steaks, rub them over with a seasoning of sweet herbs, grated nutmeg, pepper and salt; fry them slightly in butter. Line the sides and edges of a dish with puff paste, lay in the steaks, and add half a pint of rich gravy, made with the trimmings of the venison; add a glass of port wine, and the juice of half a lemon or teaspoonful of vinegar; cover the dish with puff paste, and bake it nearly two hours; some more gravy may be poured into the pie before serving it.

6. Ketchups, Sauces, Gravies, Salad Dressings

"D. Ellis having received a barl of fresh Oysters invited Joe Grigg, Tean Nut. and myself to come up and eat Oyster supper with him-So bout 10 oclock pm we went up and Mr. J. carried his bottle Tomato Catsup-Dolf. had a large pan of Stewed and with Catsup they were elegant."-Pvt. Samuel Pickens, 5th Alabama Infantry, Company D, March 6, 1863. Diary entry. During the course of the war, he was wounded once and captured twice.

Apple Sauce, for Goose and Roast Pork
From "A New System of Domestic Cookery",
By Maria Eliza Ketelby Rundell, 1807

Pare, core, and slice, some apples; and put them in a stone jar, into a sauce-pan of water, or on a hot hearth. It on a hearth, let a spoonful or two of water be put in, to hinder them from burning. When they are done, bruise them to a mash, and put to them a bit of butter the size of a nutmeg, and a little brown sugar. Serve it in a sauce-tureen.

Benton Sauce, for Hot or Cold Roast Beef
From "A New System of Domestic Cookery", By Maria
Eliza Ketelby Rundell, 1807

Grate, or scrape very fine, some horse-radish, a little made mustard, some pounded white sugar, and four large spoonfuls of vinegar. Serve in a saucer.

Bread Sauce for A Roast Fowl
From "A Plain Cookery Book for the Working Classes", By Charles Elme
Francatelli, 1852

Chop a small onion or shalot fine, and boil it in a pint of milk for five minutes; then add about ten ounces of crumb of bread, a bit of butter, pepper and salt to season; stir the whole on the fire for ten minutes, and eat this bread sauce with roast fowl or turkey.

Brown Onion Sauce
From "Directions for Cookery, in its Various Branches" By Eliza Leslie, 1840

Slice some large mild Spanish onions. Cover them with butter, and set them over a slow fire to brown. Then add salt and cayenne pepper to your taste, and some good brown gravy of roast meat, poultry or game, thickened with a bit of butter rolled in flour that has first been browned by holding it in a hot pan or shovel over the fire. Give it a boil, skim it well, and just before you take it off, stir in a half glass of port or claret, and the same quantity of mushroom catchup. Use this sauce for roasted poultry, game, or meat.

Camp Ketchup
From "The Practical Housekeeper; A Cyclopedia of Domestic Economy", By Elizabeth Fries Ellet, 1857

Take two quarts of old strong beer and one of white wine, add a quarter of a pound of anchovies, three ounces of shalots peeled, half an ounce of mace, the same of nutmeg, three large races of ginger cut in slices; put all together over a moderate fire till one third is wasted. The next day bottle it with the spice and the shalots. It will keep for many years.

Or:--A pint of claret, the same quantity of ketchup, four ounces of anchovies, one ounce of fresh lemon-peel pared thin, two cloves of garlic minced fine, half an ounce of allspice, the same of black and of red pepper, one drachm of celery-seed bruised, and half a pint of pickle-liquor. Put these ingredients into a wide-mouthed bottle; stop it close, shake it every day for a fortnight, and then strain it off.

Caper Sauce
From "A Poetical Cookbook", By Maria J. Moss, 1864

To make a quarter of a pint, take a tablespoonful of capers and two teaspoonfuls of vinegar. The present fashion of cutting capers is to mince one-third of them very fine, and divide the others in half; put them into a quarter of a pint of melted butter, or good thickened gravy; stir them the same way as you did the melted butter, or it will oil.
Some boil and mince fine a few leaves of parsley or chevrel or tarragon, and add to the sauce; others, the juice of half a Seville orange or lemon.

Celery Sauce

From "The Practical Housekeeper; A Cyclopedia of Domestic Economy", By Elizabeth Fries Ellet, 1857

Strip the outer parts of the stem, and, after carefully washing the remaining portion, cut it into small pieces; put to it a blade of mace without any other spice, and stew it in good veal broth until very tender; it will take a good deal of time, more particularly the thick hard end of the root. After this thicken it with melted butter, and flavor it with a small quantity of white wine; or it may be thickened with boiled cream without wine. It is usually served with boiled turkey, but is very delicate with any kind of white poultry or veal.

Chestnut Sauce
From "The Practical Housekeeper; A Cyclopedia of Domestic Economy", By Elizabeth Fries Ellet, 1857

Scald a score of chestnuts in hot water for ten minutes; skin them; let them stew gently for about half an hour in some good gravy seasoned with a glass of white wine, a little white pepper, salt, and mace or nutmeg; and when quite soft, serve them in the dish.

Cold Sweet Sauce
From "Directions for Cookery, in its Various Branches" By Eliza Leslie, 1840

Stir together, as for a pound-cake, equal quantities of fresh butter and powdered white sugar. When quite light and creamy, add some powdered cinnamon or nutmeg, and a few drops of essence of lemon. Send it to table in a small deep plate with a tea-spoon in it.
Eat it with batter pudding, bread pudding, Indian pudding, &c. whether baked or boiled. Also with boiled apple pudding or dumplings, and with fritters and pancakes.

Cucumber Catchup
From "The Lady's Receipt-Book; a Useful Companion for Large or Small Families", By Eliza Leslie, 1847

For a small quantity, take twelve fine full-grown cucumbers, and lay them an hour in cold water. Then pare them, and grate them down into a deep dish. Grate also six small onions, and mix them with the grated cucumber. Season the mixture to your taste, with pepper, salt, and vinegar; making it of the consistence of rich marmalade or jam. When thoroughly incorporated, transfer it to a glass jar, cover it closely, tying down over the top a piece of bladder, so as to make it perfectly air-tight.It will be found very nice (when fresh cucumbers are not in season) to eat with beef or mutton, and if properly made and tightly covered will keep well. It should be grated very fine, and the vinegar must be of excellent quality--real cider vinegar.

Egg Sauce for Roast Fowls, Etc (No. 19)
From "A Plain Cookery Book for the Working Classes", By Charles Elme Francatelli, 1852

Boil two or three eggs for about eight minutes; remove the shells, cut up each egg into about ten pieces of equal size, and put them into some butter-sauce made as follows:--viz., Knead two ounces of flour with one ounce and-a-half of butter; add half-a-pint of water, pepper and salt to season, and stir the sauce on the fire until it begins to boil; then mix in the pieces of chopped hard-boiled eggs.

A Very Fine Fish Sauce
From "A New System of Domestic Cookery", By Maria Eliza Ketelby Rundell, 1807

Put into a very nice tin sauce-pan a pint of fine port wine, a gill of mountain, half a pint of fine walnut-ketchup, twelve anchovies, and the liquor that belongs to them, a gill of walnut-pickle, the rind and juice of a large lemon, four or five shalots, some Cayenne to taste, three ounces of scraped horse-radish, three blades of mace, and two tea-spoonfuls of made mustard; boil it all gently, till the rawness goes off; then put it into small bottles for use. Cork them very close, and seal the top.

<u>Another</u>-Chop twenty-four anchovies not washed, and ten shalots, and scrape three spoonfuls of horse-radish; which, with ten blades of mace, twelve clove; two sliced lemons, half a pint of anchovy-liquor, a quart of hock, or Rhenish wine, and a pint of water, boil to a quart: then strain off; and when cold, add three large spoonfuls of walnut-ketchup, and put into small bottles well corked.

Brown Gravy for Fowl (No. 17)
From "A Plain Cookery Book for the Working Classes", By Charles Elme Francatelli, 1852

Chop up an onion, and fry it with a sprig of thyme and a bit of butter, and when it is brown, add a good tea-spoonful of moist sugar and a drop of water, and boil all together on the fire until the water is reduced, and the sugar begins to bake of a dark brown colour. It must then be stirred on the fire for three minutes longer; after which moisten it with half-a-pint of water, add a little pepper and salt; boil all together for five minutes, and strain the gravy over the fowl, etc.

Ham Gravy
From "The Practical Housekeeper; A Cyclopedia of Domestic Economy", By Elizabeth Fries Ellet, 1857

Take the wine in which the ham was steeped, and add to it the essence or juice which flowed from the meat when taken from the spit; squeeze in the juice of two lemons; put it into a saucepan, and boil and skim it; send it to table in a boat. Cover the shank of the ham (which should have been sawed short) with bunches of double parsley, and ornament it with any garnish you may think proper.

Ham Sauce
From "A New System of Domestic Cookery", By Maria Eliza Ketelby Rundell, 1807

When a ham is almost done with, pick all the meat clean from the bone, leaving out any rusty part; beat the meat and the bone to a mash with a rolling-pin; put it into a sauce-pan, with three spoonfuls of gravy; set it over a slow fire, and stir it all the time, or it will stick to the bottom. When it has been on some time, put to it a small bundle of sweet herbs, some pepper, and half a pint of beef-gravy; cover it up, and let it stew over a gentle fire. When it has a good flavour of the herbs, strain off the gravy. A little of this is an improvement to all gravies.

A L'Hollandaise
From "The Practical Housekeeper; A Cyclopedia of Domestic Economy", By Elizabeth Fries Ellet, 1857

For meat, fowl, or fish. Put six spoonfuls of water and two of tarragon vinegar, with one ounce of butter, into a stewpan; warm and thicken it with the yolks of two eggs. Make it quite hot, but do not boil it; stir it all the time; squeeze in the juice of half a lemon, and strain it through a sieve. Season with salt and cayenne. It should be quite thick.

Horseradish Sauce
From "The Practical Housekeeper; A Cyclopedia of Domestic Economy", By Elizabeth Fries Ellet, 1857

Two teaspoonfuls of mustard, two of white sugar, half a one of salt, and a little more than a wineglass of vinegar--mixed and poured over a stock of grated horseradish. This sauce is good for beef.

Kitchiner's Fish Sauce
From "Directions for Cookery, in its Various Branches" By Eliza Leslie, 1840

Mix together a pint of claret, a pint of mushroom catchup, and half a pint of walnut pickle, four ounces of pounded anchovy, an ounce of fresh lemon-peel pared thin, and the same quantity of shalot or small onion. Also an ounce of scraped horseradish, half an ounce of black pepper, and half an ounce of allspice mixed, and the same quantity of cayenne and celery-seed. Infuse these ingredients in a wide-mouthed bottle (closely stopped) for a fortnight, shaking the mixture every day. Then strain and bottle it for use. Put it up in small bottles, filling them quite full.

Lemon Catchup
From "Directions for Cookery, in its Various Branches" By Eliza Leslie, 1840

Cut nine large lemons into thin slices, and take out the seeds. Prepare, by pounding them in a mortar, two ounces of mustard seed, half an ounce of black pepper, half an ounce of nutmeg, a quarter of an ounce of mace, and a quarter of an ounce of cloves. Slice thin two ounces of horseradish. Put all these ingredients together. Strew over them three ounces of fine salt. Add a quart of the best vinegar. Boil the whole twenty minutes. Then put it warm into a jar, and let it stand three weeks closely covered. Stir it up daily.

Then strain it through a sieve, and put it up in small bottles to flavour fish and other sauces. This is sometimes called lemon pickle.

These vinegars will be found very useful, at times when the articles with which they are flavoured cannot be conveniently procured. Care should be taken to have the bottles that contain them accurately labelled, very tightly corked, and kept in a dry place. The vinegar used for these purposes should be of the very best sort.

Liver Sauce
From "The Complete Cook", By J. M. Sanderson, 1864

Scald the liver, clear away all the fibres and specky parts, pound it in a mortar, with a bit of butter, then boil it up with melted butter; season it with cayenne, and a squeeze of lemon juice. You may add catsup or anchovy.

La Magnonnaise
From "The Practical Housekeeper; A Cyclopedia of Domestic Economy", By Elizabeth Fries Ellet, 1857

Perhaps the most esteemed mode of making sauce for any sort of cold meats or fish is that known in France by this title.

Put into a round-bottomed basin the yolk of an egg and a pinch of salt; stir in very quickly, drop by drop, two table-spoonfuls of sweet oil, working the spoon very rapidly round, to work in the oil; when it is thick add a few drops of tarragon vinegar, then more oil, until there is sufficient sauce; thin it with a little more vinegar. It should be quite thick, and rather acid.

A Marinade to Baste Roast Meats
From "The Practical Housekeeper; A Cyclopedia of Domestic Economy", By Elizabeth Fries Ellet, 1857

Chop up some fat bacon with a clove of garlic and a sprig of parsley; add salt, pepper, a spoonful of vinegar, and four spoonfuls of oil; beat it up well, and baste the meat with it.

Mayonnaise
From "The Practical Housekeeper; A Cyclopedia of Domestic Economy", By Elizabeth Fries Ellet, 1857

The following receipt is contributed to "The Practical Housekeeper" by Mr. Delmonico, proprietor of the well-known establishments at the Irving House and at the corner of Beaver and William streets, New York.

In a middle-sized dish placed in cracked rice, put the yolks of two fresh eggs, a little salt, some white pepper, and some vinegar a Pestragon. Stir this mixture briskly with a wooden spoon, and as soon as it begins to thicken, mix in gradually a table-spoonful of oil and a little vinegar, taking care to beat the sauce against the sides of the dish. On this repeated beating depends the whiteness of the sauce Mayonnaise. In proportion to the bulk add oil and vinegar together, putting in but little at a time. As it comes nearer perfection it grows thick and strong-bodied. When finished add a squeeze of citron and some drops of water. This sauce is delicious for chicken salad--mayonnaise de volaille-- and serves for all kinds of fish and poultry.

Melted Butter (the French Sauce Blanche) (Author's Note: this is #378, "White Sauce")
From "The Book of Household Management", By Isabella Beeton, 1861

1/4 lb. of fresh butter, 1 tablespoonful of flour, salt to taste, 1/2 gill of water, 1/2 spoonful of white vinegar, a very little grated nutmeg.

Mode.—Mix the flour and water to a smooth batter, carefully rubbing down with the back of a spoon any lumps that may appear. Put it in a saucepan with all the other ingredients, and let it thicken on the fire, but do not allow it to boil, lest it should taste of the flour.

Time.—1 minute to simmer.

Mint Sauce for Veal or Mutton
From "The Great Western Cook Book, or Table Receipts, Adapted to Western Housewifery", By Anna Maria Collins, 1857

Take two table-spoonsful of green mint, half a tea-cupful of vinegar, and two table-spoonsful of pounded loaf sugar, and mix them well together.

Mushroom Catsup
From "The Complete Cook", By J. M. Sanderson, 1864

The juice of mushrooms approaches the nature and flavour of gravy meat more than other vegetable juices. Dr. Kitchiner sets a high value, and not without reason, upon good mushroom catsup, "a couple of quarts of which," he says, "will save some score pounds of meat, besides a vast deal of time and trouble." The best method of extracting the essence of mushrooms, is that which leaves behind the least quantity of water. In all essences, it is quality, not quantity, to which we ought to look. An excess of aqueous fluid in essences renders them less capable of keeping; while in flavouring sauces, &c. a small quantity is sufficient, so that by this means you do not interfere with the thickness or consistency of the thing flavoured. Mushrooms, that is, field mushrooms, begin to come in about September. There are several varieties of these fungi, and they differ very much, both in their wholesomeness and flavour. The best and finest flavoured mushrooms are those which grow spontaneously upon rich, dry, old pasture land. The following is the mode of making good mushroom catsup, or, as Dr. Kitchiner calls it, "double catsup."

Take mushrooms of the right sort, fresh gathered and full grown, but not maggoty or putrescent; put a layer of these at the bottom of a deep earthen pan, and sprinkle them with salt; then put another layer of mushrooms, sprinkle more salt on them, and so on alternately, mushroom and salt. Let them remain two or three hours, by whichtime the salt will have penetrated the mushrooms, and have made them easy to break; then pound them in a mortar, or break them well with your hands; then let them remain in this state for two days, not more, mashing them well once or twice a day; then pour them into a stone jar, and to each quart add an ounce and a half of whole black pepper, and half an ounce of allspice; stop the jar very close, and set it in a saucepan or stew-pan of boiling water, and keep it boiling for two hours at least. Take out the jar, and pour the juice clear from the settlings, through a hair sieve into a clean stew-pan. Let it boil very gently for half an hour; but to make good or double catsup, it should boil gently till the mushroom juice is reduced to half the quantity, or, in other words, till the more aqueous part is evaporated; then skim it well, and pour it into a clean dry jar or jug; cover it close, and let it stand in a cool place till next day, then pour it off as gently as possible (so as not to disturb the settlings at the bottom of the jug,) through a tamis, or thick flannel bag, till it is perfectly clear; add a table-spoonful of good unflavoured spirits (brandy is dear and not a whit better than common spirits of wine of equal strength) to each pint of catsup, and let it stand as before. A fresh sediment will be deposited, from which the catsup is to be poured off gently, and bottled in half pints, washed with spirit. Small bottles are best, as they are sooner used, and the catsup, if uncorked often, is apt to spoil. The cork of each bottle ought to be sealed or dipped in bottle cement. Keep it in a dry cool place; it will soon spoil if kept damp. If any pellicle or skin should appear upon it when in the bottle, boil it up again with a few peppercorns. It is a question with us, whether it would not be best to dispense with the spice altogether, and give an addition of spirits. When a number of articles are added to the catsup, such as different spices, garlic, eschalot, anchovy, &c. &c., the flavour of the mushroom is overpowered, and it ceases to be, properly speaking, mushroom catsup.

A Very Fine Mushroom Sauce for Fowls, or Rabbits From "A New System of Domestic Cookery", By Maria Eliza Ketelby Rundell, 1807

Wash and pick a pint of young mushrooms, and rub them with salt, to take off the tender skin. Put them into a sauce-pan. with a little salt, some nutmeg, a blade of mace, a pint of cream, and a good piece of butter rubbed in flour. Boil them up, and stir them till done; then pour it round the chickens, &c. Garnish with lemon. If you cannot get fresh mushrooms, use pickled ones done white, with a little mushroom-powder with the cream, &c.

A Very Rich Mushroom Sauce for Fowls or Rabbits From "The Complete Cook", By J. M. Sanderson, 1864

Pick, rub and wash a pint of young mushrooms, and sprinkle with salt to take off the skin. Put them into a saucepan with a little salt, a blade of mace, a little nutmeg, a pint of cream, and a piece of butter rolled in flour: boil them up and stir till done, then pour it into the dish with the chickens; garnish with lemon. If you cannot get fresh mushrooms, use pickled ones, done white, with a little mushroom powder with the cream.

French Mustard

From "Directions for Cookery, in its Various Branches" By Eliza Leslie, 1840

Mix together four ounces of the very best mustard powder, four salt-spoons of salt, a large table-spoonful of minced tarragon leaves, and two cloves of garlic chopped fine. Pour on by degrees sufficient vinegar (tarragon vinegar is best) to dilute it to the proper consistence. It will probably require about four wine-glassfuls or half a pint. Mix it well, using for the purpose a wooden spoon. When done, put it into a wide-mouthed bottle or into little white jars. Cork it very closely, and keep it in a dry place. It will not be fit for use in less than two days.
This (used as the common mustard) is a very agreeable condiment for beef or mutton.

To Make Mustard
From "A New System of Domestic Cookery", By Maria Eliza Ketelby Rundell, 1807

Mix the best Durham flour of mustard by degrees, with boiling water, to a proper thickness, rubbing it perfectly smooth; add a little salt, and keep it in a small jar close
covered, and put only as much into the glass as will he used soon; which should be wiped daily round the edges.

Another way, for immediate use.
Mix the mustard with new milk by degrees, to be quite smooth, and add a little raw cream. It is much softer this way, is not bitter, and will keep well.
The patent mustard is by many preferred, and it is perhaps as cheap, being always ready; and if the pots are returned, three-pence is allowed for each.
A tea-spoonful of sugar to half a pint of mustard, is a great improvement, and softens it.

Orange Gravy Sauce
From "The Practical Housekeeper; A Cyclopedia of Domestic Economy", By Elizabeth Fries Ellet, 1857

Put half a pint of veal gravy into a saucepan, add to it half a dozen basil leaves, a small onion, a roll of orange or lemon-peel, and let it boil for a few minutes, and strain it off; put to the clear gravy, the juice of a Seville orange or lemon, half a teaspoonful of salt, the same quantity of pepper, and a glass of red wine, serve it hot; shalot and cayenne may be added.

Parsley Sauce

From "Directions for Cookery, in its Various Branches" By Eliza Leslie, 1840

Wash a bunch of parsley in cold water. Then boil it about six or seven minutes in salt and water. Drain it, cut the leaves from the stalks, and chop them fine. Hare ready some melted butter, and stir in the parsley. Allow two small table-spoonfuls of leaves to half a pint of butter.
Serve it up with boiled fowls, rock-fish, sea-bass, and other boiled fresh fish.. Also with knuckle of veal, and with calf's head boiled plain.

Parsley Sauce
From "A Plain Cookery Book for the Working Classes", By Charles Elme Francatelli, 1852

Chop a handful of parsley and mix it in a stewpan with two ounces of butter, two ounces of flour, pepper and salt; moisten with half a pint of water and a table-spoonful of vinegar. Stir the parsley-sauce on the fire till it boils, and then pour it over the fish, drained free from water, on its dish.

Peach Sauce
From "Directions for Cookery, in its Various Branches" By Eliza Leslie, 1840

Take a quart of dried peaches, (those are richest and best that are dried with the skins on,) and soak them in cold water till they are tender. Then drain them, and put them into a covered pan with a very little water. Set them on coals, and simmer them till they are entirely dissolved. Then mash them with brown sugar, and send them to table cold to eat with roast meat, game or poultry.

Pink Sauce
From "Directions for Cookery, in its Various Branches" By Eliza Leslie, 1840

Mix together half a pint of port wine, half a pint of strong vinegar, the juice and grated peel of two large lemons, a quarter of an ounce of cayenne, a dozen blades of mace, and a quarter of an ounce of powdered cochineal. Let it infuse a fortnight, stirring it several times a day. Then boil it ten minutes, strain it, and bottle it for use.
Eat it with any sort of fish or game. It will give a fine pink tinge to melted butter.

Quin's Sauce
From "Directions for Cookery, in its Various Branches" By Eliza Leslie, 1840

Pound in a mortar six large anchovies, moistening them with their own pickle. Then chop and pound six small onions. Mix them with a little black pepper and a little cayenne, half a glass of soy, four glasses of mushroom catchup, two glasses of claret, and two of black walnut pickle. Put the mixture into a small sauce-pan or earthen pipkin, and let it simmer slowly till all the bones of the anchovies are dissolved. Strain it, and when cold, bottle it for use; dipping the cork in melted rosin, and tying leather over it. Fill the bottles quite full.

Roux
From "The Practical Housekeeper; A Cyclopedia of Domestic Economy", By Elizabeth Fries Ellet, 1857

<u>White</u>.--Put two ounces of butter into a stewpan over a slow fire, allow it to melt, then drain off the buttermilk: make it into a paste by dredging flour over it, and keep it on the fire for a quarter of an hour, taking care that it does not lose its color.

<u>Brown</u> is made in the same manner, only allowed to fry of a dark color. French cooks use no other kind of browning.

Sauce for a Pig
From "The Complete Cook", By J. M. Sanderson, 1864

Three quarters of a pint of good beef gravy, six or eight leaves of sage, chopped very fine, a blade of mace, a tea-cup full of bread crumbs, and eight white peppercorns; let them boil six or eight minutes, then stir into the sauce the brains, gravy, and whatever sticks about the dish on which you have split the pig, one ounce of butter rolled in flour, two table-spoonfuls of cream, and one or two of catsup, if liked; simmer a minute or two, and serve in a sauce tureen.

Scotch Sauce
From "Directions for Cookery, in its Various Branches" By Eliza Leslie, 1840

Take fifteen anchovies, chop them fine, and steep them in vinegar for a week, keeping the vessel closely covered. Then put them into a pint of claret or port wine. Scrape fine a large stick of horseradish, and chop two onions, a handful of parsley, a tea-spoonful of the leaves of lemon-thyme, and two large peach leaves. Add a nutmeg, six or eight blades of mace, nine cloves, and a tea-spoonful of black pepper, all slightly pounded in a mortar. Put all these ingredients into a silver or block tin sauce-pan, or into an earthen pipkin, and add a few grains of cochineal to colour it. Pour in a large half pint of the best vinegar, and simmer it slowly till the bones of the anchovies are entirely dissolved.

Strain the liquor through a sieve, and when quite cold put it away for use in small bottles; the corks dipped in melted rosin, and well-secured by pieces of leather tied closely over them. Fill each bottle quite full, as it will keep the better for leaving no vacancy.

This sauce will give a fine flavour to melted butter.

Superlative Sauce
From "A Poetical Cookbook", By Maria J. Moss, 1864

Claret or Port wine and mushroom ketchup, a pint of each; half a pint of walnut or other pickle liquor; pounded anchovies, four ounces; fresh lemon-peel, pared very thin, an ounce; peeled and sliced eschalots, the same; scraped horseradish, ditto; allspice and black pepper, powdered, half an ounce each; cayenne, one drachm, or curry powder, three drachms; celery seed, bruised, one drachm; all avoirdupois weight. Put these into a wide-mouthed bottle, stop it close, shake it every day for a fortnight, and strain it (when some think it improved by the addition of a quarter of a pint of soy or thick browning), and you will have "a delicious double relish." Dr. Kitchener says, this composition is one of the chefs d'oeuvres of many experiments he has made, for the purpose of enabling good housewives to prepare their own sauces; it is equally agreeable with fish, game, poultry, or ragouts, &c.; and as a fair lady may make it herself, its relish will be not a little augmented, that all the ingredients are good and wholesome.

<u>Observations-</u> Under an infinity of circumstances, a cook may be in want of the substances necessary to make sauce; the above composition of the several articles from which the various gravies derive their flavor, will be found a very admirable extemporaneous substitute. By mixing a large tablespoonful with a quarter of a pint of thickened melted butter, or broth, five minutes will finish a boat of very relishing sauce, nearly equal to drawn gravy, and as likely to put your lingual nerves into good humor as anything I know.

Tomato Catsup
From "The American Frugal Housewife", By Lydia M. Child, 1832

The best sort of catsup is made from tomatoes. The vegetables should be squeezed up in the hand, salt put to them, and set by for twenty-four hours. After being passed through a sieve, cloves, allspice, pepper, mace, garlic, and whole mustard-seed should be added. It should be boiled down one third, and bottled after it is cool. No liquid is necessary, as the tomatoes are very juicy. A good deal of salt and spice is necessary to keep the catsup well. It is delicious with roast meat; and a cupful adds much to the richness of soup and chowder. The garlic should be taken out before it is bottled.

Tomato Ketchup
From "The Great Western Cook Book, or Table Receipts, Adapted to Western Housewifery", By Anna Maria Collins, 1857

Take a gallon of skinned tomatoes, four tablespoonsful of salt, four of black pepper, and three of mustard. Grind these articles fine, and simmer them slowly in sharp vinegar, in a pewter basin, three or four hours, and then strain it through a wire sieve, and bottle for use. It may be used in two weeks, but improves much by age.
Use enough vinegar to make half a gallon of liquor when the process is over.

Tomato Ketchup
From "The Practical Housekeeper; A Cyclopedia of Domestic Economy", By Elizabeth Fries Ellet, 1857

Take six pounds of tomatoes, sprinkle them with salt and let them remain for a day or two, then boil them until the skins will separate easily; pour them into a colander or coarse sieve, and press them through, leaving the skins behind; put into the liquor a pint of Chili vinegar, half a pint of wine, pepper, cloves, ginger and allspice; boil them together until a third part has wasted--bottle them tight. The ketchup must be shaken before it is used. If it is boiled down to one-third, and the corks sealed, it will be much richer, and keep for years.

Tomato Sauce
From "The Practical Housekeeper; A Cyclopedia of Domestic Economy", By Elizabeth Fries Ellet, 1857

Fresh tomatoes; take out stalk, press them all tightly down in a stewpan, cover them, put them on the fire, strain off the liquor that is drawn from them, add to the tomatoes a slice of raw ham, two shalots, a few spoonfuls of good stock; let it stew for an hour, then rub it through a tammy sieve. Have in another stewpan a little good brown sauce, put your tomato into it, boil all together, season with cayenne, salt, sugar, and lemon-juice.

Tomata Soy
From "Directions for Cookery, in its Various Branches" By Eliza Leslie, 1840

For this purpose you must have the best and ripest tomatas, and they must be gathered on a dry day. Do not peel them, but merely cut them into slices. Having strewed some salt over the bottom of a tub, put in the tomatas in layers; sprinkling between each layer (which, should be about two inches in thickness) a half pint of salt. Repeat this till you have put in eight quarts or one peck of tomatas. Cover the tub and let it set for three days. Then early in the morning, put the tomatas into a large porcelain, kettle, and boil it slowly and steadily till ten at night, frequently mashing and stirring the tomatas. Then put it out to cool. Next morning strain and press it through a sieve, and when no more liquid will pass through, put it into a clean kettle with two ounces of cloves, one ounce of mace, two ounces of blade pepper, and two table-spoonfuls of cayenne, all powdered.
Again let it boil slowly and steadily all day, and put it to cool in the evening in a large pan. Cover it, and let it set all night. Next day put it into small bottles, securing the corks by dipping them in melted rosin, and tying leathers over them. If made exactly according to these directions, and slowly and thoroughly boiled, it will keep for years in a cool dry place, and may be used for many purposes when fresh tomatas are not to be had.

Sauce for Wild Fowl
From "A New System of Domestic Cookery", By Maria Eliza Ketelby Rundell, 1807

Simmer a tea-cupful of port wine, the same quantity of good meat-gravy, a little shalot, a little pepper, salt, a grate of nutmeg, and a bit of mace, for ten minutes; put in a bit of butter and flour, give it all one boil, and pour it through the birds. In general they are not stuffed as tame, but may be done so if liked.
<u>Another for the same, or for Ducks.</u>
Serve a rich gravy in the dish: cut the breast into slices, but don't take them off; cut a lemon, and put pepper and salt on it; then squeeze it on the breast, and pour a spoonful of gravy over before you help.

Wine Sauce
From "Directions for Cookery, in its Various Branches" By Eliza Leslie, 1840

Have ready some rich thick melted or drawn butter, and the moment you take it from the fire, stir in two large glasses of white wine, two table-spoonfuls of powdered white sugar, and a powdered nutmeg. Serve it up with plum pudding, or any sort of boiled pudding that is made of a batter.

Wine Sauce for Mutton, or Venison
From "Miss Beecher's Domestic Receipt Book", By
Catharine Esther Beecher, 1850

Take half a pint of the liquor in which the meat was cooked, and when boiling, put in pepper, salt, currant jelly, and wine to your taste; add about a teaspoonful of scorched flour, mixed with a little water.

Wow Wow Sauce, for Stewed Beef or Bouilli
From "The Complete Cook", By J. M. Sanderson, 1864

Quarter and slice two or three pickled cucumbers or walnuts, or part of each, chop fine a handful of parsley, make some melted butter in half a pint of broth in which the beef is boiled, add a tea-spoonful of made mustard and a table-spoonful of vinegar, and the same of port wine and mushroom catsup: let it simmer till thick, then stir in the parsley and pickles to get warm; pour the whole over the beef, or put in a sauce tureen. The flavour may be varied by a tea-spoonful or two of any kind of the vinegars.

A Good Sauce for Steaks
From "The Book of Household Management", By Isabella Beeton, 1861

1 oz. of whole black pepper, 1/2 oz. of allspice, 1 oz. of salt, 1/2 oz. grated horseradish, 1/2 oz. of pickled shalots, 1 pint of mushroom ketchup or walnut pickle.
Pound all the ingredients finely in a mortar, and put them into the ketchup or walnut-liquor. Let them stand for a fortnight, when strain off the liquor and bottle for use. Either pour a little of the sauce over the steaks or mix it in the gravy.

Soy
From "Miss Beecher's Domestic Receipt Book", By
Catharine Esther Beecher, 1850

One pound of salt, two pounds of sugar, fried half an hour over a slow fire, then add three pints of boiling water, half a pint of essence of anchovies, a dozen cloves, and some sweet herbs. Boil till the salt dissolves, then strain and bottle it.

Tarragon Sauce

From "The Lady's Receipt-Book; a Useful Companion for Large or Small Families", By Eliza Leslie, 1847

Take a large handful of tarragon leaves, stripped from the stalks: put them into a small sauce-pan with half a pint of boiling water, and four blades of mace. Cover the sauce-pan, and let it stew slowly till the liquid is reduced to one half, and the flavour of the tarragon is well drawn out. Then strain it; and put the liquid into a clean sauce-pan. Mix together a table-spoonful of flour, and six ounces of butter, and when it has been well-stirred, and beaten smoothly, stir it into the tarragon water. Place the sauce-pan over the fire, and watch it closely. When it has simmered well, and is just beginning to boil, take it off immediately and transfer it to a sauce-boat. Eat it with any sort of boiled meat or poultry, or with boiled fish. The tarragon will give it a fine flavour.

You may add to the tarragon, while stewing, a small white onion cut in slices. This sauce may be coloured a fine green, by pounding in a mortar a sufficient quantity of young parsley or spinach. Then take some of the juice, and add it to the liquid after you have strained it from the tarragon leaves, and before you put in the butter.

Tarragon is an herb well worth cultivating. It grows from a slip or root, and is easily raised. The leaves are fit to gather in July and August. They impart a fine and peculiar flavour to sauces, soups, and salad; and are indispensable in making French mustard. Tarragon may be kept a year or more by drying it in bunches. Also by filling a bottle half with tarragon leaves, and half with good vinegar.

Basil Vinegar or Wine (No. 397)
From "The Cook's Oracle; and Housekeeper's Manual", By William Kitchiner, 1830

Sweet basil is in full perfection about the middle of August. Fill a wide-mouthed bottle with the fresh green leaves of basil (these give much finer and more flavour than the dried), and cover them with vinegar, or wine, and let them steep for ten days: if you wish a very
strong essence, strain the liquor, put it on some fresh leaves, and let them steep fourteen days more.

Obs.-This is a very agreeable addition to sauces, soups, and to the mixture usually made for salads.

Vinegar for Salads (No. 395)
From "The Cook's Oracle; and Housekeeper's Manual", By William Kitchiner, 1830

"Take of tarragon, savoury, chives, eschalots, three ounces each; a handful of the tops of mint and balm, all dry and pounded; put into a wide-mouthed bottle, with a gallon of best vinegar; cork it close, set it in the sun, and in a fortnight strain off, and squeeze the herbs; let it stand a day to settle, and then strain it through a filtering bag."

Walnut Ketchup
From "The Book of Household Management", By Isabella Beeton, 1861

100 walnuts, 1 handful of salt, 1 quart of vinegar, 1/4 oz. of mace, 1/4 oz. of nutmeg, 1/4 oz. of cloves, 1/4 oz. of ginger, 1/4 oz. of whole black pepper, a small piece of horseradish, 20
shalots, 1/4 lb. of anchovies, 1 pint of port wine.
Procure the walnuts at the time you can run a pin through them, slightly bruise, and put them into a jar with the salt and vinegar, let them stand 8 days, stirring every day; then drain the liquor from them, and boil it, with the above ingredients, for about 1/2 hour. It may be strained or not, as preferred, and, if required, a little more vinegar or wine can be added, according to taste. When bottled well, seal the corks.

White Onion Sauce
From "Directions for Cookery, in its Various Branches" By Eliza Leslie, 1840

Peel a dozen onions, and throw them into salt and water to keep them white. Then boil them tender. When done, squeeze the water from them, and chop them. Have ready some butter that has been melted rich and smooth with milk or cream instead of water. Put the onions into the melted butter, and boil them up at once. If you wish to have them very mild, put in a turnip with them at the first boiling. Young white onions, if very small, need not be chopped, but may be put whole into the butter.
Use this sauce for rabbits, tripe, boiled poultry, or any boiled fresh meat.

7. Jams, Jellies and Preserves

"We also sampled the nice brandy peaches, I told the party that they were put up by your own fair hands, and four years ago at that. They were really very nice."-Lt. Col. James B. Griffin, Hampton's Legion, February 19, 1862. Letter to his wife, Leila.

Apple Jam
From "The Book of Household Management", By Isabella Beeton, 1861

To every lb. of fruit weighed after being pared, cored, and sliced, allow 3/4 lb. of preserving-sugar, the grated rind of 1 lemon, the juice of 1/2 lemon.

Peel the apples, core and slice them very thin, and be particular that they are all the same sort. Put them into a jar, stand this in a saucepan of boiling water, and let the apples stew until quite tender. Previously to putting the fruit into the jar, weigh it, to ascertain the proportion of sugar that may be required. Put the apples into a preserving-pan, crush the sugar to small lumps, and add it, with the grated lemon-rind and juice, to the apples. Simmer these over the fire for 1/2 hour, reckoning from the time the jam begins to simmer properly; remove the scum as it rises, and when the jam is done, put it into pots for use. Place a piece of oiled paper over the jam, and to exclude the air, cover the pots with tissue-paper dipped in the white of an egg, and stretched over the top. This jam will keep good for a long time.

About 2 hours to stew in the jar; 1/2 hour to boil after the jam begins to simmer.

Apple Jelly
From "A Poetical Cookbook", By Maria J. Moss, 1864

Pare and mince three dozen juicy, acid apples; put them into a pan; cover them with water, and boil them till very soft; strain them through a thin cloth or flannel bag; allow a pound of loaf sugar to a pint of juice, with the grated peel and juice of six lemons. Boil it for twenty minutes; take off the scum as it rises.

Apple Marmalade
From "The Lady's Receipt-Book; a Useful Companion for Large or Small Families", By Eliza Leslie, 1847

Break up four pounds of fine loaf-sugar. Put it into a preserving-kettle, and pour on a quart of clear, cold water. When the sugar has melted, stir it; set the kettle over the fire, and let it boil for a quarter of an hour after it has come to a boil; skimming it well. Have ready some fine, ripe pippin or bell-flower apples, pared, cored and sliced. There must be apple enough to weigh four pounds, when cut up. Put it into the syrup, adding the grated rinds of four large lemons. Let it simmer, stirring it well, till the apple is all dissolved, and forming a smooth mass. Then add the juice of the lemons; boil it fast; and continue boiling and stirring, till it becomes a very thick marmalade. It will generally require *simmering* an hour and a half, and *boiling fast* half an hour, or more. When it is done, put it, warm, into deep white-ware jars; cover it closely, and paste paper over the top, or tie a piece of bladder closely; and put it away in a dry, cool place. If you want any for immediate use, put some into a handsome mould, and, when cold and firm, turn it out on a glass dish; first dipping the mould in warm water.

Apricot Jam or Marmalade
From "The Book of Household Management", By Isabella Beeton, 1861

To every lb. of ripe apricots, weighed after being skinned and stoned, allow 1 lb. of sugar.

Pare the apricots, which should be ripe, as thinly as possible, break them in half, and remove the stones. Weigh the fruit, and to every lb. allow the same proportion of loaf sugar. Pound the sugar very finely in a mortar, strew it over the apricots, which should be placed on dishes, and let them remain for 12 hours. Break the stones, blanch the kernels, and put them with the sugar and fruit into a preserving-pan. Let these simmer very gently until clear; take out the pieces of apricot singly as they become so, and, as fast as the scum rises, carefully remove it. Put the apricots into small jars, pour over them the syrup and kernels, cover the jam with pieces of paper dipped in the purest salad-oil, and stretch over the top of the jars tissue-paper, cut about 2 inches larger and brushed over with the white of an egg: when dry, it will be perfectly hard and air-tight.

Time-12 hours sprinkled with sugar; about 3/4 hour to boil the jam.

Blackberry Jam
From "Miss Beecher's Domestic Receipt Book", By Catharine Esther Beecher, 1850

Allow three quarters of a pound of brown sugar to a pound of fruit. Boil the fruit half an hour, then add the sugar, and boil all together ten minutes.

Calf's Foot Jelly
From "Miss Beecher's Domestic Receipt Book", By Catharine Esther Beecher, 1850

To four nicely-cleaned calf's feet, put four quarts of water; let it simmer gently till reduced to two quarts, then strain it, and let it stand all night. Then take off all the fat and sediment, melt it, add the juice, and put in the peel of three lemons, and a pint of wine, the whites of four eggs, three sticks of cinnamon, and sugar to your taste. Boil ten minutes, then skim out the spice and lemon peel, and strain it. The American gelatine, now very common, makes as good jelly, with far less trouble, and in using it you only need to dissolve it in hot water, and then sweeten and flavor it.

Cherry Jelly
From "A Poetical Cookbook", By Maria J. Moss, 1864

Take the stones and stalks from two pounds of clear, fine, ripe cherries; mix them with a quarter of a pound of red currants, from which the seeds have been extracted; express the juice from these fruits; filter, and mix it with three quarters of a pound of clarified sugar,
and one ounce of isinglass. Replace the vessel on the fire with the juice, and add to it a pound and a half of sugar, boiled à conserve. Boil together a few times, and then pour the conserve into cases.

Clear Apple Jelly
From "The Book of Household Management", By Isabella Beeton, 1861

2 dozen apples, 1-1/2 pint of spring-water; to every pint of juice allow 1/2 lb. of loaf sugar, 1/2 oz. of isinglass, the rind of 1/2 lemon.
Pare, core, and cut the apples into quarters, and boil them, with the lemon-peel, until tender; then strain off the apples, and run the juice through a jelly-bag; put the strained juice, with the sugar and isinglass, which has been previously boiled in 1/2 pint of water, into a lined saucepan or preserving-pan; boil all together for about 1/4 hour, and put the jelly into moulds. When this jelly is nice and clear, and turned out well, it makes a pretty addition to the supper-table, with a little custard or whipped cream round it: the addition of a little lemon-juice improves the flavour, but it is apt to render the jelly muddy and thick. If required to be kept any length of time, rather a larger proportion of sugar must be used.
Time: From 1 to 1-1/2 hour to boil the apples; 1/4 hour the jelly.

Crab Apples
From "The Practical Housekeeper; A Cyclopedia of Domestic Economy", By Elizabeth Fries Ellet, 1857

Make a syrup, allowing the same weight of sugar as apples. Let it cool, then put in the apples, a few at once, so that they will not crowd, and break to pieces. Boil them till they begin to break, then take them out of the kettle. Boil the syrup in the course of three or four days, and turn it while hot upon the apples. This continue to do at intervals of two or three days, till the apples appear to be thoroughly preserved.

Cranberry and Rice Jelly
From "A New System of Domestic Cookery", By Maria Eliza Ketelby Rundell, 1807

Boil and press the fruit, strain the juice, and by degrees mix into it as much ground rice as will, when boiled, thicken to a jelly; boil it gently, stirring it, and sweeten to your taste. Put it in a basin or form, and serve to eat as the afore-directed jelly, with milk or cream.

Currant Jelly (Red)
From "The Practical Housekeeper; A Cyclopedia of Domestic Economy", By Elizabeth Fries Ellet, 1857

Strip off the currants, put them in a jar, set the jar in a kettle of hot water, let it boil an hour, then throw the cur rants and juice into a fine lawn sieve, press out all the juice, and to every pint of juice put a pound of fine sugar; put them in a preserving-pan, set it over a charcoal fire and keep it stirring till it is in a jelly, which you will know by taking a little out to cool; be careful to take off the scum as it rises, and when it is jellied and very clear pour it into glasses; when cold, cut round pieces of paper that will just cover the jelly, dipped in brandy, put white paper over the glasses, twisting round the top. Make black currant jelly the same way, using coarse sugar.

Currant Jelly
From "A Poetical Cookbook", By Maria J. Moss, 1864

Currant, grape, and raspberry jelly are all made precisely in the same manner. When the fruit is full ripe, gather it on a dry day. As soon as it is nicely picked, put it into a jar, and cover it down very close. Set the jar in a saucepan, about three parts filled with cold water; put it on a gentle fire, and let it simmer for about half an hour. Take the pan from the fire, and pour the contents of the jar into a jelly-bag, pass the juice through a second time; do not squeeze the bag. To each pint of juice, add a pound and a half of very good lump sugar pounded, when it is put into a preserving pan; set it on the fire, and boil it gently, stirring and skimming it the whole time (about thirty or forty minutes), i. e. till no more scum rises, and it is perfectly clear and fine; pour it warm into pots, and when cold, cover them with paper wetted in brandy.

Half a pint of this jelly dissolved in a pint of brandy or vinegar will give you an excellent currant or raspberry brandy or vinegar.

Observations: Jellies from the fruits are made in the same way, and cannot be preserved in perfection without plenty of good sugar. The best way is the cheapest.

Damson Jam
From "The Lady's Receipt-Book; a Useful Companion for Large or Small Families", By Eliza Leslie, 1847

Fill a stone jar with fine ripe damsons that have been washed in cold water but not dried. Cover it, set it in an open kettle with water which must not quite reach the neck of the jar, and place it over a hot fire. Let the water boil round the jar, till the stones of the damsons are all loose, and falling out from the pulp. Then transfer the damsons and their juice, to a broad pan, and carefully pick out all the stones. Next mash the pulp with a broad flat wooden ladle, or with a potatoe-masher, till it is all smooth and of an even consistence throughout. Then measure it; and to every quart of the pulp allow a pound and a half, or three large closely-packed pints of the best brown sugar. Stir the sugar and pulp well together, till it becomes a thick jam. Put the jam into a clean preserving-kettle, and boil it slowly an hour or more, skimming it well. When done, put it into broad flat stone jars, pressing it down, and smoothing the surface with the back of a large spoon. Cover the jars closely, and put them away in a cool dry place. If more convenient, you can put the jam into tumblers, pasting thick white paper closely over each.

If properly made it will be so firm that you may cut it down in slices like cheese. Plum jam may be made as above; but damsons are better for this purpose, and also for jelly, as the juice is much thicker and richer than that of plums.

It is an old-fashioned error to use unripe fruit for any sort of sweet-meat. When the fruit is thoroughly ripe it has more flavour, is far more wholesome, and keeps better.

Fruit Jelly
From "The Complete Cook", By J. M. Sanderson, 1864

Put the fruit, carefully picked, into a stone jar; cover close; set it in a kettle of cold water, which reaches not more than three parts the height of the jar. Let it boil half an hour (more or less, according to the nature of the fruit; black currants are much longer running to juice than either red currants or raspberries). Strain through a jelly-bag or lawn strainer; or the juice may be strained more quickly, by setting on the fruit in a preserving pan, and carefully stirring round the sides as it begins to heat, that it may not burn; strain through a jelly-bag or lawn strainer. To every pint of juice allow a pound of loaf-sugar. Set on the juice over a clear fire; when it boils, put in the sugar. When it has boiled some time, and the scum thickens and gathers together, skim it on to a sieve, and continue to do so while the scum rises; what runs from it may be returned to the rest. When it has boiled forty minutes, try a few drops, by putting on a plate in a cool place. If this become stiff almost immediately, the jelly is done enough. If not, it must be boiled till it will. The jelly may then be strained through a hair sieve, but if it have been properly skimmed this is not necessary, and it is a great waste. The best way is to pour it into a spouted jug that will contain the whole, and then into small jelly pots or glasses. Be very careful not to pour aside, or smear the edges, as an accident of this sort, however carefully wiped away, renders the jelly apt to turn mouldy. White currant jelly should be strained through a muslin or lawn sieve.

Four Fruit Jelly
From "The Lady's Receipt-Book; a Useful Companion for Large or Small Families", By Eliza Leslie, 1847

Take equal quantities of ripe strawberries, raspberries, currants, and red cherries. All should be fully ripe, and the cherries must be stoned, taking care to save the juice that comes from them in stoning. Add it, afterwards, to the rest. Mix the fruit together, and put it in a linen bag. Squeeze it well into a tureen placed beneath. When it has ceased to drip, measure the juice; and to every pint, allow a pound and two ounces of the best double-refined loaf-sugar, finely powdered. Mix together the juice and the sugar. Put them into a porcelain preserving-kettle; set it over the fire, and let it boil half an hour--skimming it frequently. Try the jelly by dipping out a spoonful, and holding it in the open air. If it congeals readily, it is sufficiently done. Put the jelly warm into tumblers or other wide-topped glasses. Cover it with double-tissue paper, which must be white, and cut exactly to fit the surface of the jelly. Lay it nicely and smoothly inside the top of the glass, pressing it down with your fingers all round the edge. Then paste white paper over the top, and a little way down the sides of the glass, notching it round with scissors to make it fit the better.
Set away the jelly in a cool dry closet.

Gooseberry Jelly
From "The Book of Household Management", By Isabella Beeton, 1861

Gooseberries; to every pint of juice allow 3/4 lb. of loaf sugar.
Put the gooseberries, after cutting off the tops and tails, into a preserving-pan, and stir them over the fire until they are quite soft; then strain them through a sieve, and to every pint of juice allow 3/4 lb. of sugar. Boil the juice and sugar together for nearly 3/4 hour,
stirring and skimming all the time; and if the jelly appears firm when a little of it is poured on to a plate, it is done, and should then be taken up and put into small pots. Cover the pots with oiled and egged papers, the same as for currant jelly No. 1533 (close the jars), and store away in a dry place.

Time-3/4 hour to simmer the gooseberries without the sugar; 3/4 hour to boil the juice.

Brandy Grapes
From "The Lady's Receipt-Book; a Useful Companion for Large or Small Families", By Eliza Leslie, 1847

For this purpose the grapes should be in large close bunches, and quite ripe. Remove every grape that is the least shrivelled, or in any way defective. With a needle prick each grape in three places. Have ready a sufficiency of double-refined loaf-sugar, powdered and sifted. Put some of the sugar into the bottom of your jars. Then put in a bunch of grapes, and cover it thickly with sugar. Then another bunch; then more sugar, and so on till the jar is nearly full; finishing with a layer of sugar. Then fill up to the top with the best white brandy. Cover the jars as closely as possible, and set them away. They must not go over the fire. The grapes should be of the best quality, either white or purple.

Preserved Mulberries
From "The Book of Household Management", By Isabella Beeton, 1861

To 2 lbs. of fruit and 1 pint of juice allow 2-1/2 lbs. of loaf sugar.
Put some of the fruit into a preserving-pan, and simmer it gently until the juice is well drawn. Strain it through a bag, measure it, and to every pint allow the above proportion of sugar and fruit. Put the sugar into the preserving-pan, moisten it with the juice, boil it up, skim well, and then add the mulberries, which should be ripe, but not soft enough to break to a pulp. Let them stand in the syrup till warm through, then set them on the fire to boil gently; when half done, turn them carefully into an earthen pan, and let them remain till the next day; then boil them as before, and when the syrup is thick, and becomes firm when cold, put the preserve into pots. In making this, care should be taken not to break the mulberries: this may be avoided by very gentle stirring, and by simmering the fruit very slowly.
Time-3/4 hour to extract the juice;
1/4 hour to boil the mulberries the first time, 1/4 hour the second time.

Orange Butter
From "A New System of Domestic Cookery", By Maria Eliza Ketelby Rundell, 1807

Boil six hard eggs, beat them in a mortar with two ounces of fine sugar, three ounces of butter, and two ounces of blanched almonds beaten to a paste. Moisten with orange-flower water, and when all is mixed, rub it through a colander on a dish, and serve sweet biscuits between.

Orange Jelly
From "A New System of Domestic Cookery", By Maria Eliza Ketelby Rundell, 1807

Grate the rind of two Seville and two China oranges, and two lemons; squeeze the juice of three of each, and strain, and add the juice to a quarter of a pound of lump sugar, and a quarter of a pint of water, and boil till it almost candies. Have ready a quart of isinglass-jelly made with two ounces; put to it the syrup, and boil it once up; strain off the jelly, and let it stand to settle as above, before it is put into the mould.

Peaches Preserved In Brandy
From "The Book of Household Management", By Isabella Beeton, 1861

To every lb. of fruit weighed before being stoned, allow 1/4 lb. of finely-pounded loaf sugar; brandy.

Let the fruit be gathered in dry weather; wipe and weigh it, and remove the stones as carefully as possible, without injuring the peaches much. Put them into a jar, sprinkle amongst them pounded loaf sugar in the above proportion, and pour brandy over the fruit. Cover the jar down closely, place it in a saucepan of boiling water over the fire, and bring the brandy to the simmering-point, but do not allow it to boil. Take the fruit out carefully, without breaking it; put it into small jars, pour over it the brandy, and, when cold, exclude the air by covering the jars with bladders, or tissue-paper brushed over on both sides with the white of an egg. Apricots may be done in the same manner, and, if properly prepared, will be found delicious.

Time-From 10 to 20 minutes to bring the brandy to the simmering-point.

Very Fine Preserved Peaches
From "The Lady's Receipt-Book; a Useful Companion for Large or Small Families", By Eliza Leslie, 1847

Take fine ripe free-stone peaches; pare them; cut them in half and remove the stones. Have ready a sufficiency of the best double-refined loaf-sugar, finely powdered. Weigh the sugar and the peaches together, putting the sugar into one scale and the peaches into the other, and balancing them evenly. Put the peaches into a large pan or tureen, and strew among them one-half of the sugar. Cover them, and let them stand in a cool place till next morning. Then take all the juice from them, and put it into a porcelain preserving-kettle with the remainder of the sugar. Set it over a moderate fire, and boil and skim it. When it is boiling well, and the scum has ceased to rise, put in the peaches and boil them till they are perfectly clear, but not till they break; carefully skimming them. Boil with them a handful of fresh clean peach-leaves tied in a bunch. When quite clear take the peaches out of the syrup, and put them on a flat sloping dish to drain into a deep dish placed below it. Take this syrup that has drained from the peaches, put it to the syrup in the kettle, and give it one more boil up. Then throw away the leaves. Lay the peaches flat in small glass jars. Pour an equal portion of the hot syrup into each jar, and put on the top a table-spoonful of the best white brandy. Cork the jars, and paste down paper closely over the mouth of each.

To Preserve Pears
From "The Practical Housekeeper; A Cyclopedia of Domestic Economy", By Elizabeth Fries Ellet, 1857

Pare them very thin, and simmer them in a thin syrup, allowing only one-quarter of a pound of sugar to a pound of pears. Let them lie for two days, add another quarter of a pound of sugar to each pound of pears, and simmer them again. Let them lie all night, or longer if you please, then simmer them once more, this time adding half a pound of sugar to each pound of pears, with the juice of half a lemon to every two pounds of fruit. A small portion of the lemon-peel may also be used. The fruit may then be drained and dried in the sun, so that they may be used dry; or they may be poured into the jars with the syrup over them.
Another mode of preserving pears, and a less troublesome one, is to pare, quarter and core the pears, boil them for an hour in as much water as will cover them, then add to every pound of pears a pound of white sugar and the juice of half a lemon, boil the whole and skim it. When the pears are soft, pour them into jars and the syrup over them; tie up the jars.
This is a much more expeditious way of preserving the pears, and perhaps the best for large families, where sweetmeats are in daily use; but the fruit itself does not look as clear and beautiful; as when preserved by the former method.

Pineapple Preserve
From "A Poetical Cookbook", By Maria J. Moss, 1864

Pare your pineapple; cut it in small pieces, and leave out the core. Mix the pineapple with half a pound of powdered white sugar, and set it away in a covered dish till sufficient juice is drawn out to stew the fruit in.

Stew the pineapple in the sugar and juice till quite soft, then mash it to a marmalade with the back of a spoon, and set it away to cool; pour it in tumblers, cover them with paper, gum-arabicked on.

Purple Plum.--No. 1
From "Miss Beecher's Domestic Receipt Book", By
Catharine Esther Beecher, 1850

Make a rich syrup. Boil the plums in the syrup very gently till they begin to crack open. Then take them from the syrup into a jar, and pour the syrup over them. Let them stand a few days, and then boil them a second time, very gently.

Purple Plum.--No. 2
From "Miss Beecher's Domestic Receipt Book", By
Catharine Esther Beecher, 1850

Take an equal weight of fruit, and nice brown sugar. Take a clean stone jar, put in a layer of fruit and a layer of sugar, till all is in. Cover them tightly with dough, or other tight cover, and put them in a brick oven after you have baked in it. If you bake in the morning, put the plums in the oven at evening, and let them remain till the next morning. When you bake again, set them in the oven as before. Uncover them, and stir them carefully with a spoon, and so as not to break them. Set them in the oven thus *the third* time, and they will be sufficiently cooked.

Preserved Pumpkin
From "Miss Beecher's Domestic Receipt Book", By
Catharine Esther Beecher, 1850

Cut a thick yellow pumpkin, peeled, into strips two inches wide, and five or six long.

Take a pound of white sugar for each pound of fruit, and scatter it over the fruit, and pour on two wine-glasses of lemon juice for each pound of pumpkin.

Next day, put the parings of one or two lemons with the fruit and sugar, and boil the whole three quarters of an hour, or long enough to make it tender and clear without breaking. Lay the pumpkin to cool, strain the syrup, and then pour it on to the pumpkin.

If there is too much lemon peel, it will be bitter.

Raspberry Jam.--No. 1
From "Miss Beecher's Domestic Receipt Book", By
Catharine Esther Beecher, 1850

Allow a pound of sugar to a pound of fruit. Press them with a spoon, in an earthen dish. Add the sugar, and boil all together fifteen minutes.

Raspberry Jam.--No. 2
From "Miss Beecher's Domestic Receipt Book", By
Catharine Esther Beecher, 1850

Allow a pound of sugar to a pound of fruit. Boil the fruit half an hour, or till the seeds are soft. Strain one quarter of the fruit, and throw away the seeds. Add the sugar, and boil the whole ten minutes. A little currant juice gives it a pleasant flavor, and when that is used, an equal quantity of sugar must be added.

Rhubarb Jam
From "The Book of Household Management", By Isabella Beeton, 1861

To every lb. of rhubarb allow 1 lb. of loaf sugar, the rind of 1/2 lemon.
Wipe the rhubarb perfectly dry, take off the string or peel, and weigh it; put it into a preserving-pan, with sugar in the above proportion; mince the lemon-rind very finely, add it to the other ingredients, and place the preserving-pan by the side of the fire; keep
stirring to prevent the rhubarb from burning, and when the sugar is well dissolved, put the pan more over the fire, and let the jam boil until it is done, taking care to keep it well skimmed and stirred with a wooden or silver spoon. Pour it into pots, and cover down with oiled and egged papers.
Time-If the rhubarb is young and tender, 3/4 hour, reckoning from the time it simmers equally; old rhubarb, 1-1/4 to 1-1/2 hour.

Jellies Without Fruit
From "Dr. Chase's Recipes; or, Information for Everybody", By Dr. Alvin Wood Chase, 1864

Take water 1 pt. and add to it pulverized alum 1/4 oz., and boil a minute or two; then add 4 lbs. of white crushed or coffee sugar, continue the boiling a little, strain while hot; and when cold put in half of a two shilling bottle of extract of vanilla, strawberry, or lemon, or any other flavor you desire for jelly.
This will make a jelly so much resembling that made from the juice of the fruit that any one will be astonished; and when fruit cannot be got, it will take its place

admirably. I have had neighbors eat of it and be perfectly astonished at its beauty and palatableness.

Strawberries
From "Miss Beecher's Domestic Receipt Book", By Catharine Esther Beecher, 1850

Look them over with care. Weigh a pound of sugar to each pound of fruit. Put a layer of fruit on the bottom of the preserving kettle, then a layer of sugar, and so on till all is in the pan. Boil them about fifteen minutes. Put them in bottles, hot, and seal them. Then put them in a box, and fill it in with dry sand. The flavor of the fruit is preserved more perfectly, by simply packing the fruit and sugar in alternate layers, and sealing the jar, without cooking. But the preserves do not look so well.

Preserved Strawberries In Wine
From "The Book of Household Management", By Isabella Beeton, 1861

To every quart bottle allow 1/4 lb. of finely-pounded loaf sugar; sherry or Madeira. Let the fruit be gathered in fine weather, and used as soon as picked. Have ready some perfectly dry glass bottles, and some nice soft corks or bungs. Pick the stalks from the strawberries, drop them into the bottles, sprinkling amongst them pounded sugar in the above proportion, and when the fruit reaches to the neck of the bottle, fill up with sherry or Madeira. Cork the bottles down with new corks, and dip them into melted resin.

Tomato Marmlade
From "The Virginia Housewife", By Mary Randolph, 1860

Gather full grown tomatos while quite green; take out the stems, and stew them till soft; rub them through a sieve, put the pulp on the fire seasoned highly with pepper, salt, and pounded cloves; add some garlic, and stew all together till thick: it keeps well, and is excellent for seasoning gravies, &c. &c.

To Preserve Watermelon Rind
From "The Practical Housekeeper; A Cyclopedia of Domestic Economy", By Elizabeth Fries Ellet, 1857

Pare off the outer skin and cut the rind into shapes: green them by simmer ing with vine leaves and a little alum, and allow a pound and a quarter of sugar to each pound. Make the syrup and clarify it with white of egg, and simmer the melon rind till done through and trans parent. Boil down the syrup afterwards, and pour it over the preserves.
Chips of pumpkin or muskmelon rind, cut thin, are often made into preserves,-- adding the juice and grated rind of lemons, which much improves the syrup.

Citrons may be preserved in the same manner, first paring off the outer skin, and cutting them into quarters. Also green limes.

8. Breads and Biscuits

"We have not eaten our potatoes yet. We are going to make potato bread of them this evening." —Pvt. James A. Durrett, Co. E, 18th Alabama Infantry, Nov. 12, 1863 in the Chattanooga Valley, Tennessee. Letter to his mother. He was shot through the head and died April 3, 1865 at Spanish Fort, Mobile Alabama.

"Our rations are short. We have nothing but crackers."-Pvt. Martin Van Buren Oldham, Company G of the 9th Tennessee Infantry, January 16, 1863, en route to Prison at Camp Douglas. From diary entry.

"Passed thro' little town called Flint Hill, in which David Barnum got a canteen of milk, some hot corn bread & fresh butter, & John got another Canteen of Butter milk. We camped abt. ½ mile fr. town quite early in the evening, & then made a hearty meal of the bread, butter & milk wh. of course we thought was the best thing we had ever tasted."-Pvt. Sam Pickens, Company D, Fifth Alabama Infantry, en route to Gettysburg. From diary entry.

"Times is hard here. We do not get much to eat. We have not got any bread for dinner today nor will not have any for supper, nor breakfast. We do not get much to & have not got anything to cook what we do get in." - James Andrew James, T. B. Ferguson's (South Carolina) Battery, Atlanta, Georgia, October the 20, 1863. Letter to his father

Almond Bread
From "The Practical Housekeeper; A Cyclopedia of Domestic Economy", By Elizabeth Fries Ellet, 1857

Blanch, and pound in a mortar, half a pound of shelled sweet almonds till they are a smooth paste, adding rose-water as you pound them. They should be done the day before they are wanted. Prepare a pound

of loaf-sugar finely powdered, a teaspoonful of mixed spice, mace, nutmeg and cinnamon, and three-quarters of a pound of sifted flour. Take fourteen eggs, and separate the whites from the yolks. Leave out seven of the whites, and beat the other seven to a stiff froth. Beat the yolks till very thick and smooth, and then beat the sugar gradually into them, adding the spice. Next stir in the white of egg, then the flour, and lastly the almonds. You may add twelve drops of essence of lemon. Put the mixture into a square tin pan, well buttered, or into a copper or tin-turban mould, and set it immediately in a brisk oven. Ice it when cool. It is best when eaten fresh.
You may add a few bitter almonds to the sweet ones.

Batter Bread
From "The Virginia Housewife", By Mary Randolph, 1860

Take six spoonsful of flour and three of corn meal, with a little salt--sift them, and make a thin batter with four eggs, and a sufficient quantity of rich milk; bake it in little tin moulds in a quick oven.

Biscuit
From "Confederate Receipt Book. A Compilation of Over One Hundred Receipts, Adapted To The Times", By West & Johnston, 1863

Take one quart of flour, three teaspoonfuls of cream of tartar, mixed well through the flour, two tablespoonfuls of shortening, one teaspoonful of soda, dissolved in warm water, of sufficient quantity to mould the quart of flour. For large families the amount can be doubled.

Another Reciept

Take two quarts of flour, two ounces of butter, half pint of boiling water, one teaspoonful of salt, one pint of cold milk, and half cup yeast. Mix well and set to rise, then mix a teaspoonful of saleratus in a little water and mix into dough, roll on a board an inch thick, cut into small biscuits, and bake twenty minutes.

Bread
From "The Complete Cook", By J. M. Sanderson, 1864

Put a quartern of flour into a large basin, or small pan, with two tea-spoonfuls of salt; make a hole in the middle, then put in a basin four table-spoonfuls of good yeast, stir in a pint of milk lukewarm; put it in the hole of the flour, stir just to make it of a thin batter, and then strew a little flour over the top; then set it on one side of the fire, cover it over with a cloth, let it stand till the next morning; add half a pint more of warm milk, and make it into dough, knead it for ten minutes, then set it in a warm place by the fire for one hour and a half, then knead it again, and it is ready for either loaves or bricks.

Bread
From "A Poetical Cookbook", By Maria J. Moss, 1864

Mix with six pounds of sifted flour one ounce of salt, nearly half a pint of fresh sweet yeast as it comes from the brewery, and a sufficient quantity of warmed milk to make the whole into a stiff dough, work and knead it well on a board, on which a little flour has been strewed, for fifteen or twenty minutes, then put it into a deep pan, cover it with a warmed towel, set it before the fire, and let it rise for an hour and a half or perhaps two hours; cut off a piece of this sponge or dough; knead it well for eight or ten minutes, together with flour sufficient to keep it from adhering to the board, put it into small tins, filling them three quarters full; dent the rolls all around with a knife, and let them stand a few minutes before putting them in the oven.
The remainder of the dough must then be worked up for loaves, and baked either in or out of shape.

Bread Muffins
From "The Lady's Receipt-Book; a Useful Companion for Large or Small Families", By Eliza Leslie, 1847

Take some bread dough that has risen as light as possible, and knead into it some well-beaten egg in the proportion of two eggs to about a pound of dough. Then mix in a tea-spoonful of soda that has been dissolved in a very little lukewarm water. Let the dough stand in a warm place for a quarter of an hour. Then bake it in muffin-rings. You can thus, with very little trouble, have muffins for tea whenever you bake bread in the afternoon.

Soyer's Brioche Rolls
From "The Practical Housekeeper; A Cyclopedia of Domestic Economy", By

Elizabeth Fries Ellet, 1857

Put four pounds of flour upon a dress er, one pound of which put on one side, make a hole in the middle, into which pour nearly three parts of a pint of warm water, in which you have dissolved yeast; mix it into a stiff but delicate paste, which roll up into a ball: cut an incision across it, and lay it in a basin well floured, in a warm place, until becoming very light; then make a large hole in the centre of the three pounds of flour, into which put half an ounce of salt, two pounds of fresh butter, half a gill of water, and sixteen eggs; mix it into a softish flexible paste, which press out flat, lay the leaven upon it, folding it over and working with the hands until well amalgamated; flour a clean cloth, fold the paste in it and let it remain all night. In the morning mould them into small rolls; put them upon a baking-sheet, and bake in a moderate oven. Unless your breakfast party be very large, half the above quantity will be sufficient. These rolls being a luxury, I make them only upon very especial occasions.

Common Bread
From "The Great Western Cook Book, or Table Receipts, Adapted to Western Housewifery", By Anna Maria Collins, 1857

Take two quarts of flour, rub into it two table-spoonsful of lard, a little salt; add two tablespoonsful of brewer's yeast, and work it up with warm milk. Knead it till it is very smooth, set it to rise six hours, work it over and make it into rolls. Bake in a quick oven.

Corn Muffins
From "The Great Western Cook Book, or Table Receipts, Adapted to Western Housewifery", By Anna Maria Collins, 1857

Take a quart of corn meal, an ounce of butter, rub them together. Beat it up with a quart of milk, two table-spoonsful of yeast, one of molasses, and a little salt. Let it rise four or five hours, and bake in muffin rings.

Crackers
From "The Great Western Cook Book, or Table Receipts, Adapted to Western Housewifery", By Anna Maria Collins, 1857

Rub two ounces of butter into a quart of flour. Put in a tea-spoonful of saleratus, and half a tea-spoonful of salt. Make it up with milk enough to have a stiff dough. Beat it for half an hour, or till it is quite smooth; roll it out thin, and cut it into small cakes; stick them with a fork, and bake them in a moderate oven.

Crumpets
From "The Practical Housekeeper; A Cyclopedia of Domestic Economy", By Elizabeth Fries Ellet, 1857

Beat two eggs very well, put to them a quart of warm milk and water, and a large spoonful of yeast; beat in as much fine flour as will make them rather thicker than a common batter pudding; then make the stove hot, and rub it with a little butter wrapped in a clean linen cloth; pour a large spoonful of the batter upon the iron, and let it run within a ring to the size of a teasaucer; turn them with the elastic blade of an old table-knife, and when you want to use them, toast them very quickly, but not too crisply, and butter them.

Damascus Biscuits
From "The Practical Housekeeper; A Cyclopedia of Domestic Economy", By Elizabeth Fries Ellet, 1857

Take the whites of three eggs beaten to a froth, a quarter of a pound of good beef suet chopped very fine, and half an ounce of bitter almonds blanched, chopped fine, and beaten well with the froth of the eggs. Then take the yolks of the eggs, and mix with six ounces of sifted loaf sugar, beat well, pour into the mixture of almonds and whites of egg; mix well, and shake in two ounces of flour, with sufficient lemon to flavor them. Pour into small tins, or moulded papers, and bake in a *quick* oven.

French Rolls
From "The Great Western Cook Book, or Table Receipts, Adapted to Western Housewifery", By Anna Maria Collins, 1857

Put a pint of milk into three quarts of water. In winter it should be pretty hot, but only milk-warm in summer. Lay a pint and a half of good brewer's yeast into a gallon of water, the night before. Pour the yeast off into the milk and water, and then break in rather more than a quarter of a pound of butter. Work it well, and then beat up two eggs and stir them in. Mix a peck and a half of flour with the liquor, making the dough stiffer in winter than in summer; mix it well, and the less it is worked, the better. Stir the liquor into the flour, and, after the dough is made, cover it with a cloth, and let it stand to rise while the oven is heating. When the loaves have lain in a quick oven about a quarter of an hour, turn them over and let them lay another quarter of an hour.

Ginger Crackers
From "The Lady's Receipt-Book; a Useful Companion for Large or Small Families", By Eliza Leslie, 1847

Mix together in a deep pan, a pint of West India molasses; half a pound of butter; and a quarter of a pound of brown sugar; two large table-spoonfuls of ginger; a tea-spoonful of powdered cinnamon; a small tea-spoonful of pearlash or soda, dissolved in a little warm water; and sufficient sifted flour to make a dough just stiff enough to roll out conveniently. Let the whole be well incorporated into a large lump. Knead it till it leaves your hands clean; then beat it hard with a rolling-pin, which will make it crisp when baked. Divide the dough, and roll it out into sheets half an inch thick. Cut it into cakes with a tin cutter about the usual size of a cracker-biscuit, or with the edge of a teacup dipped, frequently into flour to prevent its sticking. Lay the cakes at regular distances in square pans slightly outtered. Set them directly into a moderately brisk oven, and bake them well, first pricking them with a fork.
Ginger crackers are excellent on a sea voyage. If made exactly as above they will keep many weeks.
In greasing all cake-pans use only the best fresh butter: otherwise the outside of a thick cake will taste disagreeably, and the whole of a thin cake will have an unpleasant flavour.

Hard Biscuits
From "A New System of Domestic Cookery", By Maria Eliza Ketelby Rundell, 1807

Warm two ounces of butter in as much skimmed milk as will make a pound of flour into a very stiff paste, beat it with a rolling-pin, and work it very smooth. Roll it thin, and cut it into round biscuits; prick them full of holes with a fork. About six minutes will bake them.

Johnny Cake
From "The Great Western Cook Book, or Table Receipts, Adapted to Western Housewifery", By Anna Maria Collins, 1857

To a quart of sweet corn-meal, add a pint of warm water and a tea-spoonful of salt; beat it up very hard; spread it evenly and smoothly on the board. Place the board before a clear, moderate fire; when done, cut it in squares, and send it to table without buttering it.

Johnny Cakes
From "The Practical Housekeeper; A Cyclopedia of Domestic Economy", By Elizabeth Fries Ellet, 1857

Sift a quart of corn meal into a pan, make a hole in the middle, and pour in a pint of warm water. Mix the meal and water gradually into a batter, adding a teaspoonful of salt; beat it very quickly, and for a long time, till it becomes quite light; then spread it thick and even on a stout piece of smooth board; place it upright on the hearth before a clear fire, with something to support the board behind, and bake it well; cut it into squares, and split and butter them hot. Cakes may also be made with a quart of milk, three eggs, one teaspoonful of carbonate of soda, and one teacupful of wheat-flour; add Indian meal sufficient to make a batter like that of pancakes, and either bake it in buttered pans, or upon a griddle, and eat them with butter.

Journey or Jonny Cakes
From "Confederate Receipt Book. A Compilation of Over One Hundred Receipts, Adapted To The Times", By West & Johnston, 1863

To three spoonfuls of soft boiled rice add a small tea cup of water or milk, then add six spoonfuls of the rice flour, which will make a large Jonny cake or six waffles.

Johnny Cakes

From "A Poetical Cookbook", By Maria J. Moss, 1864

A quart of sifted Indian meal, and a handful of wheat flour sifted; mix them; three eggs, well beaten; two tablespoonfuls of fresh brewer's yeast, or flour of home made yeast, a teaspoonful of salt, and a quart of milk. *Author's Note: "The Poetical Cookbook" makes no mention of how to proceed after mixing all of the ingredients.*

Rice Journey or Johnny Cake
From "The Virginia Housewife", By Mary Randolph, 1860

Boil a pint of rice quite soft, with a tea-spoonful of salt; mix with it while hot a large spoonful of butter, and spread it on a dish to cool; when perfectly cold, add a pint of rice flour and half a pint of milk--beat them all together till well mingled. Take the middle part of the head of a barrel, make it quite clean, wet it, and put on the mixture about an inch thick, smooth with a spoon, and baste it with a little milk; set the board aslant before clear coals; when sufficiently baked, slip a thread under the cake and turn it: baste and bake that side in a similar manner, split it, and butter while hot. Small homony boiled and mixed with rice flour, is better than all rice; and if baked very thin, and afterwards toasted and buttered, it is nearly as good as cassada bread.

Kentucky Corn Dodgers
From "Miss Beecher's Domestic Receipt Book", By
Catharine Esther Beecher, 1850

Three pints of *unsifted yellow* corn meal. One tablespoonful (heaped) of lard.
One pint of milk.
Work it well, and bake in cakes the size of the hand, and an inch thick.

Light Buns
From "The Book of Household Management", By Isabella Beeton, 1861

1/2 teaspoonful of tartaric acid, 1/2 teaspoonful of bicarbonate of soda, 1 lb. of flour, 2 oz. of butter, 2 oz. of loaf sugar, 1/4 lb. of currants or raisins,—when liked, a few caraway seeds, 1/2 pint of cold new milk, 1 egg.
Rub the tartaric acid, soda, and flour all together through a hair sieve; work the butter into the flour; add the sugar, currants, and caraway seeds, when the flavour

of them latter is liked. Mix all these ingredients well together; make a hole in the middle of the flour, and pour in the milk, mixed with the egg, which should be well beaten; mix quickly, and set the dough, with a fork, on baking-tins, and bake the buns for about 20 minutes. This mixture makes a very good cake, and if put into a tin, should be baked 1-1/2 hour. The same quantity of flour, soda, and tartaric acid, with 1/2 pint of milk and a little salt, will make either bread or teacakes, if wanted quickly.

Time-20 minutes for the buns; if made into a cake, 1-1/2 hour.

Milk Biscuits
From "The Practical Housekeeper; A Cyclopedia of Domestic Economy", By Elizabeth Fries Ellet, 1857

A quarter of a pound of butter, one-quart of milk, one gill of yeast, as much flour as will form the dough, and a little salt. Stir flour into the milk, so as to form a very thick batter, and add the yeast; this is called a sponge. This should be done in the evening; in the morning cut up the butter, and set it near the fire, where it will dissolve, but not get hot; pour the melted butter into the sponge, then stir in enough flour to form a dough, knead it well and stand it away to rise. As soon as it is perfectly light, butter your tins, make out the dough in small cakes, and let them rise. When they are light, hake them in a very quick oven, and send them to the table hot.

Molasses Gingerbread
From "The Lady's Receipt-Book; a Useful Companion for Large or Small Families", By Eliza Leslie, 1847

Mix together a quart of West India molasses, and a pint of milk. Cut up in them a pound of fresh butter. Set the pan on a stove, or in a warm place till the butter becomes soft enough to stir and mix well into the molasses and milk. They must be merely warmed but not made hot. Then stir in a small teacup of ginger, and a table-spoonful of powdered cinnamon. Add, gradually, a little at a time, three pounds of sifted flour. The whole should be a thick batter. Lastly, stir in a large tea-spoonful of soda, or a smaller one of pearlash or sal-eratus, dissolved in a very little lukewarm water. Bake the mixture either in little tins, or in a large loaf. If the latter, it will require very long baking; as long as a black-cake.

Muffins
From "The Practical Housekeeper; A Cyclopedia of Domestic Economy", By Elizabeth Fries Ellet, 1857

Take two eggs, two spoonfuls of new yeast, and a little salt. Mix a little warm new milk and water into a quart of flour. Beat all well together, and let it stand to rise. Bake them for about twenty minutes, until of a light brown, either on a hot iron, or in shallow tin rings in a Dutch oven. When to be brought to table, toast them slightly on both sides, but not in the middle: then notch them round the centre, and pull them open with your fingers, without using a knife, and butter them.

Plain and Very Crisp Biscuits
From "A New System of Domestic Cookery", By Maria Eliza Ketelby Rundell, 1807

Make a pound of flour, the yolk of an egg, and some milk, into a very stiff paste; beat it well, and knead till quite smooth; roll very thin, and cut into biscuits. Bake them in a slow oven till quite dry and crisp.

Plain Buns
From "The Book of Household Management", By Isabella Beeton, 1861

To every 2 lbs. of flour allow 6 oz. of moist sugar, 1/2 gill of yeast, 1/2 pint of milk, 1/2 lb. of butter, warm milk.

Put the flour into a basin, mix the sugar well with it, make a hole in the centre, and stir in the yeast and milk (which should be lukewarm), with enough of the flour to make it the thickness of cream. Cover the basin over with a cloth, and let the sponge rise in a warm place, which will be accomplished in about 1-1/2 hour. Melt the butter, but do not allow it to oil; stir it into the other ingredients, with enough warm milk to make the whole into a soft dough; then mould it into buns about the size of an egg; lay them in rows quite 3 inches apart; set them again in a warm place, until they have risen to double their size; then put them into a good brisk oven, and just before they are done, wash them over with a little milk. From 15 to 20 minutes will be required to bake them nicely. These buns may be varied by adding a few currants, candied peel, or caraway seeds to the other ingredients; and the above mixture answers for hot cross buns, by putting in a little ground allspice; and by pressing a tin mould in the form of a cross in the centre of the bun.
Time-15 to 20 minutes.

Rocks
From "The Practical Housekeeper; A Cyclopedia of Domestic Economy", By Elizabeth Fries Ellet, 1857

Take a loaf that is half baked, pull it apart, and with two forks tear the crumb into bits about the size of a walnut; lay them on a tin, and return them to the oven, and bake of a light brown. A loaf made for the purpose with milk and a little butter makes them nicer. A sweet cake pulled in this way is very good.

Rolls
From "The Practical Housekeeper; A Cyclopedia of Domestic Economy", By Elizabeth Fries Ellet, 1857

French Rolls are usually made by the bakers, but in country houses, where families bake their own bread, they may be done as follows:--
Sift one pound of flour, and rub into it two ounces of butter; mix in the whites only of three eggs beaten to a froth, and a table-spoonful of strong yeast; to which add enough of milk, with a little salt, to make a stiff dough, and set it covered before the fire to rise--which will take about an hour; and, if cut into small rolls, and put into a quick oven, will be done in little more than ten minutes.

Rusks
From "Directions for Cookery, in its Various Branches" By Eliza Leslie, 1840

Sift three pounds of flour into a large pan, and rub into it half a pound of butter, and half a pound of sugar. Beat two eggs very light, and stir them into a pint and a half of milk, adding two table-spoonfuls of rose water, and three table-spoonfuls of the best and strongest yeast. Make a hole in the middle of the flour, pour in the liquid, and gradually mix the flour into it till you have a thick batter. Cover it, and set it by the fire to rise. When it is quite light, put it on your paste-board and knead it well. Then divide it into small round cakes and knead each separately. Lay them very near each other in shallow iron pans that have been sprinkled with flour. Prick the top of each rusk with a fork, and set them by the fire to rise again for half an hour or more. When they are perfectly light, bake them in a moderate oven. They are best when fresh.
You can convert them into what are called Hard Rusks, or Tops and Bottoms, by splitting them in half, and putting them again into the oven to harden and crisp.

Rye and Indian Bread
From "Directions for Cookery, in its Various Branches" By Eliza Leslie, 1840

Sift two quarts of rye, and two quarts of Indian meal, and mix them well together. Boil three pints of milk; pour it boiling hot upon the meal; add two tea-spoonfuls of salt, and stir the whole very hard. Let it stand till it becomes of only a lukewarm heat, and then stir in half a pint of good fresh yeast; if from the brewery and quite fresh, a smaller quantity will suffice. Knead the mixture into a stiff dough, and set it to rise in a pan. Cover it with a thick cloth that has been previously warmed, and set it near the fire. When it is quite light, and has cracked all over the top, make it into two loaves, put them into a moderate oven, and bake them two hours and a half.

Soda Biscuits
From "The Book of Household Management", By Isabella Beeton, 1861

1 lb. of flour, 1/2 lb. of pounded loaf sugar, 1/4 lb. of fresh butter, 2 eggs, 1 small teaspoonful of carbonate of soda.
Put the flour (which should be perfectly dry) into a basin; rub in the butter, add the sugar, and mix these ingredients well together. Whisk the eggs, stir them into the mixture, and beat it well, until everything is well incorporated. Quickly stir in the soda, roll the paste out until it is about 1/2 inch thick, cut it into small round cakes with a tin cutter, and bake them from 12 to 18 minutes in rather a brisk oven. After the soda is added, great expedition is necessary in rolling and cutting out the paste, and in putting the biscuits *immediately* into the oven, or they will be heavy.
Time-12 to 18 minutes.

Soda Bread
From "The Book of Household Management", By Isabella Beeton, 1861

To every 2 lbs. of flour allow 1 teaspoonful of tartaric acid, 1 teaspoonful of salt, 1 teaspoonful of carbonate of soda, 2 breakfast-cupfuls of cold milk.
Let the tartaric acid and salt be reduced to the finest possible powder; then mix them well with the flour. Dissolve the soda in the milk, and pour it several times from one basin to another, before adding it to the flour. Work the whole quickly into a light dough, divide it into 2 loaves, and put them into a well-heated oven immediately, and bake for an hour. Sour milk or buttermilk may be used, but then a little less acid will be needed.
Time-1 hour.

Spiced Gingerbread

From "The Lady's Receipt-Book; a Useful Companion for Large or Small Families", By Eliza Leslie, 1847

Sift into a deep pan a pound and a half of flour, and cut up in it half a pound of the best fresh butter. Rub them together, with your hands, till thoroughly incorporated. Then add half a pound of brown sugar, crushed fine with the rolling-pin; a table-spoonful of mixed spice, consisting of equal quantities of powdered cloves, mace, and cinnamon. Also, a table-spoonful of ground ginger, and two table-spoonfuls of carraway seeds. Mix the whole together, and wet it with a pint of West India molasses. Dissolve a small tea-spoonful of pearlash or soda in a very little warm water. Mix it into the other ingredients. Spread some flour on your paste-board, take the dough out of the pan, flour your hands, and knead the dough till it ceases entirely to be sticky. Roll it out into a very thick square sheet; cut it into long straight slips; twist every two slips together, rounding off the ends nicely. Lay them (not too closely) in buttered square pans, and bake them well. As gingerbread burns easily, take care not to have the oven too hot. Instead of forming it into twisted strips, you may cut the sheet of gingerbread-dough into round cakes with the edge of a tumbler, which, as you proceed, must be frequently dipped in flour.

Sour Milk Biscuit
From "Miss Beecher's Domestic Receipt Book", By Catharine Esther Beecher, 1850

A pint and a half of sour milk, or buttermilk, Two teaspoonfuls of salt. Two teaspoonfuls of saleratus, dissolved in four great spoonfuls of hot water.
Mix the milk in flour till nearly stiff enough to roll, then put in the saleratus, and add more flour. Mould up quickly, and bake immediately.
Shortening for raised biscuit or cake should always be worked in after it is wet up.

Tea Biscuit
From "Directions for Cookery, in its Various Branches" By Eliza Leslie, 1840

Melt a quarter of a pound of fresh butter in a quart of warm milk, and add a salt-spoonful of salt. Sift two pounds of flour into a pan, make a hole in the centre, and put in three table-spoonfuls of the best brewer's yeast. Add the milk and butter and mix it into a stiff paste. Cover it and set it by the fire to rise. When quite light, knead it well, roll it out an inch thick, and cut it into round cakes with the edge of a tumbler. Prick the top of each with a fork; lay them in buttered pans and bake them light brown. Send them to table warm, and split and butter them.

Wheat Muffins
From "The Great Western Cook Book, or Table Receipts, Adapted to Western Housewifery", By Anna Maria Collins, 1857

Beat up two eggs with a pint of sweet milk; add a table-spoonful of yeast and some salt. Beat in flour enough to make a thick batter, and let it rise five or six hours. Then bake in rings.

To Make Yeast
From "A New System of Domestic Cookery", By Maria Eliza Ketelby Rundell, 1807

Thicken two quarts of water with fine flour, about three spoonfuls; boil half an hour, sweeten with near half a pound, of brown sugar; when near cold, put into it four spoonfuls of fresh yeast in a jug, shake it well together, and let it stand one day to ferment near the fire, without being covered. There will be a thin liquor on the top, which must be poured off; shake the remainder, and cork it up for use. Take always four spoonfuls of the old to ferment the next quantity, keeping it always in succession.
A half-peck loaf will require about a gill.

Another way-Boil one pound of potatoes to a mash; when half cold, add a cupful of yeast, and mix it well. It will be ready for use in two or three hours, and keeps well.

Use double the quantity of this to what you do of beer-yeast.
To take off the bitter of yeast, put bran into a sieve, and pour it through, having first mixed a little warm water with it.

9. Drinks

Non-Alcoholic

Apple Water
From "A New System of Domestic Cookery", By Maria Eliza Ketelby Rundell, 1807

Cut two large apples in slices, and pour a quart of boiling water on them; or on roasted apples; strain in two or three hours, and sweeten lightly.

Boy's Coffee
From "Miss Beecher's Domestic Receipt Book", By Catharine Esther Beecher, 1850

Crumb bread, or dry toast, into a bowl. Put on a plenty of sugar, or molasses. Put in one half milk and one half boiling water. To be eaten with a spoon, or drank if preferred. Molasses for sweetening is preferred by most children.

Carbonated Syrup Water
From "The Lady's Receipt-Book; a Useful Companion for Large or Small Families", By Eliza Leslie, 1847

Put into a tumbler lemon, raspberry, strawberry, pine-apple, or any other *acid* syrup, sufficient in quantity to flavour the beverage very highly. Then pour in *very cold ice-water* till the glass is half full. Add *half* a tea-spoonful of bi-carbonate of soda, (to be obtained at the druggists',) and stir it well in with a tea-spoon. It will foam up to the top immediately, and must be drank during the effervescence. By keeping the syrup, and the carbonate of soda in the house, and mixing them as above with ice-water, you can at any time have a glass of this very pleasant drink; precisely similar to that which you get at the shops. The cost will be infinitely less.

To Make Chocolate
From "The Book of Household Management", By Isabella Beeton, 1861

Allow 1/2 oz. of chocolate to each person; to every oz. allow 1/2 pint of water, 1/2 pint of milk.
Make the milk-and-water hot; scrape the chocolate into it, and stir the mixture constantly and quickly until the chocolate is dissolved; bring it to the boiling-point, stir it well, and serve directly with white sugar. Chocolate prepared with in a mill, as shown in the engraving, is made by putting in the scraped chocolate, pouring over it the boiling milk-and-water, and milling it over the fire until hot and frothy. Allow 1/2 oz. of cake chocolate to each person.

Chocolate Cream
From "A New System of Domestic Cookery", By Maria Eliza Ketelby Rundell, 1807

Scrape into one quart of thick cream, one ounce of the best chocolate, and a quarter of a pound of sugar; boil and mill it; when quite smooth, take it off, and leave it to be cold; then add the whites of nine eggs. Whisk; and take up the froth on sieves, as others are done; and serve the froth in glasses, to rise above some of the cream.

Ciders-Artificial, OR Cider Without Apples
From "Dr. Chase's Recipes; or, Information for Everybody", By Dr. Alvin Wood Chase, 1864

To cold water 1 gal., put dark brown sugar 1 lb.; tartaric acid 1/2 oz.; yeast 3 tablespoons, and keep these proportions for any amount desired to make; shake it well together. Make it in the evening and it will be fit for use the next day.
I make in a keg a few gallons at a time, leaving a few quarts to make into next time--not using yeast again until the keg needs rinsing. If it gets a little sour make more into it. In hot weather draw in a pitcher with ice; or if your sales are slow, bottle it and keep in a cool cellar according to the next recipe.

<u>TO BOTTLE.</u>--If it is desired to bottle this artificial cider by manufacturers of small drinks, you will proceed as follows:
Put into a barrel, hot water 5 gals.; brown sugar 30 lbs.; tartaric acid 3/4 lb.; cold water 25 gals.; hop or brewers' yeast 3 pts.; work the yeast into a paste with flour 3/4 lb.; shake or stir all well together; fill the barrel full, and let it work 24 to 48

hours, or until the yeast is done working out at the bung, by having put in a little sweetened water occasionally to keep the barrel full.

When it has worked clear, bottle it, putting in two or three broken raisins to each bottle, and it will nearly equal champagne. Let the bottles lay in a cool place on the side--(observe also this plan of laying the bottles upon the side, in putting away apple-cider or wine)--but if it is only for your own retail trade you can make as follows in the next recipe, and have it keep until a barrel is retailed. The first recipe will last only three or or four days in hot weather, and about two weeks in winter.

Cocoa
From "The Lady's Receipt-Book; a Useful Companion for Large or Small Families", By Eliza Leslie, 1847

The cocoa which is put up solid in close packages, and usually sold at a shilling a paper, is far superior to the chocolate that is manufactured into squares or cakes, and which is too frequently adulterated with lard and meal. Baker's prepared cocoa is excellent. When you intend having it for drinking, shave down, or cut fine a sufficient quantity of the cocoa; allowing about half the contents of a paper to a quart of water, if you wish it very strong, and three pints of water for moderate strength. Then put the cocoa into a clean sauce-pan or a tin pot with a spout. Measure the water from a kettle that is boiling hard at the time; and when you have the proper quantity pour it scalding hot on the cocoa. Cover it closely; place it over the fire; and let it boil till it is all dissolved into the same consistence, and quite smooth, and free from the smallest lumps. While boiling, you must several times take off the lid, and with a spoon stir the cocoa down to the bottom. Then transfer it to your chocolate pot, which must be twice scalded with boiling water. Send it to table as hot as possible, adding milk and sugar to the cups when poured out. Eat with it dry toast; *unbuttered* rolls; milk-biscuit; or sponge-cake.

Cream Nectar, Imperial
From "Dr. Chase's Recipes; or, Information for Everybody", By Dr. Alvin Wood Chase, 1864

First, take water 1 gal.; loaf sugar 8 lbs., tartaric acid 8 oz.; gum arabic 1 oz.; put into a suitable kettle and place on the fire.

Second, take flour 4 tea-spoons; the whites of 4 eggs, well beaten together, with the flour, and add water 1/2 pt.; when the first is blood warm put in the second, and boil 3 minutes, and it is done.

DIRECTIONS: Three table-spoons of the syrup to a glass half or two-thirds full of water, and add one-third tea-spoon of super-carbonate of soda, made fine; stir well, and drink at your leisure.

In getting up any of the soda drinks which are spoken of, it will be found preferable to put about eight ounces of super-carbonate, often called carbonate of soda, into one pint of water in a bottle, and shake when you wish to make a glass of soda, and pour of this into the glass until it foams well, instead of using the dry soda as directed.

Cream Soda Without A Fountain
From "Dr. Chase's Recipes; or, Information for Everybody", By Dr. Alvin Wood Chase, 1864

Coffee sugar 4 lbs; water 3 pts.; nutmegs grated 3 in number; whites of 10 eggs well beaten; gum arabic 1 oz.; oil of lemon 20 drops; or extract equal to that amount. By using oils of other fruits you can make as many flavors from this as you desire, or prefer.

Mix all and place over a gentle fire, and stir well about thirty minutes; remove from the fire, strain, and divide into two parts; into one-half put supercarbonate of soda eight ounces; and into the other half put six ounces tartaric acid; shake well, and when cold they are ready to use, by pouring three or four spoons, from both parts, into separate glasses which are one-third full of cool water; stir each and pour together, and you have as nice a glass of cream soda as was ever drank, which can also be drank at your leisure, as the gum and eggs hold the gas.

Currant Ice Water
From "Miss Beecher's Domestic Receipt Book", By Catharine Esther Beecher, 1850

Press the juice from ripe currants, strain it, and put a pound of sugar to each pint of juice. Put it into bottles, cork and seal it, and keep it in a cool, dry place. When wanted, mix it with ice water for a drink.

Or put water with it, make it *very* sweet, and freeze it. Freezing always takes away much of the sweetness.

The juices of other acid fruits can be used in the same way.

Ginger Pop
From "A Plain Cookery Book for the Working Classes", By Charles Elme Francatelli, 1852

Put a very clean pot containing a gallon of water to boil on the fire, and as soon as it begins to boil, add twelve ounces of brown sugar, and one ounce of bruised ginger, and two ounces of cream of tartar; stir well together; pour the whole into an earthen pan, cover it over with a cloth, and let the mash remain in this state until it has become quite cold; then stir in half a gill of fresh yeast; stir all well together until thoroughly mixed, cover the pan over with a cloth, and leave the ginger-beer in a cool place to work up; this will take from six to eight
hours; the scum which has risen to the top must then be carefully removed with a spoon without disturbing the brightness of the beer; it is then to be carefully poured off bright into a jug with a spout, to enable you easily to pour it into the bottles. These must be immediately corked down tight, tied across the corks with string, and put away, lying down in the cellar. The ginger-pop will be fit to drink in about four days after it has been bottled.

Portable Lemonade
From "Miss Beecher's Domestic Receipt Book", By Catharine Esther Beecher, 1850

Mix strained lemon juice with loaf sugar, in the proportion of four large lemons to a pound, or as much as it will hold in solution; grate the rind of the lemons into this, and preserve this in a jar. If this is too sweet add a little citric acid. Use a tablespoonful to a tumbler of water.

Delicious Milk Lemonade
From "Miss Beecher's Domestic Receipt Book", By Catharine Esther Beecher, 1850

Pour a pint of boiling water on to six ounces of loaf sugar, add a quarter of a pint of lemon juice, and half the quantity of good sherry wine. Then add three quarters of a pint of cold milk, and strain the whole, to make it nice and clear.

Nectar
From "The Lady's Receipt-Book; a Useful Companion for Large or Small Families", By Eliza Leslie, 1847

Take a pound of the best raisins, seeded and chopped; four lemons, sliced thin, and the yellow rind pared off from two other lemons; and two pounds of powdered loaf-sugar. Put into a porcelain preserving-kettle two gallons of water. Set it over the fire, and boil it half an hour. Then, while the water is boiling hard, put in the raisins, lemons, and sugar; and continue the boiling for ten minutes. Pour the mixture into a vessel with a close cover, and let it stand four days; stirring it twice a-day. Then strain it through a linen bag, and bottle it. It will be fit for use in a fortnight. Drink it from wine-glasses, with a small bit of ice in each.

Pistachio Cream
From "The Lady's Receipt-Book; a Useful Companion for Large or Small Families", By Eliza Leslie, 1847

Take half a pound of pistachio nuts. Throw them into scalding water, and peel off the skins. Put the nuts (not more than two at a time) into a marble mortar, and pound them to a smooth paste, adding frequently, as you proceed, a few drops of rose-water. Sweeten a quart of cream with half a pound of powdered loaf-sugar, and stir into it, gradually, the pistachio paste. Set the mixture over the fire; and let it just come to a boil. Then take it out; stir in two table-spoonfuls of rose-water or peach-water, and set on ice to cool. Either serve it up liquid in a glass bowl, or put it into a freezer, and freeze it as ice-cream.

If you freeze it, you must substitute for the rose-water or peach-water, a table-spoonful of extract of roses, or the same quantity of extract of bitter almonds. The process of freezing diminishes the strength of every sort of flavouring; and of sweetening also.

If you serve it up as frozen, stick it all over with slips of pistachio nut, peeled and sliced.

Simple Syrup
From "Dr. Chase's Recipes; or, Information for Everybody", By Dr. Alvin Wood Chase, 1864

To make it, take 2 1/2 lbs. of the best coffee sugar, which is found not to crystalize, and water 1 pt., or what is the same, 60 lbs. sugar, water 3 gals.

Dissolve the sugar in the water by heat, removing any scum that forms upon it, and strain while hot. This can be kept in a barrel or keg, and is always ready to flavor, as desired.

Sarsaparilla
From "Dr. Chase's Recipes; or, Information for Everybody", By Dr. Alvin Wood Chase, 1864

Simple syrup, as above (See "Simple Syrup" recipe), and nice golden syrup, equal quantities of each, and mix well; then use a few drops of oils of wintergreen and sassafras to each bottle, as used.

The amounts for the desired flavors cannot be given exactly to suit every one, but all will wish different flavors; in some towns, using very high flavor, and in others sufficient to perceive it, merely. All will soon get a plan of their own, and like it better than that of others. This mixture of golden syrup makes the sarsaparilla a beautiful dark color without other coloring.

Spanish Gingerette
From "Dr. Chase's Recipes; or, Information for Everybody", By Dr. Alvin Wood Chase, 1864

To each gal. of water put 1 lb. of white sugar; 1/2 oz. best bruised ginger root; 1/4 oz. of cream of tartar, and 2 lemons sliced.

DIRECTIONS: In making 5 gals. boil the ginger and lemons 10 minutes in 2 gals. of the water; the sugar and cream of tartar to be dissolved in the cold water, and mix all, and add 1/2 pint of good yeast; let it ferment over night, strain and bottle in the morning.

This is a valuable recipe for a cooling and refreshing beverage; compounded of ingredients highly calculated to assist the stomach, and is recommended to persons suffering with Dyspepsia or Sick Headache. It is much used in European countries, and persons having once tested its virtues will constantly use it as a common drink. And for saloons, or groceries, no temperance beverage will set it aside.

For A Summer Draught
From "The Book of Household Management", By Isabella Beeton, 1861

The juice of 1 lemon, a tumbler-ful of cold water, pounded sugar to taste, 4 small teaspoonful of carbonate of soda.

Squeeze the juice from the lemon; strain, and add it to the water, with sufficient pounded sugar to sweeten the whole nicely. When well mixed, put in the soda, stir well, and drink while the mixture is in an effervescing state.

Coffees and Teas

"We only get a small piece of bread and a [ ] of coffee." – Pvt. John Calvin McAulay, Co. K, 56th North Carolina Infantry, Peace Institute Hospital, Raleigh, North Carolina, August 24th 1862. Letter to his sister, Nancy.

"Spent seventy five dollars to-day for a little tea and sugar, and have five hundred left." -Mary Boykin Chesnut, December 5, 1863. "A Diary From Dixie".

Tea Parties
From "The Lady's Receipt-Book; a Useful Companion for Large or Small Families", By Eliza Leslie, 1847

Have black tea, green tea, and coffee. Immediately after the first cups are sent in, let fresh tea be put into the pots, that the second cups may not be weaker than the first. With the cream and sugar, send round a small pot of boiling water to weaken the tea of those who do not like it strong; or for the convenience of ladies who drink only milk and water, and who otherwise may cause interruption and delay by sending out for it. When tea is handed round, it is not well to have hot cakes with it; or any thing that is buttered, or any sort of greasy relishes. Such things are frequently injurious to the gloves and dresses of the ladies, and can well be dispensed with on these occasions. It is sufficient to send round a waiter with large cakes of the *best* sort, ready sliced but the slices not taken apart. There should be an almond sponge-cake for those who are unwilling to eat cakes made with butter.

Immediately on tea being over, let the servants go round to all the company with waiters having pitchers of cold water and glasses, to prevent the inconvenience of ladies sending out for glasses of water. In less than an hour after tea, lemonade should be brought in, accompanied by baskets of small mixed cakes, (maccaroons, kisses, &c.,) which it is no longer customary to send in with the tea. Afterwards, let the blanc-mange, jellies, sweetmeats, ice-creams, wines, liquors, &c., be handed round. Next, (after an hour's interval,) the terrapin, oysters, and chicken salad, &c. These are sometimes accompanied by ale, porter, or cider; sometimes by champagne. At the close of the evening, it is usual to send round a large plum-cake.

If the plan is to have a regular supper table, it is not necessary to send in any refreshments through the evening, except lemonade and little cakes.

When the company is not very numerous, and is to sit round a tea-table, waffles or other hot articles may there be introduced. Take care to set a tea-table that will certainly be large enough to accomodate all the guests without crowding them.

<u>Tea Parties and Evening Company</u>
From "Miss Beecher's Domestic Reciept Book", By Catherine Esther Beecher, 1850

In one respect, fashion has aided to relieve a housekeeper of much care in providing evening entertainments. It is now fashionable to spread a table for evening parties, and not to serve tea and coffee, as was formerly done. As this is the easiest, and most rational way of entertaining evening company, no other method will be so minutely described.

If a lady designs to invite from forty to sixty friends to pass the evening, or even to have a much larger company invited, the following would be called a plain but genteel arrangement, for company in New York, Philadelphia, or any of our large cities.

Set a long table in the dining-room, and cover it with a handsome damask cloth. Set some high article containing flowers, or some ornamental article, in the centre. Set Champagne glasses with flowers at each corner. Set loaves of cake at regular distances, and dispose in some regular order about the table, preserves, jellies, lemonade, and any other articles that may be selected from the abundant variety offered in the collection of Receipts for Evening Parties in this book.

Where a very large company is to be collected, and a larger treat is thought to be required, then a long table is set in the centre of the room, as above, and on it are placed cakes, pastry, jellies, and confectionary. Then smaller tables are set each side of a mantle, or in corners, one of which is furnished with sandwiches, oysters, salad, celery, and wine, and the other with coffee, chocolate, and lemonade. Sometimes all are placed on one long table, and in this case, cakes, jellies, and confectionary are put in the centre, coffee and lemonade at one end, and oysters, sandwiches, celery, and wines at the other. A great deal of taste may be displayed in preparing and arranging such a table.

As it is often the case, that the old mode of serving tea and coffee will be resorted to, one modificaton is proposed, which decreases the labour and anxiety to the housekeeper, and increases the enjoyment of the company. It is this. Set a table in one of the parlors, and cover it with a damask cloth. Let the tea and coffee be served at this table, the lady of the house presiding. Then let the gentlemen wait upon the ladies around the room, and then help themselves. This is particularly convenient when it is difficult to get good waiters.

Most of the articles used for evening parties (with the exception of rich cakes, wine, and high-seasoned chicken salad) are not unhealthful, if taken moderately.

When these parties break up at seasonable hours, they may prove one of the most rational and harmless modes of securing social enjoyment; but when connected with highly exciting amusements, and late hours, they are sure to wear upon the constitution and health, and rational and conscientious persons, for these and other reasons, will avoid them.

To Make Tea
From "The Book of Household Management", By Isabella Beeton, 1861

There is very little art in making good tea; if the water is boiling, and there is no sparing of the fragrant leaf, the beverage will almost invariably be good. The old-fashioned plan of allowing a teaspoonful to each person, and one over, is still practised. Warm the teapot with boiling water; let it remain for two or three minutes for the vessel to become thoroughly hot, then pour it away. Put in the tea, pour in from 1/2 to 3/4 pint of boiling water, close the lid, and let it stand for the tea to draw from 5 to 10 minutes; then fill up the pot with water. The tea will be quite spoiled unless made with water that is actually 'boiling', as the leaves will not open, and the flavour not be extracted from them; the beverage will consequently be colourless and tasteless,—in fact, nothing but tepid water. Where there is a very large party to make tea for, it is a good plan to have two teapots instead of putting a large quantity of tea into one pot; the tea, besides, will go farther. When the infusion has been once completed, the addition of fresh tea adds very little to the strength; so, when more is required, have the pot emptied of the old leaves, scalded, and fresh tea made in the usual manner. Economists say that a few grains of carbonate of soda, added before the boiling water is poured on the tea, assist to draw out the goodness: if the water is very hard, perhaps it is a good plan, as the soda softens it; but care must be taken to use this ingredient sparingly, as it is liable to give the tea a soapy taste if added in too large a quantity. For mixed tea, the usual proportion is four spoonfuls of black to one of green; more of the latter when the flavour is very much liked; but strong green tea is highly pernicious, and should never be partaken of too freely.

Apple Tea
From "Miss Beecher's Domestic Receipt Book", By Catharine Esther Beecher, 1850

Take good pippins, slice them thin, pour on boiling water, and let it stand some time. Pour off the water, and sweeten and flavor it.

Cranberry Tea
From "Miss Beecher's Domestic Receipt Book", By Catharine Esther Beecher, 1850

Wash ripe cranberries, mash them, pour boiling water on them, and then strain off the water and sweeten it, and grate on nutmeg.

Coffee
From "The Practical Housekeeper; A Cyclopedia of Domestic Economy", by Elizabeth Fries Ellet, 1857

Take fresh roasted coffee, allow two table-spoonfuls for each person, grind it just before making, put it in a basin and break into it an egg, yolk, white, shell, and all. Mix it up with the spoon to the consistencey of mortar, put warm, not boiling water, in the coffee pot; let it boil up and break three times; then stand a few minutes and it will be as clear as amber, and the egg will give it a rich taste.

Coffee
From "The Practical Housekeeper; A Cyclopedia of Domestic Economy", By Elizabeth Fries Ellet, 1857

There are several ways of making coffee; and every housewife generally has her favorite mode. The French make excellent coffee without the aid of eggs, isinglass, or any foreign article to settle it. It consists of a sort of tin coffee-pot, with two strainers. You remove the first strainer, and pour some boiling water into the coffee-pot through the second strainer. Empty out the water, and put in a sufficient quantity of coffee for the family over the under strainer and press it flat with a little tin machine (which comes with the apparatus). Put in the other strainer, and pour in the hot water. The coffee will drain through in a few moments.

Another mode of making Coffee-Take fresh roasted coffee, allow two table-spoonfuls for each person, grind it just before making, put it in a basin and break into it an egg, yolk, white, shell, and all. Mix it up with the spoon to the consist ence of mortar, put warm, not boiling water, in the coffee pot; let it boil up and break three times; then stand a few minutes and it will be as clear as amber, and the egg will give it a rich taste.

Codfish skin, scraped, washed, and dried, and cut in pieces, an inch square, may be used to settle off, or isinglass. You may add to a pint of coffee a pint of boiling milk, and heat both together before serving.

Coffee, To Roast
From "The Practical Housekeeper; A Cyclopedia of Domestic Economy", By Elizabeth Fries Ellet, 1857

Coffee should never be roasted but when you are going to use it, and then it should be watched with the greatest care, and made of a gold color; mind and do not burn it, for a few grains burnt would communicate a bitter taste to the whole; it is the best way to roast it in a roaster over a charcoal fire, which turns with the hand, as by that means it will not be forgotten.

An Excellent Way of Making Coffee
From "The Lady's Receipt-Book; a Useful Companion for Large or Small Families", By Eliza Leslie, 1847

For this purpose you should have a percolator, or coffee-pot with strainers inside. The coffee will be much stronger and better, if roasted and ground just before it is put in the pot. There are no coffee-roasters so good as those of sheet-iron, made somewhat in the form of a large long candle-box; standing before the fire on feet; and turned round by a handle, so as to give all the coffee that is inside an equal chance of heat. When about half done, put among the coffee a piece of fresh butter. It should be roasted evenly throughout, of a fine brown colour, and not allowed to blacken or burn. Grind it while warm; and put into the percolator a sufficient quantity of coffee, placing it *between* the two strainers. Then (having stopped up the spout) pour into the upper strainer a due proportion of *cold* water; allowing a quart of water to half a pint or more of ground coffee. Cold water is now found to make a stronger infusion than hot water, as there is less evaporation, and none of the strength of the coffee is carried off in steam. As soon as the water is all in, put on the lid closely, and set away the pot. It is well to put the coffee to infuse over night, if wanted for breakfast; and in the morning, if required for evening. But, when necessary, it may be done in a much shorter time. A little before the coffee is to go to table, lift off the upper half of the percolator, (the part that contains the strainers,) transfer the lid to the lower part; set the pot over the fire, and give it one boil up-- not more. As soon as it has come to a boil it is ready for drinking; being already strained, and drawn. It will be found clear, strong, and in all respects superior to that prepared in any other manner. A short boil is sufficient to take off all taste of rawness. Long boiling weakens coffee, and frequently turns it sour.

The above method will, we are confident, be highly approved on trial. Also, it saves the expense of isinglass, white of egg, and other articles generally used in clearing coffee. Percolators for making coffee in this manner, can be obtained of all sizes at the large tin manufactory of Messrs. Williams & Co., 276 Market street, between Seventh and Eighth streets, Philadelphia.

A china or metal coffee-pot should always be scalded twice before coffee is transferred to it, from the vessel in which it has been made.

A Very Simple Method of Making Coffee
From "The Book of Household Management", By Isabella Beeton, 1861

Allow 1/2 oz., or 1 tablespoonful, of coffee to each person; to every oz. allow 1 pint of water.

Have a small iron ring made to fit the top of the coffee-pot inside, and to this ring sew a small muslin bag (the muslin for the purpose must not be too thin). Fit the bag into the pot, pour some boiling water in it, and, when the pot is well warmed, put the ground coffee into the bag; pour over as much boiling water as is required, close the lid, and, when all the water has filtered through, remove the bag, and send the coffee to table. Making it in this manner prevents the necessity of pouring the coffee from one vessel to another, which cools and spoils it. The water should be poured on the coffee gradually, so that the infusion may be stronger; and the bag must be well made, that none of the grounds may escape through the seams, and so make the coffee thick and muddy. Allow 1 tablespoonful, or 1/2 oz., to each person.

To Make Essence of Coffee
From "The Book of Household Management", By Isabella Beeton, 1861

To every 1/4 lb. of ground coffee allow 1 small teaspoonful of powdered chicory, 3 small teacupfuls, or 1 pint, of water.

Let the coffee be freshly ground, and, if possible, freshly roasted; put it into a percolater, or filter, with the chicory, and pour *slowly* over it the above proportion of boiling water. When it has all filtered through, warm the coffee sufficiently to bring it to the simmering-point, but do not allow it to boil; then filter it a second time, put it into a clean and dry bottle, cork it well, and it will remain good for several days. Two tablespoonfuls of this essence are quite sufficient for a breakfast-cupful of hot milk. This essence will be found particularly useful to those persons who have to rise extremely early; and having only the milk to make boiling, is very easily and quickly prepared. When the essence is bottled, pour another 3 tea-cupfuls of *boiling* water slowly on the grounds, which, when filtered through, will be a very weak coffee. The next time there is essence to be prepared, make this weak coffee boiling, and pour it on the ground coffee instead of plain water: by this means a better coffee will be obtained. Never throw away the grounds without having made use of them in this manner; and always cork the bottle well that contains this preparation, until the day that it is wanted for making the fresh essence.

To be filtered once, then brought to the boiling-point, and filtered again.

Milk Coffee
From "The Great Western Cook Book, or Table Receipts, Adapted to Western Housewifery", By Anna Maria Collins, 1857

Boil a table-spoonful of coffee in a pint of rich milk, a quarter of an hour; then put in a shaving or two of isinglass, and clear it; let it boil a few moments; then set it aside by the fire to settle. Sweeten to your taste, when used.

An Excellent Substitute for Milk or Cream In Tea or Coffee
From "The Book of Household Management", By Isabella Beeton, 1861

Allow 1 new-laid egg to every large breakfast-cupful of tea or coffee.

Beat up the whole of the egg in a basin, put it into a cup (or a portion of it, if the cup be small), and pour over it the tea or coffee very hot. These should be added very gradually, and stirred all the time, to prevent the egg from curdling. In point of nourishment, both these beverages are much improved by this addition.

Alcoholic Drinks

"It commenced to snow this morning at 6 o'clock, and continued until one in the afternoon. It is three inches deep. We got some whiskey into camp, which tasted very good and made us forget the cold." -Pvt. Louis Leon, Company C, First North Carolina Regiment, Wakefield, November 7, 1862, from his diary.

"You write me you are so lonesome without me. You may think how I feel. I think of you day and night. I did not get drunk for nothing that day when I wanted to leave."-Chief Musician August Rost, 17th Alabama Infantry, April 5, 1863. Letter to his wife.

How To Brew Your Own Beer

From "A Plain Cookery Book for the Working Classes", By Charles Elme Francatelli, 1852

The first preparatory step towards brewing is to gather your necessary plant together in proper working order, and thoroughly clean. Your plant or utensils must consist of the following articles, viz.:--A thirty-gallon copper, two cooling-tubs capable of holding each about thirty gallons; a mash-tub of sufficient size to contain fifty-four gallons, and another tub of smaller size, called an underback; a bucket or pail, a wooden hand-bowl, a large wooden funnel, a mash-stirrer, four scraped long stout sticks, a good-sized loose-wrought wicker basket for straining the beer, and another small bowl-shaped wicker basket, called a tapwaist, to fasten inside the mash-tub on to the inner end of the spigot and faucet, to keep back the grains when the wort is being run off out of the mash-tub. You will also require some beer barrels, a couple of brass or metal cocks, some vent-pegs, and some bungs. I do not pretend to assert that the whole of the foregoing articles are positively indispensable for brewing your own beer. I merely enumerate what is most proper to be used; leaving the manner and means of replacing such of these articles as may be out of your reach very much to your intelligence in contriving to use such as you possess, or can borrow from a neighbour, instead. Spring water, from its hardness, is unfit for brewing; fresh fallen rain water, caught in clean tubs, or water fetched from a brook or river, are best adapted for brewing; as, from the fact of their being free from all calcareous admixture, their consequent softness gives them the greater power to extract all the goodness and strength from the malt and hops.

In order to ensure having good wholesome beer, it is necessary to calculate your brewing at the rate of two bushels of malt and two pounds of hops to fifty-four gallons of water; these proportions, well managed, will produce three kilderkins of good beer. I recommend that you should use malt and hops of the best quality only; as their plentiful yield of beneficial substance fully compensates for their somewhat higher price. A thin shell, well filled up plump with the interior flour, and easily bitten asunder, is a sure test of good quality in malt; superior hops are known by their light greenish-yellow tinge of colour, and also by their bright, dry, yet somewhat gummy feel to the touch, without their having any tendency to clamminess. The day before brewing, let all your tackle be well scrubbed and rinsed clean, the copper wiped out, and all your tubs and barrels half filled with cold water, to soak for a few hours, so as to guard against any chance of leakage, and afterwards emptied, and set to dry in the open air, weather permitting; or otherwise, before the fire. Fasten the tapwaist inside the mash-tub to the inner end of the faucet and spigot, taking care to place the mash-tub in an elevated position, resting upon two benches or stools. Early in the dawn of morning, light the fire under your copper, filled with water over-night, and, as soon as it boils, with it fill

the mash-tub rather more than three-parts full; and as soon as the first heat of the water has subsided, and you find that you are able to bear your fingers drawn slowly through it without experiencing pain, you must then throw in the malt, stirring it about for ten minutes or so; then lay some sticks across the mash-tub, and cover it with sacks or blankets, and allow it to steep for three hours. At the end of the three hours, let off the wort from the mash-tub into the underback-tub, which has been previously placed under the spigot and faucet ready to receive it; pouring the first that runs out back into the mash, until the wort runs free from grains, etc.; now put the hops into the underback-tub and let the wort run out upon them. Your copper having been refilled, and boiled again while the mash is in progress, you must now pour sufficient boiling water into the grains left in the mash-tub to make up your quantity of fifty-four gallons; and when this second mashing shall have also stood some two hours, let it be drawn off, and afterwards mixed with the first batch of wort, and boil the whole at two separate boilings, with the hops equally divided; each lot to be allowed to boil for an hour and a-half after it has commenced boiling. The beer is now to be strained through the loose wicker basket into your cooling tubs and pans; the more you have of these the better the beer, from its cooling quickly. And when the beer has cooled to the degree of water which has stood in the house in summer-time for some hours, let it all be poured into your two or three largest tubs, keeping back a couple or three quarts in a pan, with which to mix a pint of good yeast and a table-spoonful of common salt; stir this mixture well together, keep it in rather a warm part of the house, and in the course of half an hour or so, it will work up to the top of the basin or pan. This worked beer must now be equally divided between the two or three tubs containing the bulk of the beer, and is to be well mixed in by ladling it about with a wooden hand-bowl for a couple of minutes. This done, cover over the beer with sacks or blankets stretched upon sticks across the tubs, and leave them in this state for forty-eight hours. The next thing to be seen to is to get your barrels placed in proper order and position for being
filled; and to this end attend strictly to the following directions, viz.:--First, skim off the scum, which is yeast, from the top or surface of the tubs, and next, draw off the beer through the spigot, and with the wooden funnel placed in the bung-hole, proceed to fill up the barrels not quite full; and, remember, that if a few hops are put into each before filling in the beer, it will keep all the better. Reserve some of the beer with which to fill up the barrels as they throw up the yeast while the beer is working; and when the yeast begins to fall, lay the bungs upon the bung-holes, and at the end of ten days or a fortnight, hammer the bungs in tight, and keep the vent-pegs tight also. In about two months' time after the beer has been brewed, it will be in a fit condition for drinking.

Anniseed Cordial
From "Directions for Cookery, in its Various Branches" By Eliza Leslie, 1840

Melt a pound of loaf-sugar in two quarts of water. Mix it with two quarts of white brandy, and add a table-spoonful of oil of anniseed. Let it stand a week; then filter it through, white blotting paper, and bottle it for use.Clove or Cinnamon Cordial may be made in the same manner, by mixing sugar, water and brandy, and adding oil of cinnamon or oil of cloves. You may colour any of these cordials red by stirring in a little powdered cochineal that has been dissolved in a small quantity of brandy.

Champagne-Cup
From "The Book of Household Management", By Isabella Beeton, 1861

1 quart bottle of champagne, 2 bottles of soda-water, 1 liqueur-glass of brandy or Curaçoa, 2 tablespoonfuls of powdered sugar, 1 lb. of pounded ice, a sprig of green borage.
Put all the ingredients into a silver cup; stir them together, and serve. Should the above proportion of sugar not be found sufficient to suit some tastes, increase the quantity. When borage is not easily obtainable, substitute for it a few slices of cucumber-rind.

Codlin Cream
From "A New System of Domestic Cookery", By Maria Eliza Ketelby Rundell, 1807

Pare and core twenty good codlins; beat them in a mortar, with a pint of cream; strain it into a dish; and put sugar, bread-crumbs, and a glass of wine, to it. Stir it well.

Corn Beer, Without Yeast
From "Dr. Chase's Recipes; or, Information for Everybody", By Dr. Alvin Wood Chase, 1864

Cold water 5 gals.; sound *[unclear]* nice corn 1 qt.; molasses 2 qts.; put all into a keg of this size; shake well, and in 2 or 3 days a fermentation will have been brought on as nicely as with yeast. Keep it bunged tight.

It may be flavored with oils of spruce or lemon, if desired, by pouring on to the oils one of two quarts of the water, boiling hot. The corn will last five or six makings. If it gets too sour add more molasses and water in the same proportions. It is cheap, healthy, and no bother with yeast.

Country Syllabub
From "Directions for Cookery, in its Various Branches" By Eliza Leslie, 1840

Mix half a pound of white sugar with a pint of fine sweet cider, or of white wine; and grate in a nutmeg. Prepare them in a large bowl, just before milking time. Then let it be taken to the cow, and have about three pints milked into it; stirring it occasionally with a spoon. Let it be eaten before the froth subsides. If you use cider, a little brandy will improve it.

Ginger Wine
From "The Virginia Housewife", By Mary Randolph, 1860

To three gallons of water, put three pounds of sugar, and four ounces of race ginger, washed in many waters to cleanse it; boil them together for one hour, and strain it through a sieve; when lukewarm, put it in a cask with three lemons cut in slices, and two gills of beer yeast; shake it well, and stop the cask very tight; let it stand a week to ferment; and if not clear enough to bottle, it must remain until it becomes so; it will be fit to drink in ten days after bottling.

Hippocras
From "The Lady's Receipt-Book; a Useful Companion for Large or Small Families", By Eliza Leslie, 1847

Put into a jar a quart of the best port wine. Beat, separately, in a mortar, a quarter of an ounce of cinnamon, two nutmegs, twelve blades of mace, and a tea-spoonful of coriander seeds. Then mix them all together; and put them into the wine. Add the yellow rind of four large lemons, pared thin, and their juice, mixed with half a pound of powdered loaf-sugar. Cover the vessel closely, and let it infuse a week, or more. Then strain the liquid through a linen bag, and bottle it.

Hydromel, Or Mead
From "The Virginia Housewife", By Mary Randolph, 1860

Mix your mead in the proportion of thirty-six ounces of honey to four quarts of warm water; when the honey is completely held in solution, pour it into a cask. When fermented, and become perfectly clear, bottle and cork it well. If properly prepared, it is a pleasant and wholesome drink; and in summer particularly grateful, on account of the large quantity of carbonic acid gas which it contains. Its goodness, however, depends greatly on the _time_ of bottling, and other circumstances, which can only be acquired by practice.

Lemon Brandy
From "Directions for Cookery, in its Various Branches" By Eliza Leslie, 1840

When you use lemons for punch or lemonade, do not throw away the peels, but cut them in small pieces, and put them into a glass jar or bottle of brandy. You will find this brandy useful for many purposes.In the same way keep for use the kernels of peach and plum stones, pounding them slightly before you put them into the brandy.

Orange Brandy
From "The Book of Household Management", By Isabella Beeton, 1861

To every 1 gallon of brandy allow 3/4 pint of Seville orange-juice, 1-1/4 lb. of loaf sugar.
To bring out the full flavour of the orange-peel, rub a few lumps of the sugar on 2 or 3 unpared oranges, and put these lumps to the rest. Mix the brandy with the orange-juice, strained, the rinds of 6 of the oranges pared very thin, and the sugar. Let all stand in a closely-covered jar for about 3 days, stirring it 3 or 4 times a day. When clear, it should be bottled and closely corked for a year; it will then be ready for use, but will keep any length of time. This is a most excellent stomachic when taken pure in small quantities; or, as the strength of the brandy is very little deteriorated by the other ingredients, it may be diluted with water.
To be stirred every day for 3 days.

Excellent Orange Cream
From "A New System of Domestic Cookery", By Maria Eliza Ketelby Rundell, 1807

Boil the rind of a Seville orange very tender; beat it fine in a mortar; put to it a spoonful of the best brandy, the juice of a Seville orange, four ounces of loaf sugar, and the yolks of four eggs; beat all together for ten minutes; then, by gentle degrees, pour in a pint of boiling cream; beat till cold; put into custard-cups set into a deep dish of boiling water, and let them stand till cold again. Put at the top small strips of orange-paring cut thin, or preserved chips.

Raspberry Brandy
From "The Complete Cook", By J. M. Sanderson, 1864

Scald the fruit in a stone jar set in a kettle of water, or on a hot hearth. When the juice will run freely, strain it without pressing: to every quart of juice allow one pound of loaf-sugar; boil it up and skim; when quite clear pour out; and when cold, add an equal quantity of brandy. Shake them well together and bottle.

Fine Raspberry Cordial
From "The Lady's Receipt-Book; a Useful Companion for Large or Small Families", By Eliza Leslie, 1847

Fill a large stone jar with ripe raspberries. Cover the jar closely, and let it stand in a corner of the hearth near the fire, or on the top of a stove, till the fruit is heated so as to break. Then put the raspberries into a linen bag, and squeeze the juice into a pan beneath. Measure the juice, and to every quart allow a pound of loaf-sugar, broken very small. Do not use the white sugar that is sold ready-powdered; it is generally so adulterated with pulverized starch, as to be unfit for any thing that is to be set away for keeping. Put the juice and sugar (well mixed) into a preserving-kettle. Give it a boil, and skim it well. When it has come to a boil, and the scum has ceased to appear, take off the kettle; measure the liquid; and pour it carefully into a large vessel; allowing an equal quantity of the best French brandy. Stir it well, and when cold, put it into a demijohn, or a large stone jug, and cork it tightly. Let it stand undisturbed a fortnight; then, if it is not perfectly clear, filter it through blotting-paper pinned inside the bottom of a sieve. Bottle it, and seal the corks. Instead of brandy, you may use the best Jamaica spirits.

Currant or cherry cordial may be made in the above manner: first stoning all the cherries, which should be fully ripe, and of the largest and best kind; either red or black, or a mixture of both. The flavour will be much improved by cracking the stones, and putting them into the demijohn before you pour on the liquid.

Peach cordial, also, may be made as above. The peaches should be fine, ripe, juicy free-stones; cut in pieces, and the stones removed. Afterwards, crack the stones, and put the kernels (broken up) into the bottom of the demijohn, to infuse with the liquid.

Rhubarb Wine
From "The Book of Household Management", By Isabella Beeton, 1861

To every 5 lbs. of rhubarb pulp allow 1 gallon of cold spring water; to every gallon of liquor allow 3 lbs. of loaf sugar, 1/2 oz. of isinglass, the rind of 1 lemon. Gather the rhubarb about the middle of May; wipe it with a wet cloth, and, with a mallet, bruise it in a large wooden tub or other convenient means. When reduced to a pulp, weigh it, and to every 5 lbs. add 1 gallon of cold spring water; let these remain for 3 days, stirring 3 or 4 times a day; and, on the fourth day, press the pulp through a hair sieve; put the liquor into a tub, and to every gallon put 3 lbs. of loaf sugar; stir in the sugar until it is quite dissolved, and add the lemon-rind; let the liquor remain, and, in 4, 5, or 6 days, the fermentation will begin to subside, and a crust or head will be formed, which should be skimmed off, or the liquor drawn from it, when the crust begins to crack or separate. Put the wine into a cask, and if, after that, it ferments, rack it off into another cask, and in a fortnight stop it down. If the wine should have lost any of its original sweetness, add a little more loaf sugar, taking care that the cask is full. Bottle it off in February or March, and in the summer it should be fit to drink. It will improve greatly by keeping; and, should a very brilliant colour be desired, add a little currant-juice.

Sassafras Beer
From "Directions for Cookery, in its Various Branches" By Eliza Leslie, 1840

Have ready two gallons of soft water; one quart of wheat bran; a large handful of dried apples; half a pint of molasses; a small handful of hops; half a pint of strong fresh yeast, and a piece of sassafras root the size of an egg.
Put all the ingredients (except the molasses and yeast) at once into a large kettle. Boil it till the apples are quite soft. Put the molasses into a small clean tub or a large pan. Set a hair sieve over the vessel, and strain the mixture through it. Let it stand till it becomes only milk-warm, and then stir in the yeast. Put the liquor immediately into the keg or jugs, and let it stand uncorked to ferment. Fill the jugs quite full, that the liquor in fermenting may run over. Set them in a large tub. When you see that the fermentation or working has subsided, cork it, and it will be fit for use next day.
Two large table-spoonfuls of ginger stirred into the molasses will be found an improvement.
If the yeast is stirred in while the liquor is too warm, it will be likely to turn sour.
If the liquor is not put immediately into the jugs, it will not ferment well.

Keep it in a cold place. It will not in warm weather be good more than two days. It is only made for present use.

Strawberry Cordial
From "Directions for Cookery, in its Various Branches" By Eliza Leslie, 1840

Hull a sufficient quantity of ripe strawberries, and squeeze them through a linen bag. To each quart of the juice allow a pint of white brandy, and half a pound of powdered loaf-sugar. Put the liquid into a glass jar or a demijohn, and let it stand a fortnight. Then filter it through a sieve, to the bottom of which a piece of fine muslin or blotting paper has been fastened; and afterwards bottle it.

Whiskey Cordial
From "The Book of Household Management", By Isabella Beeton, 1861

1 lb. of ripe white currants, the rind of 2 lemons, 1/4 oz. of grated ginger, 1 quart of whiskey, 1 lb. of lump sugar.
Strip the currants from the stalks; put them into a large jug; add the lemon-rind, ginger, and whiskey; cover the jug closely, and let it remain covered for 24 hours. Strain through a hair sieve, add the lump sugar, and let it stand 12 hours longer; then bottle, and cork well.
To stand 24 hours before being strained; 12 hours after the sugar is added.

10. Holidays

New Year's

"This is the last day in which to prepare for the dinner intended for the soldiers of General Lee's army on New-Year's day. The collection of cooked and uncooked fowls and meats, up to yesterday afternoon, at the Ballard House, was such as but few persons ever witnessed before, and yet, in the opinion of those in charge, a further supply will be needed. The Treasurer, Mr. John J. Wilson, calls for a continuance of contributions in money and provisions."-Richmond Dispatch, Dec. 31, 1864.

"The New Year's dinner has come and gone, or rather, gone, without coming"-City Under Siege, Mike Wright, Jan. 1865.

"We had a very pleasant evening and were regaled in honour of the new year, which yesterday being Sunday was celebrated today, with egg-nog, Confederate cake and pop-corn."- From the diary of Emma Florence LeConte, the daughter of scientist Joseph LeConte of Columbia, S.C., Jan 2, 1865.

"It was an amusing sight, nearly two-thirds of the soldiers were drunk, having run Memphis as they pleased for almost the last twenty four hours.....Partook of a soldier's supper, made our bed 'neath the starry canopy of Heaven and laid down, ending the year as we began it, by sleeping. Thus endeth the year 1862.....LaFayette, Tenn. Jan 1 1863 New Years' morning truly, but hard to realize. There was no cordial face of a sister or blooming face of a brother to greet me with a "Happy New Year"....But I was soon aroused from my reverie by the blunt order of Lt. Clark "Feed your horses and rub them off well!" – Pvt. Jenkin L. Jones, 6th Wisconsin Battery, from his book "An Artilleryman's Diary" .

Pound Cake
From "The Virginia Housewife", By Mary Randolph, 1836

Wash the salt from a pound of butter, and rub it till it is soft as cream--have ready a pound of flour sifted, one of powdered sugar, and twelve eggs well beaten; put alternately into the butter, sugar, flour, and the froth from the eggs--continuing to beat them together till all
the ingredients are in, and the cake quite light: add some grated lemon peel, a nutmeg, and a gill of brandy; butter the pans, and bake them. This cake makes an excellent pudding, if baked in a large mould, and eaten with sugar and wine. It is also excellent when boiled, and served up with melted butter, sugar and wine.

Broiled Fowl or Rabbit
From "The Great Western Cook Book, or Table Receipts, Adapted to Western Housewifery", By Anna Maria Collins, 1857

Cut it open down the back, wipe the inside clean with a cloth, and season it with pepper and salt. Have a clear fire, and set the gridiron at a good distance over it, lay the fowl on the inside, toward the fire, and broil it till it is a fine brown. Do not burn the fleshy side. Lay it on a hot dish, garnish it with parsley, and pour over it some melted butter.

New-Year's Cookies

From "The Practical Housekeeper; A Cyclopedia of Domestic Economy", By Elizabeth Fries Ellet, 1857

Weigh out a pound of sugar, three-quarters of a pound of butter--stir them to a cream, then add three beaten eggs, a grated nutmeg, two table-spoonfuls of caraway seed, and a pint of flour. Dissolve a teaspoonful of saleratus in a tea cup of milk, strain and mix it with half a teacup of cider, and stir it into the cookies--then add flour to make them sufficiently stiff to roll out. Bake them as soon as cut into cakes, in a quick oven, till a light brown.

Valentine's Day

"I am more than ever anxious to see you darling, but still undecided about when I shall come. Look for me when you see me, is as near as I can come to it."- Daniel Blain, a Confederate soldier in the 1st Rockbridge Artillery of Virginia, Letter to Loulie, who later became his wife.

"And how happy the thought that years increase the affection & esteem we have for each other to love & be loved. May it ever be so, and may I ever be a husband worthy of your warmest affections. May I make you happy and in so doing be made happy in return. A sweet kiss and embrace to your greeting."- Harvey Black, Surgeon to the Army of Northern Virginia, Brandy Station, Virginia. Nov. 1, 1863. Letter to his wife Mary.

"If my heart was like yours we would be united in heart you kneed not to Dout Though we are fare apart at present my heart is with you everymoment for I often think of you"-Letter from William F. Testerman (First Lieutenant Co. C of the 8thTennessee Cavalry) to Miss Jane Davis, Gallatin, Tenn. July 25, 1864.

Secrets
From "Directions for Cookery, in its Various Branches" By Eliza Leslie, 1840

Take glazed paper of different colours, and cut it into squares of equal size, fringing two sides of each. Have ready, burnt almonds, chocolate nuts, and bonbons or sugar-plums of various sorts; and put one in each paper with a folded slip containing two lines of verse; or what will be much more amusing, a conundrum with the answer. Twist the coloured paper so as entirely to conceal their contents, leaving the fringe at each end. This is the most easy, but there are various ways of cutting and ornamenting these envelopes.

Lavender Water
From "Directions for Cookery, in its Various Branches" By Eliza Leslie, 1840

Mix two ounces of essential oil of lavender, and two drachms of essence of amberis, with a pint of spirits of wine; cork the bottle and shake it hard everyday for a fortnight.

Scented Bags
From "Directions for Cookery, in its Various Branches" By Eliza Leslie, 1840

Take a quarter of a pound of coriander seeds, a quarter of a pound of orris root, a quarter of a pound of aromatic calamus, a quarter of a pound of damask rose leaves, two ounces of lavender blossoms, half an ounce of mace, half an ounce of cinnamon, a quarter of an ounce of cloves, and two drachms of musk-powder. Beat them all separately in a mortar, and then mix them well together. Make small silk or satin bags; fill each with a portion of the mixture, and sew them closely all round. Lay them among your clothes in the drawers.

Violet Perfume
From "Directions for Cookery, in its Various Branches" By Eliza Leslie, 1840

Drop twelve drops of genuine oil of rhodium on a lump of loaf-sugar. Then pound the sugar in a marble mortar with two ounces of orris root powder. This will afford an excellent imitation of the scent of violets. If you add more oil of rhodium, it will produce a rose perfume. Sew up the powder in little silk bags, or keep it in a tight box.

Chocolate Custard
From "Directions for Cookery, in its Various Branches" By Eliza Leslie, 1840

Scrape fine a quarter of a pound of the best chocolate, and pour on it a tea-cup of boiling water. Cover it, and let it stand by the fire till it has dissolved, stirring it twice. Beat eight eggs very light, omitting the whites of two. Stir them by degrees into a quart of cream or rich milk, alternately with the melted chocolate, and three table-spoonfuls of powdered white sugar. Pat the mixture into cups, and bake it about ten minutes. Send them to table cold, with sweetened cream, or white of egg beaten to a stiff froth, and heaped on the top of each custard.

St. Patrick's Day

Though Corned Beef and Cabbage is not a traditional meal in Ireland, it IS a traditional St. Patrick's Day meal of the American-Irish, here's why: During the Great Potato Famine (between 1845-1852), the Irish that had emigrated to America began making more money then they had in Ireland under British rule. With more money for food, the Irish could better afford meat. But instead of their beloved bacon, the Irish began eating beef. And, the beef they could afford just happened to be corned beef, the thing their great grandparents were famous for. Yet, the corned beef the Irish immigrants ate was much different than that produced in Ireland 200 years prior. The Irish immigrants almost exclusively bought their meat from kosher butchers. And what we think of today as Irish corned beef is actually Jewish corned beef thrown into a pot with cabbage and potatoes. The Jewish population in New York City at the time were relatively new immigrants from Eastern and Central Europe. The corned beef they made was from brisket, a kosher cut of meat from the front of the cow. Since brisket is a tougher cut, the salting and cooking process transformed the meat into the extremely tender, flavorful corned beef we know of today.

On St. Patrick's Day 1863, and after weeks of preparations, Union Gen. Meagher's Irish Brigade hosts the wildest St. Patrick's Day celebration in the Army of the Potomac. Attended by "Fighting Joe" himself, Meagher has arranged a feast complemented by horse races, weight throwing contests, Irish dancing, wheelbarrow races, and finally trying to catch a greased pig. "After the races there was an attempt to climb a greased pole to...which had been attached a ten day furlough. No one made it to the top because the grease had been applied too thickly."

To Corn Beef In Hot Weather
From "The Virginia Housewife", By Mary Randolph, 1860

Take a piece of thin brisket or plate, cut out the ribs nicely, rub it on both sides well with two large spoonsful of pounded saltpetre; pour on it a gill of molasses and a quart of salt; rub them both in; put it in a vessel just large enough to hold it, but not tight, for the bloody

brine must run off as it makes, or the meat will spoil. Let it be well covered, top, bottom and sides, with the molasses and salt. In four days you may boil it, tied up in a cloth with the salt, &c. about it: when done, take the skin off nicely, and serve it up. If you have an

ice-house or refrigerator, it will be best to keep it there. A fillet or breast of veal, and a leg or rack of mutton, are excellent done in the same way.

<u>*Interesting Irish Confederate Facts:*</u> *Although significantly fewer Irish lived in the Confederate States of America, six Confederate generals were Irish-born. Units such as the Charleston Irish Volunteers attracted Confederate Irish-Americans in South Carolina, the 24th Georgia Volunteer Infantry followed General Thomas Reade Rootes Cobb, while Irish Tennesseans could join the 10th Tennessee Infantry. A company of the Washington Blues regiment of the Missouri Volunteer Militia (later the Missouri State Guard), commanded by Colonel Joseph Kelly, was the subject of a Confederate version of a Union song, "Kelly's Irish Brigade". The Louisiana Tigers, first raised by Major Chatham Roberdeau Wheat, had a large number of Irish American members. Company E, Emerald Guard, 33rd Virginia of the Stonewall Brigade composed of Irish immigrant volunteers may have been first to initiate "rebel yell" at 1st Bull Run attacking 14th New York guns on Henry Hill.*

Professor David Gleeson has undertaken the most detailed review of the Irish in the Confederacy yet produced, which includes an attempt to accurately estimate the numbers of Irish who served the South during the war. The figure he arrives at is c. 20,000 men; although dwarfed in comparison to Irish service in the Federal forces, such a total would, in fact, represent the enlistment of just over 50% of those Irishmen of military age in the South, a proportion which significantly exceeds that seen in the North.

Major General Patrick Ronayne Cleburne-Born March 17, 1828, Killumney County, Ireland. Killed during the Battle of Franklin on November 30, 1864. He was last seen advancing on foot toward the Union line with his sword raised, after his horse was shot out from under him. Accounts later said that he was found just inside the Federal line and his body carried back to an aid station along the Columbia Turnpike. Confederate war records indicate he died of a shot to the abdomen, or possibly a bullet that went through his heart. When Confederates found his body, he had been picked clean of any valuable items, including his sword, boots and pocket watch.

Easter

"The snow is about seven or eight inches deep. I don't think we will have a very gay Easter today, as game is skearce, and we can get no eggs." -Jer Coggin, CSA Camp of the 23rd N.C. Reg., Near Guinea Station, Virginia.

Lent Potatoes
From "A New System of Domestic Cookery", By Maria Eliza Ketelby Rundell, 1807

Beat three or four ounces of almonds, and three or four bitter, when blanched, putting a little orange-flower water to prevent oiling; add eight ounces of butter, four eggs well beaten and strained, half a glass of raisin wine, and sugar to your taste. Beat all well till quite smooth, and grate in three Savoy biscuits. Make balls of the above with a little flour, the size of a chestnut; throw them into a stew-pan of boiling lard, and boil them of a beautiful yellow brown. Drain them on a sieve. Serve sweet sauce in a boat, to eat with them.

Cross-Buns
From "The Lady's Receipt-Book; a Useful Companion for Large or Small Families", By Eliza Leslie, 1847

Pick clean a pound and a half of Zante currants; wash, drain, and dry them; spreading them on a large flat dish, placed in a slanting position near the fire or in the sun. When they are perfectly dry, dredge them thickly with flour to prevent their sinking or clodding in the cakes. Sift into a deep pan two pounds of fine flour, and mix thoroughly with it a tablespoonful of powdered cinnamon, (or of mixed nutmeg and cinnamon,) and half a pound of powdered white sugar. Cut up half a pound of the best fresh butter in half a pint of rich milk. Warm it till the butter is quite soft, but not till it melts. While warm, stir into the milk and butter two wine-glasses (or a jill) of strong fresh yeast.

Make a hole in the centre of the pan of flour; pour in the mixed liquid; then, with a spoon or a broad knife, mix the flour gradually in; beginning round the edge of the hole. Proceed thus till you have the entire mass of ingredients thoroughly incorporated; stirring it hard as you go on. Cover the pan with a clean flannel or a thick towel, and set it in a warm place near the fire to rise. When it has risen well, and the surface of the dough is cracked all over, mix in a small tea-spoonful of soda, dissolved; flour your paste-board; divide the dough into equal portions, and mixing in the currants, knead it into round cakes about the size of a small saucer. Place them on a large flat dish, cover them, and set them again in a warm place for about half an hour. Then butter some square tin or iron baking-pans; transfer the buns to them; and brush each bun lightly over with a glazing of beaten white of eggs, sweetened with a little sugar. Then, with the back of a knife, mark each bun with a cross, deeply indented in the dough, and extending entirely from one edge to another. Let the oven be quite ready; set in it the buns; and bake them of a deep brown colour. In England, and in other parts of Europe, it is customary to have hot cross-buns at breakfast on the morning of Good Friday. They are very good cakes at any time; but are best when fresh.

Pancakes for Shrove Tuesday
From "A Plain Cookery Book for the Working Classes", By Charles Elme Francatelli, 1852

Twelve ounces of flour, three eggs, one pint of milk, a tea-spoonful of salt, a little grated nutmeg, and chopped lemon-peel.

First, put the flour into a basin, hollow out the centre, add the salt, nutmeg, lemon-peel, and a drop of milk, to dissolve them; then break in the eggs, work all together, with a spoon, into a smooth soft paste, add the remainder of the milk, and work the whole vigorously until it forms a smooth liquid batter. Next, set a frying-pan on the fire, and, as soon as it gets hot, wipe it out clean with a cloth, then run about a teaspoonful of lard all over the bottom of the hot frying-pan, pour in half a small teacupful of the batter, place the pan over the fire, and, in about a minute or so, the pancake will have become set sufficiently firm to enable you to turn it over in the frying-pan, in order that it may be baked on the other side also; the pancake done on both sides, turn it out on its dish, and sprinkle a little sugar over it: proceed to use up the remaining batter in the same manner.

Passover Cakes
From "The Practical Housekeeper; A Cyclopedia of Domestic Economy", By Elizabeth Fries Ellet, 1857

Make a stiff paste with biscuit-powder, milk, and water; add a little butter, the yolk of an egg, and a little white sugar. Cut into pieces, mould with the hand, and bake in a brisk oven: they should not be too thin.

Easter Fun Facts

German immigrants brought the symbol of the Easter rabbit to America. It was widely ignored by other Christians until shortly after the Civil War. In fact, Easter itself was not widely celebrated in America until after that time.

In the United States in the early nineteenth century, Dolly Madison, the wife of the fourth American President, organized an egg roll in Washington. She had been told that Egyptian children used to roll eggs against the pyramids so she invited the children of Washington to roll hard-boiled eggs down the hilly lawn of the new Capitol building! The custom continued, except for the years during the Civil War.

Dates for Easter During the Civil War:
March 31st 1861
April 20th 1862
April 5th 1863
March 27th 1864
April 16th 1865

Easter Sunday 1865, Confederate Brigadier General Robert C. Taylor was killed in action at West Point, Ga. He was the last general to be killed in the civil war one week after Robert E. Lee surrendered the Army of Northern Virginia.

Easter Sunday 1865, Jefferson Davis and the fleeing government of the Confederacy, spent the night at the rectory of St. Luke's Episcopal Church in Salisbury, North Carolina.

Election Day

Election Cake
From "Directions for Cookery, in its Various Branches" By Eliza Leslie, 1840

Make a sponge (as it is called) in the following manner:--Sift into a pan two pounds and a half of flour; and into a deep plate another pound. Take a second pan, and stir a large table-spoonful of the best West India molasses into five jills or two tumblers and a half of strong fresh yeast; adding a Jill of water, warm, but not hot. Then stir gradually into the yeast, &c. the pound of flour that you have sifted separately. Cover it, and let it set by the fire three hours to rise. While it is rising, prepare the other ingredients, by stirring in a deep pan two pounds of fresh butter and two pounds of powdered sugar, till they are quite light and creamy; adding to them a table-spoonful of powdered cinnamon; a tea-spoonful of powdered mace; and two powdered nutmegs. Stir in also half a pint of rich milk. Beat fourteen eggs till very smooth and thick, and stir them gradually into the mixture, alternately with the two pounds and a half of flour which you sifted first. When the sponge is quite light, mix the whole together, and bake it in buttered tin pans in a moderate oven. It should be eaten fresh, as no sweet cake made with yeast is so good after the first day. If it is not probable that the whole will come into use on the day it is baked, mix but half the above quantity.

Thanksgiving

In 1863, President Lincoln declared not one, but two separate Thanksgiving celebrations. The first was on Thursday, August 6, 1863 following the Union's victory at Gettysburg. The second was Lincoln's official declaration of Thanksgiving as a nationwide holiday, to be observed on the last Thursday of every November. The 1864 Thanksgiving focused heavily on honoring and thanking the Union troops, and shows early evidence of the feast being the highlight of the holiday. The Union League Club of New York made efforts to ensure that no soldier, on land, water or elsewhere, went without a Thanksgiving dinner. They asked for donations from the public, and many restaurants offered to cook the food. The soldiers feasted on turkey, cranberries and many of the other traditional foods we now associate with Thanksgiving. The response from the public was so outstanding that the list of donations in the Union League Report was 37 pages long!

The following recipes are taken from "Directions for Cookery, in its Various Branches" by Eliza Leslie, 1840. Mary Todd Lincoln taught herself to cook with this historical book.

To Roast A Turkey
From "Directions for Cookery, in its Various Branches" by Eliza Leslie, 1840

Make a force-meat of grated bread-crumbs, minced suet, sweet marjoram, grated lemon-peel, nutmeg, pepper, salt, and beaten yolk of egg. You may add some grated cold ham. Light some writing paper, and singe the hairs from the skin of the turkey. Reserve the neck, liver, and gizzard for the gravy. Stuff the craw of the turkey with the force-meat, of which there should be enough made to form into balls for frying, laying them round the turkey when it is dished. Dredge it with flour, and roast it before a clear brisk fire, basting it with cold lard. Towards the last, set the turkey nearer to the fire, dredge it again very lightly with flour, and baste it with butter. It will require, according to its size, from two to three hours roasting. Make the gravy of the giblets cut in pieces, seasoned, and stewed for two hours in a very little water; thicken it with a spoonful of browned flour, and stir into it the gravy from the dripping-pan, having first skimmed off the fat.
A turkey should be accompanied by ham or tongue. Serve up with it mushroom-sauce. Have stewed cranberries on the table to eat with it. Do not help any one to the legs, or drum-sticks as they are called.

Turkeys are sometimes stuffed entirely with sausage-meat. Small cakes of this meat should then be fried, and laid round it.

Cranberry Sauce
From "Directions for Cookery, in its Various Branches" by Eliza Leslie, 1840

Wash a quart of ripe cranberries, and put them into a pan with about a wine-glass of water. Stew them slowly, and stir them frequently, particularly after they begin to burst. They require a great deal of stewing, and should be like a marmalade when done. Just before you take them from the fire, stir in a pound of brown sugar.

When they are thoroughly done, put them into a deep dish, and set them away to get cold.

You may strain the pulp through a cullender or sieve into a mould, and when it is in a firm shape send it to table on a glass dish. Taste it when it is cold, and if not sweet enough, add more sugar.

Cranberries require more sugar than any other fruit, except plums. Cranberry sauce is eaten with roast turkey, roast fowls, and roast ducks.

Christmas

Christmas during the Civil War served both as an escape from, and a reminder of, the awful conflict rending the country in two. Soldiers looked forward to a day of rest and relative relaxation, but had their moods tempered by the thought of separation from their loved ones. At home, families did their best to celebrate the holiday, but wondered when the vacant chair would again be filled.

Civil War soldiers in camp and their families at home drew comfort from the same sorts of traditions that characterize Christmas today. Alfred Bellard of the 5th New Jersey noted, "In order to make it look much like Christmas as possible, a small tree was stuck up in front of our tent, decked off with hard tack and pork, in lieu of cakes and oranges, etc."

In one amusing anecdote, a Confederate prisoner relates how the realities of war intruded on his Christmas celebrations: "A friend had sent me in a package a bottle of old brandy. On Christmas morning I quietly called several comrades up to my bunk to taste the precious fluid of...DISAPPOINTMENT! The bottle had been opened outside, the brandy taken and replaced with water...and sent in. I hope the Yankee who played that practical joke lived to repent it and was shot before the war ended."

A Sergeant of the First Tennessee thought that Christmas Day 1861 at Bowling Green was "very dull", although some of the men "got drunk and cut up generally and were put under guard." There were similar problems at Murfreesboro the following Christmas. A member of the 154th Tennessee remarked "Eggnog was fashionable and Captains, Lieutenants and Privates was drunk and very troublesome". -Larry J. Daniel, "Soldiering In the Army of Tennessee", 1991.

"We had the pleasure of regaling ourselves Christmas on some of your cookery. It made us feel under obligation to you for so fine a treat. We will have plenty for a short time. It is said we will get a New Year's dinner from Gen. Lee. We hope o get some. I will let you know how we come out and if we fail, all will be right." –Pvt. Ephraim "Alexander" McAulay, Co. C, 37th North Carolina Infantry, Mecklenburg Salt Works, South Carolina, May 17, 1864. Letter to his mother, Nancy.

"We had for dinner oyster soup, besides roast mutton, ham, boned turkey, wild duck, partridge, plum pudding, sauterne, burgundy, sherry, and Madeira. There is life in the old land yet!" -Mary Boykin Chesnut, December 25, 1863. "A Diary From Dixie".

"We had to be "Santa Claus" ourselves this season, for cakes, apples, a little candy, & some picture books were all that could be procured for the children. We had to

tell them Santa Claus couldn't get thro' the pickets, - Jessie wanted to know why "the old fellow couldn't go to his Quartermaster & get him a pass?" They seemed to enjoy their Christmas quite as well as usual however, notwithstanding that Santa Claus was blackheaded."- Lucy Virginia Smith French, December 28, 1862, McMinnville, Tennessee. From her diary.

Egg Nog

From "The Great Western Cook Book, or Table Receipts, Adapted to Western Housewifery" By Collins, Anna Maria, Published 1857

Beat the whites of six eggs separately; add a tea-cupful of sugar to the yolks, beat them well, then pour very slowly on a half pint of brandy; stir it all the time hard, or the brandy will harden the eggs; put a quart of milk on the fire in a saucepan, let it become quite hot, but do not let it boil; pour it over the mixture, beat it all well together; then add the whites--be sure to have them very stiff, or your nogg will not be good--beat it all again, then grate a nutmeg over the top.
If you like it cold, add cold milk, instead of warming it.

A Rich Fruit Cake
From "The Virginia Housewife", By Mary Randolph, 1836

Have the following articles prepared, before you begin the cake: four pounds of flour dried and sifted, four pounds of butter washed to free it from salt, two pounds of loaf sugar pounded, a quarter of a pound of mace, the same of nutmegs powdered; wash four pounds of currants clean, pick and dry them; blanch one pound of sweet almonds, and cut them in
very thin slices; stone two pounds of raisins, cut them in two, and strew a little flour over to prevent their sticking together, and two pounds of citron sliced thin; break thirty eggs, separating the yelks and whites; work the butter to a cream with your hand-put in
alternately, flour, sugar, and the froth from both whites and yelks, which must be beaten separately, and only the froth put in. When all are mixed and the cake looks very light, add the spice, with half a pint of brandy, the currants and almonds; butter the mould well, pour in part of the cake, strew over it some raisins and citron--do this until all is in: set it in a well heated oven: when it has risen, and the top is coloured, cover it with paper; it will require three hours baking—it must be iced.

Practical Housewife's Christmas Ham
From "The Practical Housekeeper; A Cyclopedia of Domestic

Economy", By Elizabeth Fries Ellet, 1857

Soak the ham. be the weight whatever it may, half the usual time in water; remove, wash well with cold water, place in a pan large and deep enough to con tain it, cover with beer or good ale, and let it remain until the required time for soaking a ham of the size used has expired. Boil as usual until the skin can be readily removed; then place the ham in a tin or an earthenware dish, and cover with a common flour and water paste, or surround with batter. Bake in a moderately heated oven until done, remove the paste or batter, cover with bread-raspings, and serve hot.
Cooked in this manner, a ham acquires the most delicious flavor.

A Christmas Goose Pie
From "Directions for Cookery, in its Various Branches" By Eliza Leslie, 1840

These pies are always made with a standing crust. Put into a sauce-pan one pound of butter cut up, and a pint and a half of water; stir it while it is melting, and let it come to a boil.
Then skim off whatever milk or impurity may rise to the top. Have ready four pounds of flour sifted into a pan. Make a hole in the middle of it, and pour in the melted butter while hot. Mix it with a spoon to a stiff paste, (adding the beaten yolks of three or four eggs,) and then knead it very well with your hands, on the paste-board, keeping it dredged with flour till it ceases to be sticky. Then set it away to cool. Split a large goose, and a fowl down the back, loosen the flesh all over with a sharp knife, and take out all the bones. Parboil a smoked tongue; peel it and cut off the root. Mix together a powdered nutmeg, a quarter of an ounce of powdered mace, a tea-spoonful of pepper, and a tea-spoonful of salt, and season with them the fowl and the goose.
Roll out the paste near an inch thick, and divide it into three pieces. Cut out two of them of an oval form for the top and bottom; and the other into a long straight piece for the sides or walls of the pie. Brush the paste all over with beaten white of egg, and set on the bottom the piece that is to form the wall, pinching the edges together, and cementing them with white of egg. The bottom piece must be large enough to turn up a little round the lower edge of the wall piece, to which it must be firmly joined all round. When you have the crust properly fixed, so as to be baked standing alone without a dish, put in first the goose, then the fowl, and then the tongue. Fill up what space is

left with pieces of the flesh of pigeons, or of partridges, quails, or any game that is convenient. There must be no bones in the pie.

You may add also some bits of ham, or some force-meat balls. Lastly, cover the other ingredients with half a pound of butter, and pat on the top crust, which, of course, must be also of an oval form to correspond with the bottom. The lid must be placed not quite on the top edge of the wall, but an inch and a half below it. Close it very well, and ornament the sides and top with festoons and leaves cut out of paste. Notch the edges handsomely, and put a paste flower in the centre. Glaze the whole with beaten yolk of egg, and bind the pie all round with a double fold of white paper. Set it in a regular oven, and bake it four hours.

This is one way of making the celebrated goose pies that it is customary in England to send as presents at Christmas. They are eaten at luncheon, and if the weather is cold, and they are kept carefully covered up from the air, they will be good for two or three weeks; the standing crust assisting to preserve them.

A Christmas Pie
From "The Practical Housekeeper; A Cyclopedia of Domestic Economy", By Elizabeth Fries Ellet, 1857

Bone a large goose and a fowl. Parboil a smoked tongue; peel it and cut off the root. Mix together a powdered nutmeg, a quarter of an ounce of powdered mace, a tea-spoonful of pepper, the same quantity of salt, and season the fowl and goose. Roll out the paste near an inch thick, and divide it into three pieces; cut out two of them in an oval form for the top and bottom; and the other into a long straight piece for the sides or walls of the pie. Brush the paste all over with beaten white of egg, and set on the bottom the piece that is to form the wall, pinching the edges together, and cementing them with white of egg. The bottom piece must be large enough to turn up a little round the lower edge of the wall piece, to which it must be firmly joined all round. When you have the crust properly fixed, so as to be baked standing alone without a dish, put in first the goose, then the fowl, then the tongue. Fill up what space is left with pieces of the flesh of pigeons, or of partridges, quails, or any game that is convenient. There must be no bones in the pie. You may add also some bits of ham, or some forcemeat balls. Cover the ingredients with half a pound of butter, and put on the top crust which, of course, must be also of an oval form to correspond with the bottom. The lid must be placed not quite on the top edge of the wall, but an inch and a half below it; close it very well, and ornament the sides and top with festoons and leaves cut out of paste; notch the edges handsomely, and put a paste flower in the centre; glaze the whole with beaten yolk of egg, and bind the pie all round with a double fold of white paper; bake it four hours.

If the weather is cold, and the pie kept carefully covered up from the air, it will be good for two or three weeks, the standing crust assisting to preserve it.

Christmas Plum Pudding
From "A Plain Cookery Book for the Working Classes", By Charles Elme Francatelli, 1852

Two pounds of flour, twelve ounces of raisins, twelve ounces of currants, twelve ounces of peeled and chopped apples, one pound of chopped suet, twelve ounces of sugar, four eggs, one pint and a-half of milk or beer, one ounce of salt, half an ounce of ground allspice. Boil the pudding four hours. First, put the flour, suet, and all the fruit in a large pan; mix these well together, and having made a deep hole in the middle thereof with your fist, add the salt, sugar, and allspice, and half a pint of the milk, or beer, to dissolve them; next, add the four eggs, and the remaining pint of milk, or beer; mix all vigorously together with the hand, tie up the pudding in a well-greased and floured cloth, boil it for at least four hours, taking care that the water boils before the pudding is put into the pot to boil. When done,
turn the pudding out on its dish, and, if you can afford it, pour over it the following sauce (Sweet Pudding Sauce).

Sweet Pudding Sauce
From "A Plain Cookery Book for the Working Classes", By Charles Elme Francatelli, 1852

Two ounces of common flour, ditto of butter, ditto of sugar, chopped lemon-peel, half a gill of any kind of spirits, and half a pint of water. First mix the flour, butter, and sugar in a small saucepan by kneading the ingredients well together with a wooden spoon, then add the water, spirits, and lemon-peel; stir the sauce on the fire till it comes to a boil, and then pour it all over the pudding.

To Roast Chestnuts
From "Directions for Cookery, in its Various Branches" By Eliza Leslie, 1840

The large Spanish chestnuts are the best for roasting. Cut a slit in the shell of every one to prevent their bursting when hot. Put them into a pan, and set them over a charcoal furnace till they are thoroughly roasted; stirring them up frequently and taking care hot to let them burn. When they are done, peel off the shells, and send the chestnuts to table wrapped up in a napkin to keep them warm.

Chestnuts should always be roasted or boiled before they are eaten.

11. For the Sick

Author's Note: The author of this book cannot and does not vouch for, promote, nor endorse the use of any of the following "remedies" in this chapter as either safe nor effective! Readers are advised to consult with their physician before attempting any of these "remedies"! Use of these "remedies" is at your own risk!

"At the hospital at Goldsboro, there was men's wives came to see them and the doctor would not le them stay in the hospital at night. It is against the rules. There was mothers brought them something to eat and they could not get to stay in with them and let them eat it. They say that they know what to give them to eat. There is several in the hospital that has been there 6 weeks and now are not fit for service just because they do not get enough to eat. A man can never gather strength without to get something to eat." - Pvt. John Calvin McAulay, Co. K, 56th North Carolina Infantry, Peace Institute Hospital, Raleigh, North Carolina, August 24th 1862. Letter to his sister, Nancy.

"Yesterday on the train coming up to this place I got plenty of peaches and pie and watermelon but had to pay well for them. At the hospital you can not get such things without stealing them." - Pvt. John Calvin McAulay, Co. K, 56th North Carolina Infantry, Peace Institute Hospital, Raleigh, North Carolina, August 24th 1862. Letter to his sister, Nancy.

"I think we have too much wheat flour here. If we had more corn meal, I have no doubt our health would be better. As it is, the health of this regiment is bad in the extreme." –Pvt. William C. Clayton, Co. I, Fourth South Carolina Infantry, Camp near Germantown, Fairfax County, Virginia, September 29, 1861. Letter to his sister.

"The surgeons, to save their reputation, tell the ladies that we are all well fed but they know better. I ate some mushrooms today after seeing them eaten by others. They were boiled in water and should have been seasoned with butter." -Pvt. Martin Van Buren Oldham, Company G of the 9th Tennessee Infantry, October 9, 1863, Stonewall Hospital, Montogomery Alabama, after receiving a shell wound to the face on Sept. 19 near Lee's Mill. From diary entry.

"Began my regular attendance on Wayside Hospital. To-day we gave wounded men, as they stopped for an hour at the station, their breakfast. Those who are able to come to the table do so. The badly wounded remain in wards prepared for them, where their wounds dressed by nurses and surgeons, and we take bread and butter, beef, ham, and hot coffee to them." -Mary Boykin Chesnut, August 19, 1864. "A Diary From Dixie".

"I don't think there is too much danger of me eating too much. Rations are scarce or we have a small allowance. Roffe who came in the hospital with sore throat left today because he could not get enough to eat." -Pvt. Martin Van Buren Oldham, Company G of the 9th Tennessee Infantry, February 12, 1863, while prisoner at Camp Douglas. From diary entry.

Mutton Stewed and Soup for One Hundred Men
From "Directions for Cooking By Troops In Camp And Hospital, Prepared for the Army of Northern Virginia and Published By Order of the Surgeon General", By Florence Nightingale, 1861

Put in a convenient sized vessel 16 gallons water, 60 lbs. meat, 12 lbs. plain mixed vegetables, 9 lbs. pearl barley or rice (or 4½ lbs. each), 1½ lbs. salt, 1¼ lbs. flour, 1 oz. pepper. Put all the ingredients, except the flour, into the pan; set it on the fire, and

when beginning to boil, diminish the heat, and simmer gently for two hours and a half; take the meat out and keep warm; add to the soup your flour, which you have mixed with enough water to form a light batter; stir well together with a large spoon; boil another half hour; skim off the fat, and serve the meat and soup separate. The soup should be

stirred occasionally while making, to prevent burning or sticking.

Beef Soup
From "Directions for Cooking By Troops In Camp And Hospital, Prepared for the Army of Northern Virginia and Published By Order of the Surgeon General", By Florence Nightingale, 1861

Proceed the same as for mutton, only leave the meat in till serving, as it takes longer to cook than mutton. The pieces are not to be above 4 or 5 lbs. weight each.

Beef Tea, Six Pints
From "Directions for Cooking By Troops In Camp And Hospital, Prepared for the Army of Northern Virginia and Published By Order of the Surgeon General", By Florence Nightingale, 1861

Cut three pounds lean beef into pieces the size of walnuts, and break up the bones (if any); put it into a convenient sized kettle, with ½ lb. mixed vegetables (onions, celery, turnips, carrots, or one or two of these, if all are not to be obtained), 1 oz. salt, a little pepper,

2 oz. butter, ½ pint of water. Set it on a sharp fire for 15 minutes, stirring occasionally, till it forms a rather thick gravy at the bottom, but not brown; then add 7 pints of hot water; simmer gently for an hour. Skim off all the fat, strain through a sieve and serve.

Thick Beef Tea
From "Directions for Cooking By Troops In Camp And Hospital, Prepared for the Army of Northern Virginia and Published By Order of the Surgeon General", By Florence Nightingale, 1861

Dissolve a teaspoonful of arrow-root in a gill of water, and pour it into the beef tea twenty minutes before passing through the seive, or add ¼ oz. gelatine to the above quantity of beef tea, when cooking.

Mutton and veal will make good tea, by proceeding the same as above.

Chicken Broth
From "Directions for Cooking By Troops In Camp And Hospital, Prepared for the Army of Northern Virginia and Published By Order of the Surgeon General", By Florence Nightingale, 1861

Put in a stew-pan a fowl, 3 pints water, 2 teaspoonfuls of rice, 1 of salt, a little pepper and a small onion, or two ounces of mixed vegetables; boil the whole gently for one hour (if an old fowl, simmer for two hours, adding one pint more water.) Skim off the fat and serve.
A light mutton broth may be made in the same way, taking 1½ pounds mutton—neck if convenient.

Rice Water
From "Directions for Cooking By Troops In Camp And Hospital, Prepared for the Army of Northern Virginia and Published By Order of the Surgeon General", By Florence Nightingale, 1861

Put 7 pints water to boil; add 2 oz. rice, washed, 2 oz. sugar, the peel of two-thirds of a lemon, boil gently for three quarters of an hour, or till reduced to 5 pints. Strain and serve—use as a beverage.

Barley Water
From "Directions for Cooking By Troops In Camp And Hospital, Prepared for the Army of Northern Virginia and Published By Order of the Surgeon General", By Florence Nightingale, 1861

Put in a saucepan 7 pints water, 2 oz. pearl barley; stir now and then when boiling; add 2 oz. white sugar, the rind of half a lemon, thinly peeled; boil gently for two hours, and serve, either strained or with the barley left in.

Crimean Lemonade
From "Directions for Cooking By Troops In Camp And Hospital, Prepared for the Army of Northern Virginia and Published By Order of the Surgeon General", By Florence Nightingale, 1861

Put in a basin 2 tablespoonfuls of white or brown sugar, ½ a tablespoonful of lime juice, mix well together, and add one pint of water.

Citric Acid Lemonade
From "Directions for Cooking By Troops In Camp And Hospital, Prepared for the Army of Northern Virginia and Published By Order of the Surgeon General", By Florence Nightingale, 1861

Dissolve 1 oz. citric acid in one pint of cold water; add 1 lb. 9 oz. white sugar; mix well to form a thick syrup; then put in 19 pints cold water, slowly mixing well.

French Raspberry Vinegar (for a Cold)
From "The Lady's Receipt-Book; a Useful Companion for Large or Small Families", By Eliza Leslie, 1847

Take a sufficiency of fine ripe raspberries. Put them into a deep pan, and mash them with a wooden beetle. Then pour them, with all their juice, into a large linen bag, and squeeze and press out the liquid into a vessel beneath. Measure it; and to each quart of the raspberry-juice allow a pound of powdered white sugar, and a pint of the best cider vinegar. First mix together the juice and the vinegar, and give them a boil in a preserving-kettle. When they have boiled well, add gradually the sugar, with a beaten white of egg to every two pounds; and boil and skim it till the scum ceases to rise. When done, put it into clean bottles, and cork them tightly. It is a very pleasant and cooling beverage in warm weather, and for invalids who are feverish. To use it, pour out half a tumbler of raspberry vinegar, and fill it up with ice-water.
It is a good palliative for a cold, mixed with hot water, and taken as hot as possible immediately on going to bed, so as to produce perspiration.

Gargle for Sore Throat
From "Dr. Chase's Recipes; or, Information for Everybody", By Dr. Alvin Wood Chase, 1864

Very strong sage tea 1/2 pt.; strained honey, common salt, and strong vinegar, of each 2 tablespoons; cayenne, the pulverized, one rounding tea-spoon; steeping the cayenne with the sage, strain, mix, and bottle for use, gargling from 4 to a dozen times daily according to the severity of the case.
This is one of the very best gargles in use. By persevering some three months, I

cured a case of two years standing where the mouths of the Eustachian tubes constantly discharged matter at their openings through the tonsils into the patients mouth, he having previously been quite deaf, the whole throat being also diseased. I used the preparation for "Deafness" also as mentioned under that head. Remembering always to breath through nature's channel for the breath, the nose. Besides the foregoing, you will wash the whole surface twice a week with plenty of the "Toilet Soap," in water, wiping dry, then with a coarse dry towel rub the whole surface for ten minutes at least, and accomplish the coarse towel part of it every night and morning until the skin will remain through the day with its flushed surface, and genial heat; this draws the blood from the throat and other internal organs, or in other words, equalizes the circulation; know, and act, upon this fact, and no inflammation can long exist, no matter where it is located. Blood accumulates in the part inflamed, but let it flow evenly through the whole system, and of course there can be no inflammation.

Rice Gruel (for Bowl Complaints)
From "The Complete Cook", By J. M. Sanderson, 1864

This is principally used for bowel complaints, but is not so good as arrow-root. A table-spoonful of ground rice will thicken a pint of milk or water. Mix it in the same manner as oatmeal gruel; boil in a bit of dried orange or lemon peel, and a bit of cinnamon. Let it boil about ten minutes, sweeten with loaf-sugar, and add two glasses of port, or one brandy, as may be required.

Chronic Gout-To Cure
From "Dr. Chase's Recipes; or, Information for Everybody", By Dr. Alvin Wood Chase, 1864

"Take hot vinegar, and put into it all the table salt which it will dissolve, and bathe the parts affected with a soft piece of flannel. Rub in with the hand, and dry the foot, &c., by the fire. Repeat this operation four times in the 24 hours, 15 minutes each time, for four days; then twice a day for the same period; then once, and follow this rule whenever the symptoms show themselves at any future time."
The philosophy of the above formula is as follows: Chronic gout proceeds from the obstruction of the free circulation of the blood (in the parts affected) by the deposit of a chalky substance, which is generally understood to be a carbonate and phosphate of lime. Vinegar and salt dissolve these; and the old chronic compound is broken up. The carbonate of lime, &c., become acetate and muriate, and these being soluble, are taken up by the circulating system, and discharged by secretion.

This fact will be seen by the gouty joints becoming less and less in bulk until they assume their natural size. During this process, the stomach and bowels should be occasionally regulated by a gentle purgative. Abstinence from spirituous libations; exercise in the open air, and especially in the morning; freely bathing the whole surface; eating only the plainest food, and occupying the time by study, or useful employment, are very desirable assistants.

Lemonade, Nourishing, For Fever Patients
From "Dr. Chase's Recipes; or, Information for Everybody", By Dr. Alvin Wood Chase, 1864

Arrow-root 2 or 3 tea-spoons rubbed up with a little cold water, in a bowl or pitcher, which will hold about 1 qt.; then squeeze in the juice of half of a good sized lemon, with 2 or 3 table-spoons of white sugar, and pour on boiling water to fill the dish, constantly stirring whilst adding the boiling water.

Cover the dish, and when cold, it may be freely drank to allay thirst, as also to nourish the weak, but some will prefer the following:

Prof. Hufeland's Drink for Fever Patients OR Excessive Thirst
From "Dr. Chase's Recipes; or, Information for Everybody", By Dr. Alvin Wood Chase, 1864

Cream of tartar 1/2 oz.; water 3 qts.; boil until dissolved; after taking it from the fire add a sliced orange with from 1 1/2 to 3 ozs. of white sugar, according to the taste of the patient; bottle and keep cool.

To be used for a common drink in fevers of all grades, and at any time when a large amount of drink is *craved* by the *invalid*. Neither is there any bad taste to it for those in health.

3 Ways To Purify Air In A Sick Room
From "Dr. Chase's Recipes; or, Information for Everybody", By Dr. Alvin Wood Chase, 1864

1) To purify the air from noxious effluvia in sick rooms, not of a contagious character, simply slice three or four onions, place them on a plate upon the floor, changing them three or four times in the twenty-four hours.

2) Coffee, dried and pulverized, then a little of it sprinkled upon a hot shovel, will, in a very few minutes, clear a room of all impure effluvia, and especially of an animal character.
3) Chloride of Lime--Half a saucer of it, moistened with an equal mixture of good vinegar and water, a few drops at a time only, will purify a sick-room in a few minutes.

Camphor Ice-For Chapping Hands or Lips
From "Dr. Chase's Recipes; or, Information for Everybody", By Dr. Alvin Wood Chase, 1864

Spermaceti tallow 1 1/2 ozs.; oil of sweet almonds 4 tea-spoons; gum camphor 3/4 oz.; made fine. Set on the stove until dissolved, constantly stirring. Do not use only just sufficient heat to melt them.
Whilst warm, pour into moulds if desired to sell, then paper and put up in tin foil. If for your own use, put up in a tight box. Apply to the chaps or cracks two or three times daily, especially at bed time.

Warts and Corns-To Cure In Ten Minutes
From "Dr. Chase's Recipes; or, Information for Everybody", By Dr. Alvin Wood Chase, 1864

Take a small piece of potash and let it stand in the open air until it slacks, then thicken it to a paste with pulverized gum arabic, which prevents it from spreading where it is not wanted.
Pare off the seeds of the wart or the dead skin of the corn, and apply the paste, and let it remain on ten minutes; wash off, and soak the place in sharp vinegar or sweet oil, either of which will neutralize the alkali. Now do not jam nor squeeze out the wart or corn, like "street-corner pedlers," but leave them alone, and nature will remove them without danger of taking cold, as would be if a sore is made by pinching them out. Corns are caused by pressure; in most cases removing the pressure cures the corn. Nine of every ten corns can be cured by using twice, daily, upon it, any good liniment, and wearing loose shoes or boots.

A Soothing Ointment
From "The American Frugal Housewife", By Lydia M. Child, 1832

Plantain and house-leek, boiled in cream, and strained before it is put away to cool, makes a very cooling, soothing ointment. Plantain leaves laid upon a wound are cooling and healing.

For A Headache
From "The American Frugal Housewife", By Lydia M. Child, 1832

Half a spoonful of citric acid, (which may always be bought of the apothecaries,) stirred in half a tumbler of water, is excellent for the head-ache.

For A Cold
From "The American Frugal Housewife", By Lydia M. Child, 1832

Water-gruel, with three or four onions simmered in it, prepared with a lump of butter, pepper, and salt, eaten just before one goes to bed, is said to be a cure for a hoarse cold. A syrup made of horseradish-root and sugar is excellent for a cold.

Relief of Sore Throat
From "The American Frugal Housewife", By Lydia M. Child, 1832

Loaf sugar and brandy relieves a sore throat; when very bad, it is good to inhale the steam of scalding hot vinegar through the tube of a tunnel. This should be tried carefully at first, lest the throat be scalded. For children, it should be allowed to cool a little.

The following poultice for the throat distemper, has been much approved in England: The pulp of a roasted apple, mixed with an ounce of tobacco, the whole wet with spirits of wine, or any other high spirits, spread on a linen rag, and bound upon the throat at any period of the disorder.

Corns
From "The American Frugal Housewife", By Lydia M. Child, 1832

A corn may be extracted from the foot by binding on half a raw cranberry, with the cut side of the fruit upon the foot. I have known a very old and troublesome corn drawn out in this way, in the course of a few nights.

Egg Gruel for Dysentery
From "The American Frugal Housewife", By Lydia M. Child, 1832

This is at once food and medicine. Some people have very great faith in its efficacy in cases of chronic dysentery. It is made thus: Boil a pint of new milk; beat four new-laid eggs to a light froth, and pour in while the milk boils; stir them together thoroughly, but do not
let them boil; sweeten it with the best of loaf sugar, and grate in a whole nutmeg; add a little salt, if you like it. Drink half of it while it is warm, and the other half in two hours.

12. Dishes The Soldiers Ate

"We got orders to march this morning. Left here with two days' rations of corn meal and bacon in our haversacks."-Pvt. Louis Leon, Company C, First North Carolina Regiment, at Drewry's Bluff, July 6, 1862, from his diary.

"I will tell you something about our rations at present. We have not drawn any meat of any kind for the past four days but we have drawn sugar in its place which makes a splendid mess. I like it better than the beef but some of the boys do not."- Pvt. James A. Durrett, Co. E, 18th Alabama Infantry, Nov. 12, 1863 in the Chattanooga Valley, Tennessee. Letter to his mother. He was shot through the head and died April 3, 1865 at Spanish Fort, Mobile Alabama.

"'Tis nothing here but march and countermarch & that on short rations. Corn meal & beef is the standard ration. Once in a while — say every ten days — bacon is circulated in very small quantities and that with the few wasting ears that they are able to gather in the fields on the roadside is all that can be had for the inner man." – Pvt. Smith G. Homan of Co. F, 29th Georgia Infantry, July 21, 1863 at Morton, Mississippi. Letter to Amelia McCorkle.

"We have to pay one dollar per pound for butter milk & some will give us milk. We are faring fine here in the way of eatables." -Pvt. James F. Currie (of Lauderdale County, Tennessee) of Co. M, 7th Tennessee (Confederate) Cavalry (a.k.a. "Duckworth's Cavalry"), Abbeville, Mississippi, June 2, 1864. Letter to his wife, Kate.

"The most experienced men discuss the situation and decide that "somebody" must go foraging. Though the stock on hand is small, no one seems anxious to leave the small certainty and go in search of the large uncertainty of supper from some farmer's well filled table. But at last several comrades start out, and as they disappear the preparations for immediate consumption commence. The meat is too little to cook alone, and the flour will scarcely make six biscuits. The result is that "slosh" or "coosh" must do. So the bacon is fried out till the pan is half full of boiling grease. The flour is mixed with water until it flows like milk, poured into the grease and rapidly stirred till the whole is a dirty brown mixture. It is now ready to be served."-Pvt. Carlton McCarthy, Second company Richmond Howitzers, Cutshaw's Battalion from *Detailed Minutiae Of Soldier Life In The Army Of Northern Virginia.*

Coffee for One Hundred Men, One Pint Each
From "Directions for Cooking By Troops In Camp And Hospital, Prepared for the Army of Northern Virginia and Published By Order of the Surgeon General", By Florence Nightingale, 1861

Put 12 gallons water into a suitable vessel (or divide if necessary), on the fire; when boiling, add 3 lbs. ground coffee, mix well with a spoon; leave on the fire a few minutes longer; take it off, and pour in ½ a gallon cold water; let it stand till the dregs subside, say from 5
to 10 minutes; then pour off and add 6 lbs. sugar. If milk is used, put in 12 pints, and diminish the water by that amount.

Fresh Beef Soup for One Hundred Men
From "Directions for Cooking By Troops In Camp And Hospital, Prepared for the Army of Northern Virginia and Published By Order of the Surgeon General", By Florence Nightingale, 1861

Take 75 lbs. beef; cut into pieces of about ¼ lb. each; 15 gallons water; 8 lbs. mixed vegetables; 10 small tablespoonfuls salt; 2 small tablespoonfuls ground pepper; some cold bread, crackers, or 3 lbs. rice, to thicken; place on the fire; let it come to a boil; then simmer for 3 hours. Skim off the fat and serve.

Soyer's Stew For One Hundred Men
From "Directions for Cooking By Troops In Camp And Hospital, Prepared for the Army of Northern Virginia and Published By Order of the Surgeon General", By Florence Nightingale, 1861

Cut 50 lbs. fresh beef in pieces of about ¼ lb. each, and with 18 quarts of water put into the boiler; add 10 tablespoonfuls of salt, two of pepper, 7 lbs. onions, cut in slices, and 20 lbs. potatoes peeled and sliced; stir well, and let it boil for 20 or 30 minutes; then add
1½ lbs. flour previously mixed with water; mix well together, and with a moderate heat simmer for about two hours. Mutton, veal or pork can be stewed in a similar manner, but will take half an hour less cooking. A pound of rice or plain dumplings may be added with great advantage.

Suet Dumplings
From "Directions for Cooking By Troops In Camp And Hospital, Prepared for the Army of Northern Virginia and Published By Order of the Surgeon General", By Florence Nightingale, 1861

Take 10 lbs. flour, 15 teaspoonfuls of salt, 7 of ground pepper, 7 lbs. chopped fat pork or suet, 5 pints water; mix well together; divide into about 150 pieces; which roll in flour, and boil with meat for 20 or 30 minutes.—If no fat or suet can be obtained, take the same ingredients, adding a little more water, and boil about 10 minutes. Serve with the meat.

To Fry Meat
From "Directions for Cooking By Troops In Camp And Hospital, Prepared for the Army of Northern Virginia and Published By Order of the Surgeon General", By Florence Nightingale, 1861

Place your pan on the fire for a minute or so; wipe it clean; when the pan is hot, put in either fat or butter (fat from salt meat is preferable); then add the meat you are going to cook; turn it several times, to have it equally done; season to each pound a small teaspoonful of salt and a quarter of pepper. A few onions in the remaining fat, with the addition of a little flour, a quarter pint of water, two tablespoonfuls of vinegar, or a few chopped pickles, will be very relishing.

To Cook Salt Beef or Pork
From "Directions for Cooking By Troops In Camp And Hospital, Prepared for the Army of Northern Virginia and Published By Order of the Surgeon General", By Florence Nightingale, 1861

Put the meat, cut in pieces of from 3 to 4 lbs., to soak the night before; in the morning wash in fresh water, and squeeze well with the hands to extract the salt; after which, put in your kettle with a pint of water to each pound, and boil from 2 to 3 hours.

Salt Beef or Pork, With Mashed Beans, For One Hundred Men
From "Directions for Cooking By Troops In Camp And Hospital, Prepared for the Army of Northern Virginia and Published By Order of the Surgeon General", By Florence Nightingale, 1861

Put in two vessels 37½ lbs. meat each; divide 24 lbs. beans in four pudding cloths, loosely tied; putting to boil at the same time as your meat, in sufficient water; let all boil gently for two hours; take out the meat and beans; put all the meat into one boiler, and remove the
liquor from the other; into which turn out the beans; add to them two teaspoonfuls of pepper, a pound of fat, and with the wooden spatular mash the beans, and serve with the meat. Six sliced onions fried and added improves the dish.
[NOTE-In cooking all kinds of meat, be careful to preserve the grease, which can be easily done by putting the liquor in which it is boiled, by till it cools; then skim off and place in a clean covered vessel. It is an excellent substitute for butter; is useful for cooking purposes,
and will burn in a common lamp or tin plate with a piece of old cotton twisted up for a wick.]

Measurements and Definitions

<u>Bain Marie</u>- A container holding hot water into which a pan is placed for slow cooking. Used for melting chocolates, etc. Similar to a Double-Boiler.

<u>Bitter Almonds</u>-A variety of the common almond, and is injurious to animal life, on account of the great quantity of hydrocyanic acid it contains, and is consequently seldom used in domestic economy, unless it be to give flavour to confectionery; and even then it should he used with great caution. A single drop of the essential oil of bitter almonds is sufficient to destroy a bird, and four drops have caused the death of a middle-sized dog. (From "The Book of Household Management").

<u>Burdock</u>-An herb. The entire plant is edible and is a popular vegetable in Asia, particularly in Japan.

<u>Bushel</u>-Eight Gallons.

<u>Cochineal</u>-A red color additive derived from a scale insect called the cochineal scale (*Dactylopius coccus*). Cochineal is a naturally occurring compound, used for hundreds of years. Today, it is still used in many food and cosmetic products and is known by different names, including cochineal, carmine, carminic acid, Natural Red 4, and E120.

<u>Codlin</u>- A small immature apple, any of several elongated greenish English cooking apples.

<u>Demijohn</u>-A bulbous narrow necked bottle holding from 3 to 10 gallons of liquid.

<u>Desiccated Vegetables</u>- Dehydrated vegetables. Carrots, onions, and celery were dehydrated and compressed into pucks that were then boiled and eaten in camp.

Dorure-Yolks of eggs well beaten.

Drachm- A unit of weight formerly used by apothecaries, equivalent to 60 grains or one eighth of an ounce.

Faggot-A small bunch of parsley and thyme and a bay-leaf tied up.

Fortnight-Two weeks.

Gill or Jill-One quarter pint (Liquid Measure) or Eight Tablespoons.

Green Borage- Known as the bee plant, used to prepare green sauce, garnish salads, etc., adding a "cucumber-like" aroma to recipes.

Gum-Arabicked- Acacia gum. A natural gum consisting of the hardened sap of various species of the acacia tree.

Half-Bushel-Four Gallons.

Hot Oven-400-425 degrees F.

Indian Meal-Corn meal.

Isinglass-A pure, transparent or translucent form of gelatin, obtained from the air bladders of certain fish, especially the sturgeon: used in glue and jellies and as a clarifying agent.

Jelly Bag-"How to Make A Jelly-Bag-The very stout flannel called double-mill, used for ironing-blankets, is the best material for a jelly-bag: those of home manufacture are the only ones to be relied on for thoroughly clearing the jelly. Care should be taken that the seam of the bag be stitched twice, to secure it against unequal filtration. The most convenient mode of using the big is to tie it upon a hoop the exact size of the outside of its mouth; and, to do this, strings should be sewn round it at equal distances. The jelly-bag may, of coarse, be made any size; but one of twelve or fourteen inches deep, and seven or eight across the mouth, will be sufficient for ordinary use. The form of a jelly-bag is the fool's cap." (From "The Book of Household Management").

Loaf Sugar- Refined sugar molded into loaves or small cubes or squares. A large conical mass of hard refined sugar.

Moderately Hot Oven-375 degrees F.

Moderate Oven-350 degrees F.

Moderately Slow Oven-325 degrees F.

Nasturtion-Seed- From a genus of roughly 80 species of annual and perennial herbaceous flowering plants. It has a slightly peppery taste reminiscent of watercress. The unripe seed pods can be harvested and dropped into spiced vinegar to produce a condiment and garnish, sometimes used in place of capers.

Neats- A cow or other domestic bovine animal.

Patna Rice-A variety of long-grain rice, used for savoury dishes.

Peck-Two gallons (Dry Measure).

Pestragon-Vinegar flavoured with tarragon.

Quart (Dry Measure)- Generally about equal in quantity to a pound avoirdupois, (sixteen ounces.).

Quartern-A quarter of any given measurement. For example, a quartern milk equals a quart.

Quick Oven- 375-400 degrees, F.

Race (as in "of ginger")-A root or sprig.

Salamander-A tool made of cast iron with a round, flat, but relatively thick plate attached to a long handle which made it possible to grasp the cooler end of the handle without getting so close to the heat of an open hearth fire. The plate could rest on the two short legs while pushed into the hot coals so that the cook did not have to hold up its ample weight during the heating process. It resembles a metal bread or oven peel except that they are much smaller and shorter than a peel.

Saleratus-Sodium bicarbonate (or sometimes potassium bicarbonate) as the main ingredient of baking powder.

Sal-Prunel- Potassium nitrate fused and cast in balls, cakes, or sticks.

Salt Petre (or "Salt Peter")- Nitrate crystals. No longer used commercially because it is toxic in quantity. Instead, sodium nitrate or sodium nitrite is used. Saltpetre was also used for gunpowder. You must instead use Prague Powder #1 and #2. You can find them on any website that sells sausage making supplies (casings, stuffers, etc). #1 is also known as pink curing salt, and is a mixture of 1 oz sodium nitrite per pound of salt.

Sauter-To fry very lightly.

Savoury Herbs-Examples include celery, rosemary, parsley, thyme, sage, oregano and marjoram.

Scrag- The lean end of a neck of mutton or veal.

Slow Oven-300 degrees, F.

Spikenard Root-Known commonly as wild or false sarsaparilla, in part for the ROOT'S mild, pleasant, licorice like flavor, and has been often used as a substitute for sarsaparilla. It can be purchased on-line.

Subcarbonate of Soda-Also known as "Washing Soda". It is not to be confused with baking soda, despite being closely related.

Suet- A form of animal fat, similar to lard, but usually sold in shredded form. SUET is the solid white fat found around the kidneys and loins of beef, sheep and other animals. Your butcher should be able to get this for you.

Tamis or "Tammy"-A strainer of thin woollen canvas, or silk, used for straining soups and sauces.

Tartaric Acid-A white crystalline diprotic organic acid. The compound occurs naturally in many plants, particularly in grapes, bananas, and tamarinds. It is also one of the main acids found in wine. Tartaric Acid can be added to food when a sour taste is desired. It can be purchased at grocery stores or on-line.

Tin Kitchen-A type of roaster.

Tincture-Liquid extracts.

Treacle, or Molasses-Treacle is the uncrystallizable part of the saccharine juice drained from the Muscovado sugar, and is either naturally so or rendered uncrystallizable through some defect in the process of boiling. As it contains a large quantity of sweet or saccharine principle and is cheap, it is of great use as an article of domestic economy. Children are especially fond of it; and it is accounted wholesome. It is also useful for making beer, rum, and the very dark syrups.

Unbolted Flour-Whole grain flour.

Very Slow-Oven-Below 300 degrees F.

Vinegar a Pestragon-Vinegar flavored with tarragon.

Volatile Salt- Ammonium carbonate is a salt with the chemical formula $(NH_4)_2CO_3$. Since it readily degrades to gaseous ammonia and carbon dioxide upon heating, it is used as a leavening agent and also as smelling salt. It is also known as "Baker's Ammonia" and was a predecessor to the more modern leavening agents baking soda and baking powder. It is a component of what was formerly known as sal volatile and salt of hartshorn. Baker's Ammonia can be purchased on-line.

<u>Wine Glass</u>-Four Tablespoons.

<u>Yelk</u>-Yolk of an egg.

<u>Yellow Dock</u>-A perennial flowering plant in the family Polygonaceae, native to Europe and Western Asia. It can be purchased on-line.

<u>Bibliography</u>

Beecher, Catherine Esther, *Miss Beecher's Reciept Book: Designed As A Supliment To Her Treastise On Domestic Economy*, Third Edition. New York: Harper & Brothers, 1850.

Beeton, Isabella. *The Book of Household Management*. London: S. O. Beeton Publishing, 1861.

Bury, Charlotte Campbell. *The Lady's Own Cookery Book*, Third Edition. London, 1844.

Chase M.D., Alvin Wood. *Dr. Chase's Recipes, or Information for Everybody*. Ann Arbor, MI: Chase, 1864.

Chesnut, Mary Boykin. *A Diary From Dixie*. New York: D. Appleton and Company, 1905.

Child, Lydia M. The *American Frugal Housewife*. Boston: Carter, Hendee and Co., 1832.

Collins, Angelina Maria. *The Great Western Cook Book*. New York: A.S. Barnes & Company, 1857.

Confederate Receipt Book. A Compilation of over One Hundred Receipts, Adapted to the Times. Richmond: West and Johnston, 1863.

Daniel, Larry J. *Soldiering In The Army of Tennessee.* Chapel Hill: The University of North Carolina Press, 1991.

Ellet, Elizabeth Fries. *The Practical Housekeeper.* New York: Stringer and Townsend, 1857.

Francatelli, Charles Elmé. *A Plain Cookery Book for the Working Classes.* London: Routledge, Warne, and Routledge, 1852.

Hubbs, G. Ward. *Voices From Company D.* Athens, Georgia: University of Georgia Press, 2003.

Jones, Jenkin Lloyd. *An Artilleryman's Diary.* Wisconsin Historical Commission, 1914.

Kitchiner, Dr. William. *The Cook's Oracle and Housekeeper's Manual.* New York: J. and J. Harper, 1830.

Leon, Louis. *Diary of a Tar Heel Confederate Soldier.* Charlotte: Stone Publishing Company, 1913.

Leslie, Eliza. *Directions for Cookery, in its Various Branches.* Philadelphia, H.C. Baird, 1840.

Leslie, Eliza. *The Lady's Receipt-Book; a Useful Companion for Large or Small Families.* Philadelphia: Carey and Hart, 1847.

McArthur, Judith N. and Burton, Orville Vernon, eds.. *"A Gentleman and an Officer": A Military and Social History of James B. Griffin's Civil War* New York: Oxford University Press, 1996.

Moss, Maria J. *A Poetical Cook-Book.* Philadelphia: Caxton Press of C. Sherman, Son & Co., 1864.

Nightingale, Florence. *Directions for Cooking By Troops In Camp And Hospital, Prepared for the Army of Northern Virginia and Published By Order of the Surgeon General.* Richmond, Virginia: J. W. Randolph, 1861.

Randolph, Mary. *The Virginia Housewife Or Methodical Cook.* Baltimore: John Plaskitt, 1836.

Rundell, Maria Eliza Ketelby. *A New System of Domestic Cookery.* Philadelphia : Benjamin C. Buzby, 1807.

Sanderson, J. M. *The Complete Cook*. Philadelphia: J. B. Lippincott, 1864.

"Civil War Diaries of Van Buren Oldham" Dieter C. Ullrich, ed. Originals at Special Collections/University Archives, Univ. of Tennessee at Martin. https://www.utm.edu/departments/special_collections/E579.5%20Oldham/text/vboldham_1863.php (Accessed 18 January 2018).

"Billy Yank and Johnny Reb Letters" Wordpress.com. https://billyyankjohnnyreb.wordpress.com/ (Accessed 18 January 2018).

"Diary of a Confederate Soldier" Southern Historical Society Papers, Volume 10. http://www.perseus.tufts.edu/hopper/text?doc=Perseus%3Atext%3A2001.05.0123%3Achapter%3D7.66 (Accessed 18 January 2018).

"Contributions To A History of the Richmond Howitzer Battalion". https://www.civilwardigital.com/CWDiaries/Diary%20of%20T.%20Roberts%20Baker,%20of%20the%20Second%20Howitzer%20Company,%20of%20Richmond,%20Va..pdf (Accessed 15 February 2019).

"1864: Augustus Alexander Clewell Family Letters" Wordpress.com. https://sparedshare7.wordpress.com/2014/09/14/1864-augustine-a-clewell-family/
(Accessed 15 February 2019).

"Capt. Henry A. Chambers Diary".
http://nccivilwar.lostsoulsgenealogy.com/ownwords/diarycapthachambers.htm
(Accessed 2 January 2018).

"Detailed Minutiae Of Soldier Life In The Army Of Northern Virginia (Part 4)" Southern Historical Society Papers, Volume VI.
http://www.civilwarhome.com/minutiae4.html (Accessed 20 August 2018).

"The Letters of James A. Durrett" Wordpress.com. https://durrettblog.wordpress.com/ (Accessed 15 February 2019).

"1863: Charles Abram Rutledge to Harriet Matilda Rutledge" Wordpress.com. https://sparedshared9.wordpress.com/2015/11/07/1863-charles-abram-rutledge/
(Accessed 15 February 2019).

"1862: George Washington Brummett to Pleasant Brummett" Wordpress.com. https://sparedshared9.wordpress.com/2014/12/23/1862-george-washington-brummett-to-pleasant-brummett/ (Accessed 15 February 2018).

"War Letters From Confederate Soldiers" The In-Depth Genealogist. http://theindepthgenealogist.com/war-letters-from-confederate-soldiers/(Accessed 26 April 2019).

"1862-1864: James Andrew James to John James" Wordpress.com. https://sparedshared9.wordpress.com/2015/11/28/1864-james-a-james-to-john-james/
(Accessed 18 October 2018).

"1862-1863: John Calvin McAulay to Nancy Keziah McAulay" Wordpress.com. https://sparedshared14.wordpress.com/2017/01/10/1862-john-calvin-mcaulay-to-nancy-keziah-mcaulay/ (Accessed 13 February 2018).

"1863-1864: August Rost to Mary Rost" Wordpress.com. https://sparedshared10.wordpress.com/2016/03/07/1861-august-rost/ (Accessed 22 November 2018).

"1864: Ephraim Alexander McAulay to Nancy D. (Alexander) McAulay" Wordpress.com. https://sparedshared14.wordpress.com/2017/01/10/1864-ephraim-alexander-mcaulay-to-nancy-d-alexander-mcaulay/ (Accessed 13 February 2018).

"Letters to Santa" Tennessee State Library and Archives Blog. http://tslablog.blogspot.com/2014/12/ (Accessed 22 November 2018).

"1861-62 Clayton Letters" Wordpress.com. https://sparedshared10.wordpress.com/2016/03/06/1861-clayton-letters/ (Accessed 26 April 2019).

"1863: Smith G. Homan to Amelia McCorkle" Wordpress.com. https://sparedshared9.wordpress.com/2015/03/26/1863-smith-g-homan-to-amelia-mccorkle/
(Accessed 26 April 2019).

"1864: James F. Currie to Kate Currie" Wordpress.com. https://sparedshared9.wordpress.com/2015/12/18/1864-james-currin-to-wife/ (Accessed 26 April 2019).

"Burr J. Caldwell to Sarah Rebecca (Mounts) Caldwell" Wordpress.com. https://sparedshared4.wordpress.com/letters/1864-burr-j-caldwell-to-sarah-rebecca-mounts-caldwell/ (Accessed 13 February, 2019).

Index

3 Ways To Purify Air In A Sick Room, 210, 211

A Good Sauce for Steaks, 133
A L'Hollandaise, 122
A Nice Way of Cooking Game, 105
A Soothing Ointment, 211, 212
Almond Bread, 149
Anchovy Toast, 75
Anniseed Cordial, 181
Apple Jam, 136
Apple Jelly, 136
Apple Marmalade, 136
Apple Pancakes, 15
Apple Sauce, for Goose and Roast Pork, 118
Apple Tea, 173
Apple Water, 163
Apricot Jam or Marmalade, 137
Asparagus Loaves, 87
Asparagus Pudding, 88

Bacon and Cabbage Soup, 28
Bake A Ham, 60
Bake Pike, 84
Bake Smelts, 85, 86
Baked Beans-Yankee Fashion, 88
Baked Carp, 76
Baked Fish, 76
Baked Goose, 110
Baked Potatoes, 89
Baked Salmon, 84
Baked Salmon-Trout, 84
Baked Soups, 28
Baked Tomatoes, 89
Barley Soup
Barley Water
Basil Vinegar or Wine, 134
Batter Bread, 150
Bean Soup, 29
Beef À La Braise, 48
Beef a-la-Mode, 42

Beef Bouilli, 43
Beef Ragout, 53
Beef Soup, 206
Beef Steaks, 54
Beef Steaks A La Parisienne, 49
Beef Steaks Rolled and Roasted, 50
Beef Steaks With Mushrooms, 50
Beef Steaks, A La Francaise, 49
Beef Stew, 44
Beef Tea, Six Pints, 206
Beef With Baked Potatoes, 43
Beef, or Veal Stewed with Apples, 55
Beef-Collops, 43
Beef-Steak Pie, 52
Beef-Steaks with Fried Potatoes, 51
Beet Roots, 89
Benton Sauce, for Hot or Cold Roast Beef, 118
Biscuit, 150
Black Puddings, 57
Blackberry Jam, 137
Boil Ducks With Onion Sauce, 105
Boil Fowl with Rice, 108
Boiled Cauliflowers, 89, 90
Boiled Lobster, 80
Boiled Rabbit, 114, 115
Boiled Salad, 99
Boned Turkey, 115
Bouillabaisse Soup, 29
Bouillon, 30
Boy's Coffee, 163
Brain Balls, 90
Braise (Fowl), 108
Brandy Grapes, 142
Bread, 150, 151
Bread Muffins, 151
Bread Sauce for A Roast Fowl, 118, 119
Brew Your Own Beer, 178-180
Broil Beef Steaks, 45, 54
Broiled Beef-Steaks or Rump Steaks, 44
Broiled Fowl or Rabbit, 188
Broiled Rashers of Bacon, 58
Broth Made From Bones for Soup, 30
Brown Gravy for Fowl, 121
Brown Onion Sauce, 119
Buckwheat Cakes, 16
Buttered Parsnips, 90

Buttered Swedish Turnips, 90

Cabbage, 90, 91
Cabbage Soup, 30
Calf's Heart, 49
Calf's Foot Jelly, 137
Camp Ketchup, 119
Camphor Ice-For Chapping Hands or Lips, 211
Caper Sauce, 119
Carbonated Syrup Water, 163
Carp, To Stew, 76
Carrot Soup, 30
Carrots In The German Way, 91
Catfish Soup, 31
Cauliflower Dressed Like Macaroni, 92
Cauliflower in White Sauce, 93
Cauliflower Maccaroni, 92
Cauliflowers With Parmesan Cheese, 92
Celery Sauce, 119, 120
Celery Soup, 31
Champagne-Cup, 181
Chantilly Soup, 32
Cherry Jelly, 138
Chestnut Sauce, 120
Chicken Broth, 32, 207
Chicken Croquets and Rissoles, 68
Chicken Gumbo, 69
Chicken or Fowl Patties, 69
Chicken Pudding, A Favourite Virginia Dish, 73
Chickens Stewed Whole, 70
Chitterlings or Calf's Tripe, 44
Chocolate Cream, 164
Chocolate Custard, 190, 191
Chowder, 32, 77
Christmas Goose Pie, 201
Christmas Pie, 202
Christmas Plum Pudding, 203
Chronic Gout-To Cure, 209
Ciders-Artificial, OR Cider Without Apples, 164
Citric Acid Lemonade, 208
Clam Pie, 77
Clam Soup, 32
Clear Apple Jelly, 138
Cocoa, 165

Cocoa-Nut Soup, 33
Cod's Head and Shoulders, 77, 78
Codlin Cream, 181
Coffee, 174-176
Coffee for One Hundred Men, One Pint Each 215
Coffee, To Roast, 175
Cold Slaw, 93
Cold Sweet Sauce, 120
Common Bread, 152
Common Pancakes, 25
Cook Pigeons, 114
Corn Beer, Without Yeast, 182
Corn Muffins, 152
Corns, 212-213
Cottage Soup, 34
Country Syllabub, 182
Crab Apples, 138
Crackers, 152
Cranberry and Rice Jelly, 139
Cranberry Sauce, 198
Cranberry Tea, 173
Crayfish Soup, 34
Cream Nectar, Imperial, 165
Cream Pancakes, 16
Cream Soda Without A Fountain, 166
Crepes, 16
Crimean Lemonade, 207-208
Cross-Buns, 194
Crumpets, 153
Cucumber Catchup, 120
Cucumbers A La Poulette, 93
Cucumbers Stewed, 94
Cure Hams, 59
Currant Ice Water, 166
Currant Jelly, 139
Currant Jelly (Red), 139
Curried Fowl, 70

Damascus Biscuits, 153
Damson Jam, 140
Davenport Fowls, 109
Delicious Milk Lemonade, 167
Dutch Pancakes, 17

Economical Dish, 60
Egg Balls, 94

Egg Gruel for Dysentery, 213
Egg Nog, 200
Egg Plant, 94
Egg Sauce for Roast Fowls, 121
Egg Soup, 34
Eggs A La Maitre D'Hotel, 18
Eggs and Bread, 17
Eggs Stewed with Cheese, 18
Eggs with Brown Butter, 18
Election Cake, 96
English Dish of Beefsteak and Onions, 47
Essence of Coffee, 177
Excellent Orange Cream, 184

Fillet of Pork to Resemble Veal, 61
Fine Pancakes, 25
Fish Sauce, 121
Fish Stock No. 192, 34
For A Cold, 212
For A Headache, 212
Four Fruit Jelly, 141
Fowl A La Hollandaise, 72
Fowl and Oysters, 109
French Beef, 46
French Chicken Cutlets, 71
French Chicken Pie, 72
French Ham Pie, 61
French Mustard, 126-127
French Raspberry Vinegar (for a Cold), 208
French Rolls, 153
French Spinach, 94-95
French Vegetable Soup, 35
Fresh Beef Soup for One Hundred Men, 215
Fricaseed Rabbits, 115
Fricassee of Parsnips, 95
Fricasseed Chickens, 71
Fried Artichokes, 95
Fried Cauliflower, 95
Fried Celery, 96
Fried Eggs and Bacon, 17
Fried Fowls, 71
Fried Ham and Eggs, 19
Fried Oysters, 80-81
Fried Rump-Steak, 50
Fried Steaks, 48

Fried Steaks and Onions, 49
Fruit Cake, 200
Fruit Jelly, 140
Fry Beefsteaks, 49
Fry Calf's Liver, 47
Fry Fish78, 79
Fry Potatoes, 96
Fry Smelts, 86
Fry Trout, 86

Game Soup, 109
Gargle for Sore Throat, 208
Ginger Crackers, 154
Ginger Pop, 166, 167
Ginger Wine, 182
Gooseberry Jelly, 141
Green Corn Pudding, 97
Green Peas A La Francaise, 97
Green-Peas Soup, 35
Greens, 97

Halibut Cutlets, 78
Ham and Eggs Fried, 19
Ham Gravy, 122
Ham Sauce, 122
Ham, To Stuff A, 60
Hard Biscuits, 154-155
Hare, Rabbit, or Partridge Soup, 110
Hashed Beef, 20
Hashed Duck, 105-106
Hessian Soup, 36
Hippocras, 182-183
Horseradish Sauce, 122
Hydromel, Or Mead, 183

Indian Batter Cakes, 21
Italian Beef-Steaks, 51

Jellies Without Fruit, 146
Jerked Beef, 51
Johnny Cake, 155-156
Jugged Hare, 111

Kedgeree, 21
Kentucky Batter Cakes, 21
Kentucky Corn Dodgers, 156
Kitchiner's Fish Sauce, 123

La Magnonnaise, 123
Larded Calf's Liver, 52
Lavender Water, 190
Leg of Pork Roasted, 62
Lemon Brandy, 183
Lemon Catchup, 123
Lemonade, Nourishing, For Fever Patients, 210
Lent Potatoes, 193
Lettuce Peas, 98
Light Buns, 156
Liver Pudding, 62
Liver Sauce, 123
Lobster, 79

Macaroni As Usually Served, 98
Macaroni Gratin, 98
Macaroni Soup (Mrs. F.'s Receipt), 36
Maccaroni Soup, 36
Making Coffee,
Marinade to Baste Roast Meats, 124
Matelote of Fish (English), 80
Mayonnaise, 124
Medium Stock (No. 105), 36
Melted Butter, 124
Melt Lard, 61
Milk Biscuits, 157
Milk Coffee, 177
Mint Sauce for Veal or Mutton, 125
Mock Hare, 52
Molasses Gingerbread, 157
Muffins, 157-158
Mullagatawny Soup, 37
Mushroom Catsup, 125
Mustard, 127
Mutton Stewed and Soup for One Hundred Men, 205-206

Nectar, 167
New-England Pancakes, 26
New-Year's Cookies, 188-189

Ochra Soup, 37
Oeufs Au Plat, or Au Miroir, 22
Omlette, 22
Omlette Souffle, 24
Onion Custard, 99
Onion Sauce, 105

Onion Soup, 38
Orange Brandy, 183
Orange Butter, 142-143
Orange Gravy Sauce, 127
Orange Jelly, 143
Oyster Loaves, 82
Oyster Omelet, 22
Oyster Pie, 82

Pancakes for Shrove Tuesday, 195
Pancakes of Rice, 26
Parsley Sauce, 127, 128
Partridges In Pears, 112
Passover Cakes, 195
Peach Sauce, 128
Peaches Preserved In Brandy, 143
Peas and Bacon, 99
Perch Stewed With Wine, 83
Perch With Wine, 83
Pheasant Cutlets, 113
Pig's Feet Fried, 63
Pigeons, 114
Pineapple Preserve, 144-145
Pink Sauce, 128
Pistachio Cream, 168
Plain and Very Crisp Biscuits, 158
Plain Buns, 158
Plain Green Pea Soup, 38
Plain Omelet, 23
Plum Broth, 38
Poach Eggs, 25
Pork Cheese, 64
Pork Chops, 65
Pork Chops Grilled or Broiled, 65
Pork Cutlets, 65, 66
Pork Cutlets, 65, 66
Pork Steaks, 66
Portable Lemonade, 167
Potato Omelette, 27
Potato Salad, 100
Potato Soup, 38
Poulet A La Marengo, 73
Pound Cake, 188
Practical Housewife's Christmas Ham, 200-201

Preserve Pears, 144
Preserve Watermelon Rind, 147
Preserved Mulberries, 142
Preserved Pumpkin, 145
Preserved Strawberries In Wine, 147
Prof. Hufeland's Drink for Fever Patients OR Excessive Thirst, 210
Pull Chickens, 73
Purple Plum.--No. 1, 145
Purple Plum.--No. 2, 145

Quin's Sauce, 128-129

Ragout A Duck Whole, 106
Raspberry Brandy, 184
Raspberry Cordial, 184
Raspberry Jam.--No. 1, 146
Raspberry Jam.--No. 2, 146
Relief of Sore Throat, 212
Rhubarb Jam, 146
Rhubarb Wine, 185
Rice Chicken Pie, 74
Rice Gruel (for Bowl Complaints), 209
Rice Journey or Johnny Cake, 156
Rice Water, 207
Rich Brown Soup, 39
Richer Pancakes, 26
Roast A Loin of Pork, 62
Roast a Spare Rib, 63
Roast a Sucking Pig, 64
Roast Beef, 55
Roast Chestnuts, 203
Roast Chickens, 74
Roast Ducks, 106
Roast Goose, 110
Roast Hare, 111-112
Roast Onions, 100
Roast Pheasants, 114
Roast Shad-(Sea-Shore Receipt), 85
Roasted Hare,
Roasted Salmon, 85
Rocks, 158
Rolls, 159
Roux, 129

Rump of Beef Stew, 55, 56
Rusks, 159
Russian or Swedish Turnips, 100
Rye and Indian Bread, 158
Rye Batter Cakes, 26

Salmis of Wild Duck, 107
Salmon Baked In Slices, 85
Salt Beef, 56
Salt Beef or Pork, With Mashed Beans, For One Hundred Men, 217
Sarsaparilla, 168, 169
Sassafras Beer, 185
Sauce for a Pig, 129
Sauce for Wild Fowl, 132
Sausage to Eat Cold, 67
Sausages, 67
Scented Bags, 190
Scotch Kail, 56
Scotch Sauce, 129
Secrets, 189-190
Simple Syrup, 168
Slices of Ham or Bacon, 19
Sloosh (Coosh)
Soda Biscuits, 160
Soda Bread, 160
Soft Crullers, 16
Soup à-la-sap, 39
Soup De L'Asperge, 39
Soup Italienne, 40
Soup Maigre, 40
Sour Kraut, 101
Sour Milk Biscuit, 161
Soused Mackerel, 80
Soy
Soyer's Brioche Rolls, 151
Soyer's Stew For One Hundred Men, 216
Spanish Gingerette, 169
Spare Rib, 63
Spiced Gingerbread, 160, 161
Spinach, 101
Spinach Soup, 40
Squashes, 100-101
Stew a Rump of Beef, 53
Stew Canvas-Back Ducks, 107
Stew Celery, 101

Stew Cold Corned Beef, 56
Stew Ducks, 107
Stew Fish White, 81
Stew Oysters, 82
Stew Pigeons, 113
Stew Pork, 64
Stewed Eggplant, 102
Stewed Green Peas, 102
Stewed Red Cabbage, 102
Stewed Rump Another Way
Stewed Trout, 86
Stewed Venison, 117
Stewed Wild Ducks, 108
Strawberries, 147
Strawberry Cordial, 186
Substitute for Milk or Cream In Tea or Coffee, 177
Succotash, 103
Succotash, á La Tecumsah, 103
Suet Dumplings, 216
Summer Draught, 169
Superlative Sauce, 130
Sweet Pudding Sauce, 203

Tarragon Sauce, 133-134
Tea, 172
Tea Biscuit, 161, 162
Tea Parties, 170
Tea Parties and Evening Company, 171
Thick Beef Tea, 206
To Cook Salt Beef or Pork, 217
To Corn Beef In Hot Weather, 192
To Fry Meat, 216
To Make Chocolate, 164
To Make Yeast, 162
To Roast A Turkey, 197
To Stuff and Roast A Calf's Liver,
Tomata Soy, 132
Tomato Catsup, 130-131
Tomato Ketchup, 131
Tomato Marmlade, 147
Tomato Sauce, 131
Tomato Soup, 41
Tongue Pie, 62
Tongue Toast, 67
Turnips, 103

Vegetable Soup, 41
Venison, 116
Venison Pasty, 117
Very Fine Mushroom Sauce for Fowls, or Rabbits, 126
Very Fine Preserved Peaches, 143
Very Rich Mushroom Sauce for Fowls or Rabbits, 126
Very Simple Method of Making Coffee,
Vinegar for Salads (No. 395), 135-136
Violet Perfume, 190

Walnut Hill's Doughnuts, 17
Walnut Ketchup, 135
Warm Slaw, 103
Warts and Corns-To Cure In Ten Minutes, 211
Wheat Muffins, 162
Whiskey Cordial, 186
White Onion Sauce, 135
Wine Sauce, 132-133
Wine Sauce for Mutton, or Venison, 133
Winter Vegetable Soup, 41
Wow Wow Sauce, for Stewed Beef or Bouilli, 133

Young Corn Omelet, 24

About the Author

David W. Flowers earned his Bachelor's of Science, with a Minor in Sociology and additional hours in Education from Illinois State University. In 2016, 2017 and 2018, David was honored with the "Grand Cook of the Year" award from Civil War Talk (civilwartalk.com) for his research in original Civil War era recipes. The American Civil War has been a passion, culminating in a lifetime of study, travel to battlefields and actively participating in Civil War reenactments on the local and National levels since 2005 with Scott's Tennessee Battery. Since the 1980's, he has taught classes ranging from Career Counseling, Pre-K, Junior High School and GED/HiSET coursework to youth involved in the Criminal Justice system. Combining a love of cooking, reenacting and Civil War history, it came natural for his kitchen and backyard fire pit to exude the smells and tastes of the 1860's. In 2018, the first volume of "Voices From the Kitchen" was published. He resides in Aledo, Illinois with his wife, Monica, son, David, dog, Molly and cat, Lucky Charms.

Made in the USA
Coppell, TX
17 January 2020